Gothic
& Gender

For my mother

Margaret O'Brien

Gothic & Gender

An Introduction

Donna Heiland

Blackwell Publishing

BLACKWELL PUBLISHING

350 Main Street, Malden, MA 02148-5020, USA
108 Cowley Road, Oxford OX4 1JF, UK
550 Swanston Street, Carlton, Victoria 3053, Australia

First published 2004 by Blackwell Publishing Ltd

Library of Congress Cataloging-in-Publication Data

Heiland, Donna.
Gothic and gender : an introduction / Donna Heiland.
p.   cm.
Includes bibliographical references and index.
ISBN 0-631-20049-5 (hardcover : alk. paper) – ISBN 0-631-20050-9
(pbk. : alk. paper)
1. Horror tales, English – History and criticism.   2. Gothic revival (Literature) – Great Britain.   3. English fiction – 19th century – History and criticism.
4. English fiction – 18th century – History and criticism.   5. English fiction –
Women authors – History and criticism.   6. Feminism and literature – Great
Britain.   7. Women and literature – Great Britain.   8. Patriarchy in
literature.   9. Sex role in literature.   I. Title.
PR830.T3H37 2005
823′.0872909 – dc22
2003026894

A catalogue record for this title is available from the British Library.

Set in 10/12$\frac{1}{2}$ pt Dante by SNP Best-set Typesetter Ltd., Hong Kong
Printed and bound in the United Kingdom by MPG Books Ltd,
Bodmin, Cornwall

The publisher's policy is to use permanent paper from mills that operate a sustainable forestry policy, and which has been manufactured from pulp processed using acid-free and elementary chlorine-free practices. Furthermore, the publisher ensures that the text paper and cover board used have met acceptable envirnmental accreditation standards.

For further information on
Blackwell Publishing, visit our website:
http://www.blackwellpublishing.com

Contents

Acknowledgments

I have been lucky in my communities, and without their support could not have written this book. Vassar College, and especially the Vassar English Department, gave me a wonderful intellectual home for many years. I am especially grateful to Robert DeMaria, Jr. for suggesting to Blackwell that I write this book, and for always supporting my work. To my many students at Vassar I also owe special thanks. They taught me a great deal.

The American Council of Learned Societies gave me my next academic home, and I am especially grateful to ACLS President Emeritus Francis Oakley and Vice-President Steven C. Wheatley for agreeing that I could take a summer leave to finish this book. To the staff of the ACLS Fellowships Office I owe a great deal. Suzy Beemer has been a wonderful colleague and friend from the day she arrived at ACLS, and that she did my job as well as her own while I was away from the office still astonishes me. Cynthia Mueller and Karen Mathews have done every-thing they could – even after I returned to the office – to take responsibilities off my shoulders so that I would be able to finish what I had started. Ruth Waters has been a lifeline.

My life at ACLS had a complement during Spring 2003 in my life at Barnard College. Thanks to James G. Basker for inviting me into this community, and to the students who took my course on "Eighteenth-Century Gothic." I learned much from them, and our time together blended seamlessly into a summer of writing.

Others in these communities and beyond also have my thanks for their wise guidance and sympathetic support. Susan Bianconi, Tita Chico, Jennifer Fleis-chner, Wendy Graham, and Heather Weidemann listened, advised, agreed, disagreed, and were wonderful interlocutors every step of the way. Peter Antelyes, Pinar Batur, Heesok Chang, Mita Choudhury (the historian), Mita Choudhury (the literary critic), Carolyn Dever, Leslie Dunn, Maggie Fusco, Kim Hall, Mary Loeffeholz Ellen Martin, Elizabeth Medina, James Mendelsohn, Uma Narayan, Brock Pennington, Karen Robertson, Kathe Sandler, David Schacher, Marvin J. Taylor, Randolph Trumbach, and Susan Zlotnick all contributed to this project in different ways. David L. Clark, Sharon Mazer, and Laura J. Rosenthal read the manuscript at crucial moments, and responded with exactly the combination of generosity and rigor that I needed. The editorial staff at Blackwell made this a better book, and I am particularly indebted to Janet Moth, whose attentive copy-editing saved me from many an error.

Finally, I am grateful to my father, Philip Heiland, and to Gwenlyn Setterfield. I also owe much to my brother Patrick and his family: Christy Sneddon, Emma Heiland, and Michael Heiland. Equally important has been my connection to my brother Michael and his family: Sheri, Branden, and Karen Heiland. They provided bedrock support and a refuge in Toronto whenever I needed or wanted it.

* * *

My discussions of Walpole in chapter 1, of Burke and Lewis in chapter 2, of Radcliffe in chapter 3, and of Atwood in chapter 8 were initially published – in sometimes substantially different form – as part of "Postmodern Gothic: *Lady Oracle* and its Eighteenth-Century Antecedents," *Recherches Sémiotiques / Semiotic Inquiry*, 12 (Spring 1992), 115–36. I am grateful to the editor of the journal for permission to reprint.

Parts of chapter 7 were initially published – in a slightly different form – as "The *Unheimlich* and the Making of Home: Matthew Lewis's *Journal of a West India Proprietor*," in Laura Rosenthal and Mita Choudhury (eds.), *Monstrous Dreams of Reason* (Lewisburg: Bucknell University Press, 2001). I am grateful to the Associated University Press for permission to reprint.

Introduction

The setting is the Empire Theater. A piano accompanies the film unfolding silently on the screen. The audience watches, "breathless, eager for the next terror," and what do they see?

A man in evening clothes has cornered a young woman in a slinky nightgown halfway up a clock tower. No narrative preamble required, *all ist klar*, the shadows lurk, the tower lists, the music creeps the winding stair, the villain spies a grace-note of silken hem and he's on the chase in six-eight time up to where our heroine clings to a snatch of girlish melody, teetering on the precipice of high E, overlooking the street eight octaves below. Villain struggles with virgin in a macabre waltz, Strauss turned Faust, until, just when it seems she'll plummet, dash her brains on the bass clef and die entangled in the web of the lower stave, a vision in tenor crescendos on to save the day in resolving chords.

This scene from Ann-Marie Macdonald's novel *Fall on Your Knees* (p. 50) may or may not be known to you, but its melodramatic story of an innocent young woman trapped by one man and rescued by another will almost certainly be familiar. For this is the plot of a classic gothic novel, compressed into three wonderful sentences. Reduce the pressure, let the three sentences open out into three volumes, and you'll see what stories like this generally looked like when they emerged in the late eighteenth century. Now ask yourself some questions. Why is the girl being chased and why is she in a tower? What does the man in the suit want from her, and is it he who transformed the romance of a waltz (Strauss) into this dance with a devil (Faust)? Who is the savior, and why is he showing up so late? Will the woman be better off with him than she would be with death or the devil? And why is their story told in the language of music? Answer them and you will have the beginnings of an introduction to gothic and gender.

Gothic fiction constitutes one of our most enduring and seemingly ubiquitous forms of popular literature. Not every gothic tale looks exactly like the one in the passage cited above, but they all bear a family resemblance to it. Film might be the best-known purveyor of gothic narrative in our time: a representative but hardly comprehensive list might include slasher movies on the order of the *Halloween* series, classic horror films such as *Rosemary's Baby* and *The Exorcist*, more quietly frightening ghost stories like *The Sixth Sense* and *The Others*, even scary but not supernatural stories like *Single White Female*. Television is equally enthralled with gothic narratives: witness the long run of the *X-Files*. Mainstream presses make huge profits from the work of such well-known authors as Stephen King, Anne Rice, and many others. All of these cultural productions have their origins in mid-eighteenth-century Europe and especially England, where fascination with what would eventually be defined as gothic first took hold.

The tremendous appeal of gothic narratives merits explanation, for it is far from obvious that readers should keep returning to these highly formulaic and therefore highly predictable stories. Why are they so popular and what cultural function do they serve? Their accomplishment is double-edged, for they at once entertain and terrify us. They fill us with relief at our exemption from the dangers they represent, but force us to look at those dangers all the same. They feel like escapist fantasy, but can tell us a great deal about what William Godwin called "things as they are." All we need is the patience to read them well, to account for their complicated appeal, and to do so is my principal aim in this book. Because the broad outlines of the genre and most of its principal transformations emerged in England between the mid-eighteenth and the mid-nineteenth centuries, I have chosen to focus primarily on material from this time and place (though my final chapter moves more than a century ahead to look at recent work in the gothic tradition). My second aim is to provide a critical framework for understanding the gothic that will be useful to anyone trying to come to terms not just with the works discussed here, but with other works as well. My approach to the novels is feminist in its intent, by which I mean that I wish to think through gothic fiction's engagement with the social structures that shape gender relations. I do this through an analysis that is historically informed, but theoretical in its emphasis, bringing together a broad but related range of theoretical and critical sources to demonstrate the genre's ever more complicated but fundamentally consistent concerns over time. While this study is historically based, then, it provides not so much a history of gothic fiction as a particular theoretical path through this body of literature.

That said, a brief discussion of the historical and literary contexts in which gothic fiction emerged is certainly in order. The word "gothic" literally refers to the Gothic people, and yet, as Robin Sowerby has commented, it has been understood that "the use of the term 'Gothic' to describe the literary phenomenon that began in the later eighteenth century has little, if anything, to do with the people from whom it is derived" (2000: 15). Sowerby notes that Edward Gibbon was writing his *Decline and Fall of the Roman Empire* at roughly the same time as gothic fiction emerged on the literary scene, and is right to suggest that this concurrence of events merits further thought. The Goths did much to bring about the fall of the Roman empire (of which Britain had been a part), and while gothic fiction does not literally depict the Goths' repeated incursions into Roman territory, or the sack of Rome in A.D. 410, gothic fiction *does* tell stories of "invasions" of one sort or another. Gothic fiction at its core is about transgressions of all sorts: across national boundaries, social boundaries, sexual boundaries, the boundaries of one's own identity. But why were people in Britain thinking so much about transgression in the late eighteenth century, and how were they thinking about it? Was it something to worry about or something to celebrate?

On the question of why transgression was on people's minds one could write volumes. Considered in political terms, the "long eighteenth century" (1660–1800) was a period framed by revolutions. The English civil wars had seen Charles I beheaded in 1649 and the monarchy replaced by Oliver Cromwell's "Protectorate," which lasted until the restoration of Charles II to the throne in 1660; the "bloodless revolution" of 1688 had seen James II abdicate because of issues raised by his conversion to Catholicism, and William of Orange (husband of James's daughter Mary) take his place; the period from 1789 through the mid-1790s – arguably the high point of gothic fiction – was dominated by the French Revolution, which initially garnered the support of radical thinkers such as William Godwin and Mary Wollstonecraft. In terms of intellectual history, the eighteenth century is generally seen as a period of "enlightenment," a "modern" era that privileged the powers of reason, experience, and the individual over superstition, an unquestioning adherence to the teachings of the "ancients," and willing submission to the dictates of authority. In terms of economic history, capitalism was on the rise, as was a middle class capable of challenging the authority of the ruling aristocracy. At the same time, there was a shift in the organization of family structures, as men were drawn into the workplace, women were increasingly confined to the home, and gender roles were insistently codified even as they were insistently resisted. It was a period characterized by massive instabilities in its socio-political structures. If people could have avoided thinking about transgression, it would have been astonishing.

While there were myriad reasons to turn one's attention to what would come to be seen as the gothic possibilities of everyday life, then, how to think about those possibilities was still a question. And here again, the historical meanings – or better, uses – of the term "gothic" again guide us to an understanding of the range of responses. Eighteenth-century England had self-consciously modeled itself on Greek and Roman culture (the first half of the eighteenth century was known as the Augustan age, after the Roman emperor Augustus), and from this neo-classical perspective, the term "gothic" suggested one of two things. On the one hand, it conjured up the barbarism and savagery of unlawful invading forces, and was understood as all that threatens civilized life. On the other hand, it took one back to the "dark ages" of the English medieval period, viewing it as a purer expression of English national identity than the neo-classical present. Thus the gothic represents a return to a national ideal (Duncan 1992: 21–2; Miles 1995: 30, 39–43). Robert Miles has noted as well that this second vision of the gothic was particularly empowering to women, opening the way to literary accomplishment as it elevated English literature above the classics. Further – and here Miles makes a somewhat unexpected claim – "the gothic myth insisted upon female equality," viewing women not just as objects of "chivalrous devotion," but as "partners and equals" in their relationships with men (1995: 30, 42).

When Horace Walpole's *Castle of Otranto* burst on the scene in the final week of 1764,[1] the term "gothic" would have resonated in complex ways, and yet the historical circumstances of its use do not tell the whole story. What of the literary circumstances of its use? What kinds of things were people writing in eighteenth-century England when Walpole inaugurated this tradition? The genre with which gothic fiction has the clearest connection is, of course, the novel. This seemingly obvious point becomes less so if one considers the way in which eighteenth-century authors themselves talked about their work. Horace Walpole and Clara Reeve did not speak of their gothic fictions as novels but as romances (Duncan 1992: 2–6, 20–7; Miles 1995: 35–43). The genre of the novel was (as the name implies) new in the eighteenth century, was generally taken to include works written in a realistic idiom (think of *Robinson Crusoe*), and has generally been discussed as both symptomatic of and instrumental in the emergence of the middle classes. Romances were seen as something quite different. They were generally understood to be sentimentalized tales of times past that focused on the aristocracy, "the product of the Gothic societies of the Middle Ages" (Miles 1995: 36). Recent scholarship on the history of the novel has taught us that there were in fact close ties between the two forms (McKeon 1987; Moglen 2001), and certainly eighteenth-century authors were aware of those ties as well. Walpole's *Castle of Otranto* was intended to combine the two forms (identified in his preface as "ancient" and "modern" forms of romance), and the gothic tradition includes within it not only novels that are quite fantastic, but also novels whose realism has led critics to question whether they belong in the tradition at all (William Godwin's *Caleb Williams*, for example).

If gothic novels do not need to "look" gothic – if they do not need the "trappings" (as they are often called) of castles, ghosts, corrupt clergy, and so on –

then what exactly defines the genre? The answer would still point to a series of conventions, just slightly different ones. As I noted above, the stories of gothic novels are always stories of transgression. The transgressive acts at the heart of gothic fiction generally focus on corruption in, or resistance to, the patriarchal structures that shaped the country's political life and its family life, and gender roles within those structures come in for particular scrutiny. Further, and importantly, these acts are often violent, and always frightening. For gothic novels are above all about the creation of fear – fear in the characters represented, fear in the reader – and they accomplish this through their engagement with the aesthetic of the sublime or some variant of it. The sublime is the aesthetic category through which eighteenth-century critics understood the disruptive, irregular, transgressive energies I have been discussing, and an understanding of how this aesthetic shapes the gothic's handling of its stories of social transgression is crucial to an appreciation of its literary accomplishment.

This book argues that, from their origin in the eighteenth century, gothic novels explored the workings of patriarchal politics through an aesthetic based in the subjective realities of sensibility and the sublime. My first chapter begins with a theoretical discussion of the term "patriarchy" as it has been understood by the political scientist Carol Pateman, then moves on to discuss how patriarchal principles are seemingly naturalized in the eighteenth-century aesthetic discourse of sensibility. From there, the chapter considers novels by Horace Walpole, Clara Reeve, and Sophia Lee that show how the basic "formula" of gothic fiction anatomizes and explores the workings of a patriarchal society. The second chapter considers gothic's fascination with the sublime, which is by definition an experience so overwhelming that it holds the promise of breaking through the boundaries of patriarchy and every other social structure, but which often does just the reverse and upholds those structures by quenching opposition to them. Readings of eighteenth-century theoretical writing about the sublime open into discussion of how Matthew Lewis's *The Monk*, Charles Maturin's *Melmoth the Wanderer*, and Charlotte Dacre's *Zofloya, or, The Moor* deploy the sublime in order to contain perceived threats – from women, and from some men too – to the status quo. The third chapter is tightly tied to the second in its reading of Ann Radcliffe as a writer who rejects the sublime as a mode of social control, implicitly recognizing its tendency to oppress women and others who threaten the structure of patriarchy, and who in fact takes pains – as critics have noted from the start – to offer rational explanations for anything that is initially terrifying. Those who would otherwise have been controlled by fear – and they are women above all – are thus enabled to fight back in ways that let them strengthen their place in the patriarchy.

The fourth and fifth chapters shift their theoretical underpinnings from the eighteenth-century concept of the sublime to what a number of critics have identified as the twentieth-century version of the same thing: Freud's concept of the *Unheimlich* or uncanny. This movement in the argument is not meant to suggest either that gothic fiction suddenly lost interest in the sublime, or that out of the blue it developed an altogether new interest in the uncanny. Rather, it responds to particular emphases of the novels discussed under this rubric, and builds on the work of the preceding chapters by exploring the relationship of the sublime to the uncanny. The two experiences are indeed alike in their capacity to create fear in those who undergo them, though I read them as differing importantly in both their causes and effects. Where the sublime breaks down boundaries between a perceiving subject and something outside herself, the uncanny confronts the subject with something long repressed or forgotten, but does not allow that breakdown of boundaries. Instead the person is literally or figuratively "haunted" by this reminder of a past that she cannot identify and cannot escape. From an introductory discussion of the uncanny, chapter 4 moves to discuss William Godwin and Mary Wollstonecraft, who are inheritors of Radcliffe in their use of an increasingly realistic idiom to describe social injustice, and innovators in their understanding of how that injustice can manifest itself as a pattern of uncanny encounters between the empowered and the disempowered. Mary Shelley's *Frankenstein*, discussed in chapter 5, thinks still more radically about how social injustice shapes individuals with its portrait of a "monster" who is the uncanny double of his maker. The sixth chapter maintains a focus on the uncanny in its discussion of Emily and Charlotte Brontë, whose development of what we might call "domestic gothic" focuses particularly on ways in which uncanny relationships disrupt the very possibility of a functional "home."

The seventh chapter considers how gothic fiction opens up into stories of national and colonial identity. Freud's *Unheimlich* gradually metamorphoses into Homi Bhabha's "unhomely," a term that for Bhabha describes the inevitably doubled sense of "home" that characterizes the life of a colonial subject. Charlotte Smith's efforts to define English identity at the very moment of the American colonies' rebellion sit interestingly alongside Charles Brockden Brown's efforts to define American identity in a novel set just a little before the rebellion (though written just after it). *The Old Manor House* and *Wieland* both show us nations whose identities are defined but to some degree also undermined by their (past) colonial ties, and the double-edged nature of those connections are but a prelude to the painfully unsettling experience portrayed in Matthew Lewis's *Journal of a West India Proprietor*. Lewis's *Journal* is a nonfictional text, yet it without question has a place in this discussion, for it demonstrates clearly how gothic fiction shaped eighteenth- and nineteenth-century understandings of lived experience and vice versa.

My final chapter discusses novels by the Canadian writers Margaret Atwood and Ann-Marie Macdonald, whose responses to the gothic engage the tradition and at the same time show us ways to move beyond it. Feminist, postmodern, and post-colonial, these writers envision a world in which differences – of gender, of race, of nationality – are eventually embraced rather than eradicated. A coda provides an overview of the movement by which gothic gradually became a major focus for literary critics, paying particular attention to the feminist reinvigoration of gothic studies that began in the 1970s and continues today, as discussions of gender come into dialogue with discussions of race, class, nationalism, imperialism and more.

1

Patriarchal Narratives in the Work
of Horace Walpole, Clara Reeve,
and Sophia Lee

The Structure of Patriarchy

Early gothic novels make absolutely clear the genre's concern with exploring, defining, and ultimately defending patriarchy.[1] Patriarchy is a term
that can seem to lack critical force, perhaps because it has so often been
used to talk rather impressionistically about any sort of social structure that
seems to be run by men. Such uses of the term are not entirely inaccurate, but
they flatten out the historical specificity and richness that it should rightly conjure
up. When Walpole published the "first" gothic novel in the mid-1760s, he was
writing at the end of nearly a century of debates about whether human society
was intrinsically patriarchal or whether it was in fact the result of a social contract among its members.

Carol Pateman has forcefully summarized and critiqued the debate between
the patriarchalists and the contract theorists, and in the following pages I present
those parts of her argument that are most salient to a reading of gothic novels.[2]
As Pateman reminds us, the most extreme version of the patriarchal argument
had been put forward in Sir Robert Filmer's *Patriarcha* (1680). Published at the

height of the Exclusion Crisis in Britain, when Parliament had made repeated efforts to ensure that the Catholic James II would not succeed to the throne, and written much earlier, probably during the period leading up to the beheading of Charles I, this treatise is an unwavering argument for the divine right of kings to rule over their people.[3] Filmer locates the derivation of monarchy in literal patriarchy or fatherhood, reaching back to the Bible for his precedents, and citing Adam as the first patriarchal ruler. Adam's patriarchal authority was that of a father first and king second; as Filmer writes, "not only Adam but the succeeding patriarchs had, by right of fatherhood, royal authority over their children" (1991: 6). Logic dictates that the roles of father and king would become distinct from each other when a king's subjects began to include more than his biological descendants, and Filmer himself acknowledges that by the time he is writing it "may seem absurd to maintain that kings now are the fathers of their people" (1991: 10). He clings to the connection, however, arguing that kings "either are, or are to be reputed as the next heirs to those progenitors who were at first the natural parents of the whole people, and in their right succeed to the exercise of supreme jurisdiction" (1991: 10). Scholars of Filmer have argued that, where "traditional patriarchal argument" made an analogy between the roles of king and father, he went further, "claiming that paternal and political power were not merely analogous but *identical*" (Pateman 1988: 24).[4] This conflation of the roles of father and king creates logical problems, however, for "if fathers were the same as kings, wielding the same absolute power, then there could be no 'king', merely a multitude of father-kings" (Pateman 1988: 84).

Alternatives to what Pateman describes as Filmer's "classic patriarchalism" came most powerfully in the work of those philosophers who argued that human society was the result of a social contract. Thomas Hobbes, John Locke, and Jean-Jacques Rousseau were among the principal proponents of contract theory, and over time they succeeded in shifting radically the ways in which social organization was understood. Pateman credits Locke with formulating the "historically decisive" response to Filmer when he proposed distinguishing between "paternal power" and "political power" (Pateman 1988: 85), and so doing away with the problem of the "father-kings."

Where Filmer had insisted that people were born subject to a patriarchal rule that went as far back as Adam, Locke, in his *Second Treatise on Government* (1690), argued that they existed in "a *State of perfect Freedom* to order their Actions, and dispose of their Possessions, and Persons, as they think fit, within the bounds of the Law of Nature, without asking leave, or depending upon the Will of any other Man" (Locke 1988: 269 [II, §4]). The individual's movement from this state of nature into a civil society occurs with the making of a "Compact" among people "agreeing together mutually to enter into one Community, and make one Body Politick" (1988: 276–7 [II, §14]). While this "body politic" is composed

9

entirely of men, it marks an advance on Filmer's vision of society because it is recognized as a cultural rather than a natural formation, because it is egalitarian, and because it is seen as distinct from the domestic sphere of the family. Locke articulates a seemingly revisionist view of domesticity as well, arguing that the *"first Society* was between Man and Wife" and resulted from a "voluntary Compact" whose "chief End" is "Procreation" (1988: 319 [II, §§77–8]), while the family they produce is one which is shaped not by "Paternal Power" but by "Parental Power" (1988: 303f [II, §§52f]), in which "the *Mother* too has her share with the *Father*" (1988: 310 [II, §64]). A second look at his redefinitions of both the political and domestic spheres shows that patriarchy had not been so much left behind, however, as redefined.

Pateman argues convincingly that Filmer's classic patriarchalism is not abandoned but modified in the contract theory defined by Locke and others. Filmer was aware that "[s]ons do not spring up like mushrooms" (cited in Pateman 1988: 87), and that men's domination of women is therefore founded in *"sex-right or conjugal right"* even more than in the *"right of fatherhood"* (Pateman 1988: 87). He did his best to downplay women's role in procreation, however, presenting the father as the parent who gives life and the mother as simply the "vessel" who enables him to do so. The contract theorists necessarily modified this view of male (pro)creative power when they ceased to see the state as a family, though perhaps not with the consequences one might have expected. In their view, men were no longer perpetuating a social order through their sexual relations with women, but, rather, were producing it without the help of women at all. Seeking to wrest power from the single father/king and vest it in all men, the contract theorists created a model of civil society based not in paternal but in fraternal authority: not fatherhood but brotherhood provides the conceptual frame for Locke's civil society (Pateman 1988: 102–3). Thus came about what Pateman has called "perhaps the greatest tale of men's creation of new political life" (1988: 36), and a social vision that is even more masculinist than the one it replaced. Women are no longer needed even as vessels in the birthing of this new state order, and are important only as vessels of birthing in the domestic order, where Locke's vision of the father and mother as equal partners is severely undercut by his assertion of a husband's "Conjugal Power" over his wife (Locke 1988: 174 [I, §48]).

Considering Pateman's analysis of late seventeenth- and eighteenth-century debates about the nature of social and self-government, a reader of gothic novels cannot but notice her insistence on the fact that patriarchy persists – albeit with changes – from the seventeenth century to the eighteenth, and, still more importantly, that it changes in ways that ever more effectively exclude women from participation in the social order.[5] For gothic novels are all about patriarchies, about how they function, what threatens them, what keeps them going. And what becomes ever clearer as one reads these novels is that patriarchy is not only the subject of gothic novels, but is itself a gothic structure. Patriarchy inevitably celebrates a male creative power that demands the suppression – and sometimes the outright sacrifice – of women.

The Tie to Sensibility

The second half of the eighteenth century has long been known as the "age of sensibility" (Frye 1956), with "sensibility" referring to a capacity for strong and generally sympathetic feeling. "Sensibility" is sufficiently imprecise in its connotations that it often slides over into its near synonym, "sentimentality" (Todd 1988: 6–10), though sufficiently precise that its opposition to the term "sense" – meaning "common sense" or "good sense" or rational thought – is always clear. While *"sensibility* is associated with the body" and *"sentiment* with the mind" (Van Sant 1993: 4), that distinction tends to blur when one studies how the terms were generally used, and even current criticism does not always keep the two rigorously distinct.

The period's fascination with the "sensible" and the "sentimental" stems from a range of well-researched sources, usefully summarized by Claudia Johnson, whose work I draw on here. In part the interest came from medicine, which was increasingly interested in the nervous system of the human body, and believed that we register experience in the very fibres of our being. In part it came from religious debates about the innate "goodness or badness of human nature" (Johnson 1995: 12). And in part it came from the political contexts in which those debates were taking place, arguing for "sociable man's sensitivity. . . . Because the subjects of the state are sensitive to each other's approval and disapproval – craving the former and avoiding the latter – they observe and sustain shared customs without requiring the intervention of authoritarian rule" (Johnson 1995: 13). The explicit politics of the sensible and sentimental shade into the politics of what Johnson describes as " 'polite culture,' where 'polite' refers principally to the increased presence of and deference to women in social life, and to the belief that the sociable commingling of the sexes promoted the polish and refinement of men' " (Johnson 1995: 13).

For the reader of gothic novels, what is particularly interesting about sensibility is its relationship to gender. Insofar as it has been seen as a democratizing force (everyone has feelings), sensibility might be seen as a potential means of levelling the ground between men and women. More often it has been read as the province of women, while "men of feeling" risked being seen as feminized. Recent work on this topic has usefully complicated our vision, however.

Claudia Johnson has argued that sentimentality did not feminize men so much as it masculinized feeling. Focusing her analysis on novels of the 1790s, she argues that "the affective practices associated with [sentimentality] are valued *not* because they are understood as feminine, but precisely and only insofar as they have been recoded as masculine" (1995: 14). Thus women are left "without a distinct gender site" and are in effect "equivocal beings" (1995: 11). They may occupy an important position in sentimental culture, but their "presence . . . is not to be confused with [their] empowerment there" (1995: 14). Yet George Haggerty suggests that not just women, but also men, can become "equivocal beings" in a world defined by sensibility and sentimentality, and that "equivocation" may not be such a bad thing if what it does is disrupt the binary gender system that defines patriarchal culture (1998: 14). Where Johnson and other recent critics see sensibility and sentimentality as forces that maintain the status quo, Haggerty is more interested in the ways in which they threaten established social structures. Building on the work of Slavoj Žižek, Haggerty argues that sensibility is in effect a "symptom" of what a culture has repressed (1998: 3, 1999: 83–4). And what has been repressed is pleasure, desire, the possibility of social change. Sensibility can point the way to the dissolution of the self (in male writers), to the restructuring of gender relations (in female writers), and to different ways of being male and female (in both) (Haggerty 1998: ch. 3, 1999: introduction).

Pateman's work on patriarchy resonates alongside this recent work on sensibility and sentimentality. On the one hand, sensibility can be deployed to support patriarchal structures. Indeed, to support a political structure by emotional means seems particularly canny, for while emotions are in fact highly codified forms of cultural expression, they do not look like they are. They look natural, and thus the structure they support seems all the more inevitable. On the other hand, sensibility has the potential to disrupt not just patriarchal structures but the gender definitions in which patriarchy is grounded. In the remainder of this chapter, I will discuss three early gothic novels that explore the structure of patriarchy with increasing reference to sensibility.

The Castle of Otranto and *The Old English Baron*

Horace Walpole's *Castle of Otranto* (1764) and Clara Reeve's *The Old English Baron* (1777) are usefully paired.[6] Both portray what Pateman would describe as classic patriarchal societies and both focus explicitly on the question that is central to the survival of those societies: the passage of power through the male line. *The Castle of Otranto* was written first, and does much to establish what might be called the formula of gothic fiction. The novel opens with Manfred, the heir to a usurped kingdom, learning that a giant helmet has fallen from the sky and crushed his only son on his wedding day. Manfred struggles from that point on to retain his power over Otranto, seeking to control the women who can in various ways affect the line of succession: his wife Hippolita, his daughter Matilda, and the woman who was nearly his daughter-in-law, Isabella. His tyranny over these women is thwarted by a series of supernatural interventions, however, and by the end of the novel the rule of Otranto passes back to the rightful heir. Reeve's novel tells a similar story, but with considerably less supernatural apparatus. While both authors anatomize the basic principles of patriarchal government, making clear their interest in its structure, its workings, and its means of self-perpetuation, they do so in ways that suggest significantly different understandings of why and how it has come to exist.

The Castle of Otranto imagines a society much like those described in Filmer's *Patriarcha*. The identification between state and familial power is complete in Manfred, who rules both with the same iron hand. The conflict in *Otranto* is not over whether this form of patriarchy should exist, but over how corruption in such a patriarchy can be rooted out, how a patriarchy based on "might" can be replaced by one based on "right." Manfred's power has come down to him from his ancestor Ricardo, who had himself poisoned his master Alfonso and then taken on his role. Manfred's power stems from his ancestor's act of violence, in other words, and the events of the novel focus on his desperate attempts to maintain that power through further violence. Manfred's violence initially directs itself against the supernatural disasters that repeatedly threaten his rule, and especially against the peasant Theodore. When Theodore observes that the helmet on the statue of Alfonso the Good resembles the helmet that killed Conrad, inadvertently suggesting that the legitimate ruler of the house of Otranto has killed an illegitimate heir, Manfred responds by trying to kill Theodore in turn. Far more importantly, however, Manfred's violence directs itself against the seemingly natural world of the novel, and especially against the women who populate it. Manfred has to rely on women to perpetuate his rule, and works to control them in any way he can.

From the moment that Conrad is killed, Manfred knows that his family's hold on the throne of Otranto is jeopardized, for he has no male heir. When he is reminded of the wife who provided him with his one sickly and now dead son, he cries out, "Curse on Hippolita!. . . . forget her from this moment, as I do" (p. 22). When his daughter Matilda tries to comfort him following the death of Conrad, he responds only by saying, "Begone, I do not want a daughter" (p. 21). Even as he had tried to kill Theodore, so he rhetorically does away with both his daughter and his wife in order to make room for the one woman who can give him an heir: Isabella, who was to have married his son and whom he now decides to pursue himself, shifting from prospective father-in-law to prospective husband in an instant. The violence he directs at Isabella is the most extreme we have seen yet, for when his arguments for their marriage draw only horrified rejections

from her, he literally chases her through the castle and into a series of subterranean tunnels by which she eventually escapes. The confusion at the end of the
novel, when Manfred stabs a woman whom he believes to be Isabella but who
in fact turns out to be Matilda, makes clear the terrible cost of his actions. The
figuratively incestuous penetration of his daughter kills her and ends his rule as
well. His world literally collapses around him.[7]

Manfred needs women to perpetuate his line of descent, but does not want
to accord them any power. Were there a way to perpetuate the patriarchy
without women, Manfred might be happy, and while Manfred cannot accomplish
this miracle, Walpole can. When the walls of the castle come down around
Manfred, and "the form of Alfonso, dilated to an immense magnitude, appear[s]
in the centre of the ruins" to set things to rights, one understands that the patriarchal order will be perpetuated not by living women but by dead men (p. 108).
Alfonso's ghost appears to tell the story of his ancestor's death, as well as to pro-
claim Theodore his rightful heir. By the time Theodore ventures to produce his
own mother's written testimony to all that has been said, even that has been
deemed superfluous.

Importantly, Walpole knows that this effacement of women is a literal impossibility, even as he knows that his turn to the supernatural is incredible, and he
takes pains to draw attention to these facts. Alfonso's appearance is the last in a
series of notably two-dimensional supernatural events that begins with the
appearance of the giant helmet on the first page of the novel, and the gradual
re-membering of the body of Alfonso the Good is also a remembering of his
story. This act of remembering is arguably intended to do justice to the rightful
heirs of Otranto, even as it just as arguably does an injustice to the women who
bore them. In the context of the plot, in other words, it would seem to be an act
of high seriousness, and so one must wonder why it tends to appear to readers
as something akin to comedy. Why should the body of the patriarch "excite
laughter," to use Clara Reeve's phrase? (p. 5). Because patriarchy is laughable?
Perhaps, but a little more subtlety is in order. What provokes a smile here is the
obviously artificial nature of the construct.[8] The more clearly one sees the body
of Alfonso – the body of the patriarch, and, by extension, the body of patriarchy
– the more comprehensible it becomes. And the more comprehensible it
becomes, the less frightening it becomes. One might think here of Edmund
Burke's observation that fear – hallmark of those experiences that he called
sublime – grows out of obscurity, while "a clear idea is . . . a little idea" (1968:
63). By the end of the novel, the big body of patriarchy may still be terrifying to
the characters within the novel, but it has been brought well within the grasp of
the novel's readers, who have the advantage of contemplating that body in its
entirety.

Clara Reeve was one of the first readers of Walpole, and she found his practice of building up suspense only to subvert it with a ludicrously literal supernatural event disconcerting. Perhaps she did not see Walpole's interest in how the supernatural enabled but also exposed the paradoxes of a patriarchal social order that wanted to do away with women, or perhaps she was simply not willing to understand the exposure of patriarchy as a convincing critique of it. Feeling that Walpole should have produced terror through and through, Reeve responded to him by writing *The Champion of Virtue; a Gothic Story*, which appeared in 1777, and a year later was republished with the title by which most readers know it today, *The Old English Baron*. She acknowledges her novel to be "the literary offspring of the Castle of Otranto, written upon the same plan, with a design to unite the most attractive and interesting circumstances of the ancient Romance and modern Novel, at the same time it assumes a character and manner of its own, that differs from both" (p. 3). Her aim is to bring together "a sufficient degree of the marvellous, to excite the attention; enough of the manners of real life, to give an air of probability to the work; and enough of the pathetic, to engage the heart in its behalf" (p. 4). In her view, Walpole had accomplished two out of three, but had a "redundancy" of the marvellous thanks to "machinery . . . so violent, that it destroys the effect it is intended to excite" (p. 4). Where Walpole had used an overblown supernatural to at least hint that patriarchy could be seen as a comically imaginative construct, Reeve's insistence that the supernatural be "kept within the utmost *verge* of probability" (p. 4) results in a far less laughable, and so far more conservative, view of the patriarchal politics that are also at the heart of her novel.

Like Walpole's novel, Reeve's tells a story of patriarchy disrupted, showing us one man who has come to power through crimes not his own, and another who has been deprived of that power through those same crimes. Where Walpole relies on the supernatural from the start, however, Reeve – true to her own principles – invokes it seldom and with relative subtlety. She relies on a vocabulary that moves in small degrees from realism, through what one might call the surreal, to the supernatural in telling the story of how Edmund – counterpart to Walpole's Theodore – comes to be recognized as the true heir of Lovel.[9]

When Reeve's novel opens, the Baron Fitz-Owen reigns in the castle of Lovel, having purchased it from his brother-in-law, who had in turn inherited it from his deceased brother. Fitz-Owen has taken Edmund into his household, and while Edmund is but the "son of a cottager" (p. 17), he nonetheless outshines everyone else in the family. Reeve emphasizes the fact that Edmund's noble blood manifests itself in both his good looks and his temperament. His striking resemblance to his father gains him the immediate attention of Sir Philip Harclay, who had been a close friend of the deceased Lord Lovel; the Baron Fitz-Owen comments that Edmund's "uncommon merit, and gentleness of manners, distinguishes him from those of his own class" (p. 17); even the servant Joseph says to Edmund, "I cannot help thinking you were born to a higher station than you now hold" (p. 25). When the time comes for Edmund to prove his identity, these inborn qualities – along with the solid empirical evidence provided by his adoptive mother, and discovered in the castle itself – do much to help him make his case.

Empirical evidence alone does not restore Edmund's patrimony, however. Reeve turns from the rational to the irrational – but not yet the supernatural – when she assigns to dreams some of the revelations that Walpole gave to supernatural agents. Only a few pages into the novel, Sir Philip Harclay has "strange and incoherent dreams" that foretell much of the novel's plot (p. 14). Similarly, Edmund's first clue that he really is the heir of Lovel comes to him during the first night he spends in a supposedly haunted chamber, when he dreams that he is visited by "a Warrior, leading a Lady by the hand," who identify him as their child, announce that they are "employed in [his] preservation," and then leave him to visions that again predict what actually happens in the novel (pp. 44–5). Reeve's use of dreams recalls but revises Walpole's account of writing *The Castle of Otranto*:

> Shall I even confess to you what was the origin of this romance? I waked one morning in the beginning of last June from a dream, of which all I could recover was, that I had thought myself in an ancient castle (a very natural dream for a head filled like mine with Gothic story) and that on the uppermost bannister of a great staircase I saw a gigantic hand in armour. In the evening I sat down and began to write, without knowing in the least what I intended to say or relate. (p. ix)[10]

Both Walpole and Reeve connect the supernatural with dreams. Walpole simply does away with the framework of the dream, thereby exposing the irrationality and implausibility of human experience. In contrast, Reeve holds on to that framework for at least a while, straddling the boundary between the rational world she wishes to depict and the irrational qualities she knows it to include, and perhaps even stretching or blurring our definitions of rational and irrational in the process.[11]

Reeve does not rest in that half-way position for ever, but aids Edmund's progress toward self-knowledge as well as power by allowing him to be guided by a series of supernatural signs that help lead him to the truth about his heritage. Collapsing armor "calls" him to the room in which his parents will later prove to be buried (p. 52); a groan from beneath the floorboards where his father's body lies inspires him to go out and seek empirical evidence of who his parents really were (pp. 52–4); the groans and ghostly appearance of the murdered Lord Lovel drive those who would thwart Edmund's purposes from the room (p. 78);

the doors of the castle of Lovel fly open of their own accord when Edmund finally enters the castle with proof of his heritage (pp. 130–1). As if to qualify even these minor supernatural incidents, however, Reeve takes pains elsewhere in the novel to render them ever so slightly ironic. When Edmund leaves the castle to seek the assistance of Sir Philip Harclay in proving his lineage, he deliberately mystifies his departure so that the supposedly haunted room in which he has been staying – and which really does hold the secret of his paternity – will not be disturbed by other members of the household. He disappears "in the dead of night" in a way that is meant to "terrify and confound all the family" (p. 64), leaving a note for the Baron from the "guardian of the haunted apartment" along with the key and instructions to protect it "until the right owner shall come" (p. 71). That some of the family immediately suspect Edmund of writing the note further emphasizes Reeve's tendency to bring common sense to bear on the seemingly supernatural.

Reeve takes care to distinguish her work from Walpole's, though in the end Walpole's supernatural and Reeve's dreams and other irrational events serve very similar purposes. Like Walpole, Reeve uses these supernatural events to establish the proper shape of patriarchy, reconstructing and ensuring the continuance of the system almost entirely without the help of women. Indeed, Reeve is even more conservative than Walpole in her imagining of this possibility, for where Walpole clearly made fun of it even as he indulged himself in imagining it, Reeve does no such thing. Hers is a world in which female authority is not even a problem to be handled, but is simply not there at all, at least not to any appreciable degree. Reeve's novel makes the relationships between men and women that will be so fundamental to the action of later gothic novels secondary to the relationships between men who structure the patriarchy.

In its focus on male–male relationships, Reeve's novel describes a world like those discussed by Eve Kosofsky Sedgwick (1985), who has argued that "large-scale social structures" – like patriarchal societies – function much like erotic triangles in which two men are interested in a single woman who stands between them. The relationship that matters most in the triangle is not either of the male–female relationships that one sees at first glance. Rather, it is the relationship between the two men, who are rivals for the one woman, and have what Sedgwick describes as a "homosocial" connection with each other (1985: 25). Sedgwick's discussion of the relationship between the homosocial and the homosexual makes clear that the two exist on a not always obvious continuum with each other, and so opens the way to a reading of desire focused on same-sex as well as opposite-sex relations in Reeve's novel.[12]

While one can argue that the most important relationships in *The Castle of Otranto* are the father–son ties that perpetuate patriarchy, their primacy emerges clearly only at the end of the novel. In contrast, *The Old English Baron* focuses on relationships between men from the start (Haggerty 1998). These relationships at times take the form of rivalry, even of enmity, yet those at the heart of the novel are notable above all for being built on great affection. Edmund's connection to his servant Joseph is one such tie; his attachment to the priest Oswald is another. Among the most important are those with his "two paternal friends," Baron Fitz-Owen and Sir Philip Harclay (p. 146). Early in the novel, Edmund responds to the possibility that he will have to leave the Baron's household with a speech so expressive of his heartfelt desire to stay where he is that he moves himself, the Baron, and Sir Philip to tears. The Baron comments on how "this boy engages the heart" (p. 20), even as Sir Philip had earlier described how Edmund's "strong resemblance . . . to a certain dear friend" had initially "touched [his] heart in [Edmund's] favor" (p. 19). These men are linked through affective bonds that only grow stronger as the novel progresses, reaching a peak when Edmund goes to Sir Philip with evidence that he is in fact the son of that "dear friend" he so much resembles.

> Sir Philip grew every moment more affected by the recital; sometimes he clasped his hands together, he lifted them up to heaven, he smote his breast, he sighed, he exclaimed aloud; when Edmund related his dream, he breathed short, and seemed to devour him with attention; when he described the fatal closet, he trembled, sighed, sobbed, and was almost suffocated with his agitations: But when he related all that passed between his supposed mother and himself, and finally produced the jewels, the proofs of his birth, and the death of his unfortunate mother – he flew to him, he pressed him to his bosom, he strove to speak, but speech was for some minutes denied: He wept aloud . . . (p. 86)

The remarkable intensity of this scene is not matched elsewhere in the novel. Its portrait of the relationship between Sir Philip and Edmund suggests the primacy of father–son bonds, whose importance in the novel is also marked simply by the fact that Edmund has no fewer than four father figures (in addition to the Baron and Sir Philip, there are also Andrew Twyford, the cottager who discovers him as an abandoned infant and takes him into his household, and the murdered Lovel, who was Edmund's biological father).

Insofar as Sir Philip's strong tie to Edmund derives from the latter's strong resemblance to his deceased father, one can also read their connection as one that testifies to the importance of male friendship,[13] and a similarly intense friendship between men is seen in the relationship between Edmund and William, the second son of Baron Fitz-Owen. Early in the novel we read that the Baron Fitz-Owen's sons "doat upon" Edmund, "especially Master William, who is about his own age," and that connection only deepens over time (p. 15). William goes to fight the French with Edmund as his "attendant," "treat[ing] him in public as his principal domestic, but in private as his chosen friend and brother" (p. 26). His "dear friend William" is the only person with whom Edmund communicates individually when he leaves the Baron's castle to seek Sir Philip's support in regaining the Lovel estate, and when he has finally acceded to the estate, we read that "William and Edmund renewed their vows of everlasting friendship" in the same moment that we learn of the "mutual vows" that guarantee Edmund's marriage to William's sister Emma.

That pairing of the vows between Edmund and William with those between William and Emma is not accidental. Female characters figure minimally in this novel (as Haggerty 1998 also notes), and only when their appearance will help to ensure the reproduction and maintenance of the patriarchal line. We read briefly of Edmund's biological mother, the late Lady Lovel, who is remembered above all for dying at the moment she gave birth to her son; Margery Twyford, Edmund's adoptive mother, functions primarily to legitimate his claim to the Lovel estate; Lord Clifford's daughter, otherwise unnamed, is in part a bargaining chip that helps resolve the political tangles brought about by Edmund's claiming of his title. Emma's place in this limited world of women reinforces this general pattern but is somewhat more complex.

Heterosexual relationships facilitate but also screen the homosocial relationships that are more primary, and one does not have to look hard to see that Edmund's relationship with Emma is linked to his relationship with William. When Edmund requests Emma's hand in marriage, he states, "I never loved any woman but her; and, if I am so unfortunate as to be refused her, I will not marry at all. . . . Give me your lovely daughter! Give me also your son, my beloved William!" (p. 126). He will have Emma or no one, perhaps because only with Emma can he have William. In wrapping up the stories of its various characters, the novel tells us that Edmund's "third son was called William; he inherited the fortune of his uncle of that name, who adopted him, and he made the castle of Lovel his residence, and died a batchelor" (p. 152). William the uncle is figuratively identified with his nephew of the same name, and in that merged figure we see Edmund's beloved, his son, his heir, and in some sense a double for himself.

By its conclusion, *The Old English Baron* demonstrates the shaping of not one but two patriarchal lines. Edmund's discovery of his paternity and his marriage to Emma ensures the production of biological successors. At the same time, Edmund's friendship with William creates a successor of another kind, for William junior is in a sense their child as well. Insofar as he represents both his father (biologically) and his uncle (in his name), he is their offspring, and a testimony to the productive power of male relationships in a patriarchal society that relies less on women than on dreams, ghosts, and otherworldly revelations for its survival.

Finally, it is useful to consider how Reeve and Walpole think about their projects, specifically about how their discussions of their own literary lineage relate to their thinking on the subject of lineage more generally. Walpole's self-presentation is the more obviously complicated, given that his novel initially appeared as an anonymous translation of an existing Italian manuscript written by one Onuphrio Muralto, and only in the second edition was claimed by Walpole as his own. Walpole's reluctance to reveal himself as the author of *Otranto* speaks in part of his concern about how the novel would be received, but also plays into the novel's interest in the fragility of patriarchal stories and the little reason we have to trust the lineages they work so hard to preserve. What Walpole could not do, Reeve can, however. Like Walpole, she does not reveal herself as author of her novel until the publication of the second edition, though her reasons for doing so are somewhat different. Reeve's decision suggests her understanding of how difficult it was to be both a "proper lady" and a "woman writer" (Poovey 1984) in the patriarchal world in which she lived. It is ironic that, in emulating the strengths and correcting what she takes to be the weaknesses in Walpole's story, her novel shows us just how to render patriarchy secure.[14]

The Recess

While both Walpole and Reeve expose but also endorse the workings of patriarchal society, Sophia Lee's *The Recess* does not.[15] Published over the years 1783–5, *The Recess* is a stunning accomplishment. Relatively early in the gothic tradition, it brings together a number of what would over time became identified as its signature issues: an overarching interest in the workings of a patriarchal society, the haunting of the present by the past, the entrapment of women, and an interest in the extent to which sensibility contributes to or alleviates that entrapment.[16] It explores all of these issues in a more explicitly political context than most of its successors, through a narrative that is rooted in the historical rivalry between Elizabeth I and Mary Queen of Scots for the throne of England, and develops into a fictional narrative about the making of both English history and women's authority.[17]

In focusing her novel on Elizabeth I and Mary Stuart, Lee ensured that her readers would direct their thinking about patriarchy, women, and power to a particular set of questions. At the most general level, the fact that Elizabeth and Mary are both women asks readers to consider the relationship between England's explicitly patriarchal system of government and the women who contended for the role of "patriarch." More specifically, the fact that Elizabeth was Protestant while Mary was Catholic asks readers to think about Renaissance England's uneasy positioning between these two religions (a timely issue, given the violence of the anti-Catholic "Gordon Riots" in 1780),[18] and to consider the relationship between the identity of the nation and the identity of its ruler. Most specifically, given that Elizabeth's and Mary's stories emerge in and alongside first-person narratives supposedly written by Mary's fictional daughters, we are asked to consider what it might mean to talk about public and private identity in the lives of women who could imagine themselves in positions of political power.

The Recess begins from the fictional premise that, during her imprisonment by Elizabeth, Mary secretly took as her husband the duke of Norfolk and by him had twin daughters, Matilda and Ellinor. Because their mother remains imprisoned while their father first fights and then dies in his battle against Elizabeth, the infant girls are spirited off to the recess of the title – in actuality a secret dwelling built in the ruins of a convent (p. 22) – to be raised in safety. They learn the story of their birth just a little while before they leave the recess to live in a larger world, and, once in that larger world, they are plagued by a series of disasters.

The sisters' problems all begin with their connection to Mary. Mary's claim to the English throne means that they have one too, and, as Lee tells it, Elizabeth's execution of Mary is just the beginning of her effort to contain the threat that they pose. Political relationships between and among women thus motivate the novel's action at its deepest level, yet they are overlaid by romantic relationships that complicate and to an extent screen the novel's politics, as the sisters develop connections with Elizabeth's two favorites, the earl of Leicester and the earl of Essex. When Leicester secretly marries Matilda, he marries a woman whom he knows to be both a political and a sexual rival to Elizabeth, and the first half of the novel turns on the complications caused by this marriage. When Essex forms a secret attachment to Ellinor, he does basically the same thing, and much of the novel's second half turns on the problems caused by this situation. In both cases, the straightforward political contest between Elizabeth and the sisters is transformed into a sexual contest that shifts attention away from state politics to personal life.

The first generation: Mary and Elizabeth

The historical figures of Mary Stuart and Elizabeth Tudor have been imagined and reimagined over time, and *The Recess* participates in this effort. As one would expect in a story told by the supposed daughters of Mary Queen of Scots, Lee's narrative is one that glorifies Mary and villainizes Elizabeth. Jayne Elizabeth Lewis has written of the eighteenth century's transformation of Mary into a sentimental heroine who was understood more as an icon of "vulnerable femininity" (1998: 130) than as a Catholic queen who posed a significant threat to the

English throne (1998: 103–23). In contrast to the sentimental Mary, whose helpless situation inspires sympathy in all those around her, Elizabeth emerges as a passionate woman whose power inspires those around her with fear, approaching the stature of what in the next chapter I will discuss as a sublime figure.

Mary's story is told by Mrs. Marlow, the woman who has functioned as a surrogate mother to Mary's daughters, and it is above all a tale of successive imprisonments. We first read of Mary "imprisoned by her subjects as an accessory to the murder of her husband" (p. 24). She manages to escape her prison and throws herself on Elizabeth's mercy, only to find herself "in a worse condition than if she had still remained in her own country" (pp. 24–5), imprisoned at Bolton Castle in Yorkshire. Finally, we read of her courtship by the duke of Norfolk, whose ambition to marry her because of her rank is seemingly transformed into a desire to marry her for love, yet the marriage – accomplished in secret – is judged an "error, which heightened every affliction, and gave new pangs to a long, long captivity" (p. 28). All of these "misfortunes" are said to have "had their source in love" (p. 28), and Mary's captivity is thus defined as a product of sensibility. She is a true gothic heroine.

As Lewis has argued, Mary not only acts on the basis of her own sensibility, but inspires equally feeling responses in others. When Matilda sees her mother walking in the garden that is a part of her prison, supported by her maids, with "beads and cross . . . her only ornaments," she reports that Mary "mingled the Saint with the Queen," and that she and Ellinor "wept – we incoherently exclaimed – and striking ourselves eagerly against the bars, seemed to hope some supernatural strength would break them" (p. 75). It is as if Matilda and Ellinor are the prisoners, rather than Mary, and while they attract her attention by putting their hands through the bars of the window, the connection lasts only a moment before she walks away.

As this exchange shows, Mary's legacy to her daughters is not only their royal blood, which guarantees their imprisonment in the recess, at Kenilworth, at court, and in their lives beyond the court. That legacy consists also of their conventionally defined femininity, their propensity to act on and so eventually be trapped by their feelings.[19] As if she understands the danger of legacies for women, Elizabeth does her best to detach herself from the dangers of inheritances, and to define herself in isolation from those around her.

Susan Frye (1993) has written about how the historical Elizabeth grappled with the seeming disjunction between her roles as a public ruler and private citizen, tracing Elizabeth's efforts to redefine what it meant to be a patriarchal ruler, and elucidating the "competition for representation" that followed her death. Lee participates in this "competition for representation" of Elizabeth, yet shifts the ground of debate significantly when she questions the legitimacy of

Elizabeth's reign not because she is a woman, but because of the kind of woman she is.

Elizabeth does not appear in the novel until near the end of the first volume, though she is discussed from early on. First to mention her is Mrs. Marlow, who portrays the queen as a woman who was motivated by fear to order the sisters' father beheaded and their mother imprisoned, a woman whose court the girls – according to their father's command – were never to see. Robert Dudley, the earl of Leicester and a long-time favorite of Elizabeth, predictably offers a more sympathetic account of the queen. He does not so much deny Elizabeth's penchant for power as contextualize it, talking about the time she herself spent imprisoned by the order of her predecessor Mary Tudor, and her subjection during that time to the unwanted attentions of the earl of Devonshire (whom Leicester helped her to fend off) (pp. 44–8). Elizabeth here looks like another gothic heroine in the making, and yet she refuses the role. She is neither helpless nor desirous of being ruled by her feelings, and, having acceded to the throne, she purports to be ruled by politics above all. As Leicester recalls, she had told him:

> that although she preferred me to all men existing, she could not by marrying make me happy, or be so herself; that in yielding to this weakness of her heart, she should forever sully her reputation for wisdom, which would always, while single, teach her how to manage other potentates, either by hope or fear; and that such a degradation in general opinion would too sensibly affect her. (p. 52)

When she later changes her mind and announces her desire to marry him, she leads into the topic by explaining that "now, when I have no potent enemy to fear, I may crown thy passion and indulge my own" (p. 94). The suggestion is that, because her political house is in order, she is at last free to act according to her affections, yet this vision is quickly recast: "A new plot I have discovered to release Mary, renders it absolutely necessary I should, by marrying, cut off her hopes and those of her party" (p. 94). Politics not only precede but also subsume personal affections, so fully that one is not even sure those affections really exist. Elizabeth's overt refusal to be ruled by her heart differentiates her from Mary, and could be seen as explaining her success as England's monarch. The rest of the novel tells another story, however, for if Lee's Elizabeth does not want to be ruled by her heart, Lee suggests that, to some degree, she is.

The single most notable characteristic of Lee's Elizabeth is her jealousy, which reveals itself in her dealings with her two favorites, the earl of Leicester and the earl of Essex. That jealousy surfaces when she first sees Mary as her rival for Leicester's affections, though all he has done is admire a miniature portrait of her, and while Leicester at that point describes Elizabeth as "jealous to excess of her power" (p. 50), he understands that her jealousy has a sexual basis as well.

This becomes clear when he conceals from her his his marriage to Lady Essex, having acknowledged that Elizabeth has "rigidly maintained over [him] the rights of a jealous lover, while she disclaimed the title" (p. 54). And when he conceals from her his subsequent marriage to Matilda, along with the far weightier secret that Matilda has a claim to the English throne, he is clearly motivated by a desire to evade both forms of jealousy.

Mary and Elizabeth thus offer two approaches to the shaping of history. In spite of her rank, Mary follows the dictates of patriarchy and plays the woman's traditional role. Using her rank, Elizabeth manipulates the patriarchy, but does not do away with it. The more severe critiques of the patriarchy come from the younger women of the novel, Matilda and Ellinor, whose repeated efforts to claim their place in that order ironically challenge it at the same time, albeit unsuccessfully. By the conclusion of the novel, all proofs of Matilda's and Ellinor's connections to the Queen of Scots have been destroyed, and the sisters' place in official history has been thoroughly effaced. Yet their autobiographical statements remain, providing an alternative version to official records, and making clear that the sisters have claimed agency and identity through their writing.

The second generation: Matilda and Ellinor

Part of the power of Lee's novel comes from her creation of the distinct and often opposed voices of Matilda and Ellinor. Matilda's narrative can seem to have greater authority, primarily because the novel as a whole takes the form of a letter that Matilda writes to a friend, in which Ellinor's narrative is embedded, and also because Ellinor's narrative trails off into madness. However, it would be a mistake to put more weight on the words of one sister than on those of the other, for their stories complement each other in their portraits of two very different experiences of – and responses to – oppression. Matilda tries to assert an identity built on her connections to her mother, her daughter, and the community of women that helps her to survive.[20] In contrast, Ellinor increasingly seeks to escape an identity that has functioned to oppress her.

The sisters begin life together, living partly in the "recess" of the title and partly in the abbey attached to it. The recess and the abbey together recall the once dominant Catholic culture that their imprisoned mother still represents, and clearly genders that culture as well. The recess itself is built on the ruins of a convent "once inhabited by nuns of the order of St. Winifred" (p. 22), which even then was linked to the monastery that was the precursor to the current abbey. The religious affiliations of these structures change over time, as the recess remains Catholic, while the abbey becomes the property of the Protestant Lord Scrope. The gender connotations of these spaces also grow more complicated, as the recess is taken over and enlarged by Catholic fathers, though I want to argue that its primary association with women persists into the time represented by the novel.

Its existence hidden even from those who inhabit the abbey to which it is attached, this subterranean home is the female and arguably maternal domain of Mrs. Marlow, sister to Lord Scrope as well as the only mother the sisters have ever known. The feminized character of the space is enhanced by its physical configuration, which Matilda recalls as the novel opens:

> This Recess could not be called a cave, because it was composed of various rooms; and the stones were obviously united by labor; yet every room was distinct, and divided from the rest by a vaulted passage with many stairs, while our light proceeded from small casements of painted glass, so infinitely above our reach we could never seek a world beyond; and so dim, that the beams of the sun were almost a new object to us when we quitted this retirement. (pp. 7–8)

Lest the identification of the recess as maternal still seem too easy, a reflexive linking of enclosed spaces with the enclosed space of the womb, Lee goes out of her way to make this connection still clearer.[21] When the sisters are forced to return to the recess after three years spent in the abbey, they enter through a secret passage. A storeroom in the abbey leads to stairs, passages, and at last into the recess through "a door the size of that portrait which first gave [Matilda] such singular sensations" (p. 15). The portrait in question could perhaps be that of the sisters' father, the duke of Norfolk, which they had earlier regarded with "veneration" and "surprising softness" (p. 9), but seems more likely to be that of Mary, Queen of Scots, which had inspired a far stronger reaction: "a thousand melting sensations," involuntary tears, and the certainty that the portrait "is but part of one great mystery" which will one day be revealed to them (p. 10). Without doubt, however, the portrait in question is one associated with the girls' parentage, and the most important thing about their parents is their maternal lineage – their connection with the Queen of Scots. Thus the physical entry into the recess is also the entry into that maternal history.

Throughout the novel, Matilda tries unceasingly to gain public recognition of the fact that Mary Stuart is her mother, and her life comes to seem merged with that of her mother in the process. That merging begins with the fact that she looks exactly like her mother (even as Ellinor looks exactly like their father), and is helped along by the fact that her way out of the recess comes when she meets Lord Leicester. Leicester is first mentioned in the novel as the person on whom the duke of Norfolk most relied in his efforts to free Mary and have Elizabeth recognize his marriage to her, and – as I mentioned above – he himself is at one point seen as a suitor to Mary. When the sisters meet him as he flees through the forest near the recess, Matilda offers him shelter in their underground home, and from that moment on is attached to him. The fact that he has just poisoned his wife and her lover should perhaps cast a pall over his speedy marriage to Matilda, which at the insistence of Father Anthony – the girls' guardian follow- ing the death of Mrs. Marlow – takes place before he leaves that sanctuary. In Matilda's eyes, however, the match is made for love, and she willingly agrees to keep it a secret in order to protect herself and her husband from the wrath of Elizabeth.

In linking her fate to that of Leicester, Matilda has in one sense found a way to move from the recess to a larger world, though in another she is perhaps still more confined than she has been. When she and Ellinor take up residence in Leicester's home at Kenilworth, fears of Elizabeth lead them to hide not only the fact of Matilda's marriage, but their very identities. Disguised as "young women educated in a Convent, who, not finding a call to the monastic life, came . . . to embellish the retirement of Lord Leicester by [their] musical talents" (p. 66), they appear before Elizabeth. Like Walpole's Theodore and Reeve's Edmund, however, they are unable to hide fully their noble blood. In a memorable scene, Matilda sings while Ellinor accompanies her on the lute, both hidden from the view of the company. The performance is so marvelous that the queen orders the curtain to be drawn aside to reveal the performers, and when she becomes suspicious about their identities Leicester tells a story about them that can do nothing to alleviate whatever fears Elizabeth may have. While he does not admit that they are the daughters of Mary Stuart, he does say that they are the chil- dren of his brother and Lady Jane Grey, hidden away in the now dead hope of again succeeding to the throne;[22] to this already complicated story, he adds that they should be told they are his illegitimate daughters. As Matilda quickly sees, his story places them "almost as near to the throne as [they] really stood" (p. 82), and she knows that Elizabeth is not taken in by the story when she says nothing, but simply makes them her maids of honor. There, thinks Matilda, she can bring about their "safe and silent ruin" (p. 82).

For Leicester and Matilda, that ruin comes when Elizabeth's offer to marry Leicester renders the discovery of his marriage imminent. At this point Matilda's need to protect herself from Elizabeth's persecution renders her life still more like her mother's, and her success in doing so renders the difference between them more palpable as well. She and Leicester flee, first back to the recess, where they are betrayed by one of Leicester's enemies (a former servant), but, helped by one of Matilda's friends (Rose Cecil), they go on to France, where they are betrayed by Matilda's Catholic relations, the Mortimer family. Leicester is killed, while the pregnant Matilda is forcibly taken by John Mortimer, son of the woman from whom she had expected protection, and put on a boat to Jamaica, where he owns a plantation.

As Matilda's horizons broaden to include not just England, but also France and Jamaica, so do those of the novel, becoming more explicitly political than they have been. The flight to France brings to the surface the religious tensions that have been lurking throughout the novel. While the sisters have a Catholic mother, were raised by the Catholic Mrs. Marlow and Father Anthony, and spent their early lives in a "recess," whose history as first a Catholic convent and then a Catholic monastery is well known to them, explicit questions of religious affiliation do not surface until Matilda actually finds herself in France. For a number of reasons, what she describes as her "fluctuating religious principles" (p. 128) here become firmly aligned with Protestantism.

The most obvious reason that Matilda turns from Catholicism to Protestantism concerns her husband. Her relation Lady Mortimer represents the marriage as invalid because it "want[s] the sanction of the Pope," then addresses this problem by arranging the murder of Lord Leicester in his bed, in the hope that Matilda will then renounce her errors and claim her place as the "head of the English Catholic party" (p. 127). Predictably, Matilda does just the reverse, responding to this conjunction of events by condemning a religion that would rely on "midnight tapers, suspended black, or waving plumes" to "relieve those eyes which seek in vain their only object" (p. 128). As important as these events, if not more so, is the fact that Matilda's embrace of Protestantism coincides with the execution of her mother at Elizabeth's command. Catholicism in this novel is the religion of the mother, and when she dies, so does all explicit allegiance to her faith. Implicitly, however, Matilda's Catholicism continues to surface at moments in the novel when she is most like the mother whose death she mourns.

Matilda's entrapment by Lady Mortimer is followed by similar treatment at the hands of Lady Mortimer's son, John, who abducts her, puts her on a boat, and takes her to his estate in Jamaica with the aim of forcing her to marry him. Matilda's unwanted interaction with the French is thus complicated by an even more unwanted interaction with the Spanish, who occupied Jamaica at the end of the sixteenth century, and with whom Mortimer is allied by marriage. Lee more or less conflates the Spanish and the French here, both Catholic countries and both known for their interest in gaining the throne of England, and initially seems to set both in opposition to the English Protestant Matilda.[23] The clear dichotomy quickly breaks down, however.

Matilda is saved from a forced marriage by a rebellion of Mortimer's slaves, who kill their master and would have killed his mistress too, had she not been saved by two of the rebels themselves: a Spaniard named Emmanuel (who timed the rebellion to free her) and a slave named Aimor. When the rebels are in turn defeated, Matilda is pictured sitting at the foot of a tree, the child she bore Lord Leicester on her lap, her hands reaching out to Emmanuel on the one hand and Aimor on the other. She describes herself as the "Queen of Sorrow" (p. 142), and her physical position echoes that of the Virgin Mary in her guise as the "Mater Dolorosa." In this moment of extreme vulnerability, she is strongly identified with both the Catholic Mary who is the mother of God, and with that other Catholic Mary who was her own mother.[24]

Matilda's identity thus continues to waver between Catholic and Protestant, but is now further complicated by her positioning between cultures and races as well. When the colonial governor imprisons her for what he takes to be her role in the rebellion, she spends eight years in jail, and is freed only through the intervention of the governor's mistress, a well-to-do black woman named Anana. Anana initially shows great kindness to Matilda's daughter Mary, and eventually – following the death of the governor – buys the freedom of the mother and daughter. This vision of interracial solidarity is perhaps fanciful, for white European women in the late eighteenth century were as much part of the colonial project as anyone, yet it makes clear Lee's sense that such solidarity is needed if women are to find a way past the constraints of the patriarchal society in which they live.[25]

The notion that female solidarity is necessary for women to escape the literal and figurative constraints on their lives pervades the book (Isaac 1996). Matilda relies on a series of women over the course of the novel – Mrs. Marlow, her sister, Lady Arundell at court, Rose Cecil in her flight to France, and Anana in the West Indies. These women are not immortal, however, and they die off one by one. By the time she returns to England, only her sister and Lady Arundell are still alive from among this group, and neither of them lives much longer. Matilda is at this point left with her daughter as her sole hope and support, and that bond breaks too in the novel's final movement, when her daughter is poisoned by the wife of a lover. Add to that the fact that this last crisis takes place in yet another prison, where Matilda's brother – who is also Elizabeth's successor – has confined them after destroying all evidence of their kinship to Mary Stuart, and the future seems bleak indeed. Yet, when there would seem to be no alternative to her entrapment and isolation, and finally the effacement of both herself and her story, Matilda finds a way. She retires to France – once again implicitly turning to the Catholicism that the novel officially rejects – and writes her story, addressing it to the daughter of the French ambassador to England. She thus ensures the existence of an alternative to the official narratives of the period, and a critique of England's patriarchy, if not a way out of it.

Matilda's life imitates that of her mother more than she might wish it to, and if neither she nor her daughter ever gains official recognition as Mary's heir, she at least survives her many trials. Her survival comes in part because she behaves so much like a typical gothic heroine.[26] While she transgresses a basic rule when she allows Leicester into the recess, she is thereafter fairly passive, finding her way out of one disastrous situation after another only because someone comes along to rescue her; the single exception to this pattern comes in her efforts to free herself and her daughter from their final incarceration at the earl of Somerset's castle. Ellinor's story is the more dire as well as the more radical, for she resists the role of gothic heroine far more than Matilda does. She is at times more active on her own behalf, while at others she is far more inclined to give up hope altogether. If she succeeds in escaping the literal as well as the figurative prisons in which she finds herself, the price is very high: she pays first with her sanity and finally with her life.

Ellinor's narrative picks up at the point at which the sisters' lives began to diverge – that is, at the point at which Matilda marries Leicester – and is remarkable for its reinterpretation of events already laid out by Matilda. In Ellinor's account, the admirable Leicester emerges as an ambitious and self-serving man who is not to be trusted, and is contrasted to the man with whom she forms an alliance – the earl of Essex. Ellinor's relationship with Essex is always tumultuous, for the two are attracted to each other from the start, but kept apart by a series of circumstantial problems. Their continued separation causes Ellinor to move in and out of states of madness, while Essex gradually ceases to behave as the queen wishes him to, and instead comes to be ruled by his heart.

The story of Ellinor's separation from Essex begins in earnest when Elizabeth has discovered Ellinor's connection to Mary Queen of Scots, and just after Matilda has fled to France with Leicester. Elizabeth's desire to protect her crown thus merges with her jealousy of both Leicester and Essex to determine the initial motive for her treatment of Ellinor. This conflation of the political with the personal persists, as Elizabeth has her agents trick Ellinor into signing a document disavowing her connection to Mary Queen of Scots, the reward for which was to have been Mary's life, though Elizabeth later has Mary executed anyway. Tied to this manipulation is Ellinor's forced marriage to the insipid Lord Arlington, which she is told will keep Essex from the death to which he would be sentenced for having been involved in a plot to free Mary. That Essex never was in any such danger is something Ellinor does not discover until much later.

This series of events precipitates Ellinor's madness, which finally emerges as a way of escaping the confines of her bodily existence. She describes her initial loss of sanity in this way: "the deep melancholy which had seized upon my brain soon tinctured my whole mass of blood – my intellects strangely blackened and confused, frequently realized scenes and objects that never existed, annihilating many which daily passed before my eyes" (p. 182). For the rest of her life, Ellinor will pass in and out of such states, fleeing the various traps by which she is confined. Her marriage, court politics, the circumstances of the moment disappear as she leaves behind the most fundamental of all traps, her embodied self. That self – female, forced to conform to the rules of the world in which she lives – is finally only a prison for Ellinor. And so, as Essex says, her "soul . . . like a frightened bird, forsakes its home when misery hovers over it" (p. 264).

With this pattern in mind, one understands why her encounters with Essex – fraught with danger as they always are – consistently result in her losing her identity in some way. At times, that self-loss takes the relatively conventional form of simply losing self-consciousness. Thus, when she sees Essex for the first time after her marriage to another man, she gradually loses control: "They told me, I suffered myself to be led to the chair of the Queen, who no sooner in the common form presented me her hand, than I haughtily repelled it, and fixing my eyes on her with a dreadful meaning, gave a deep groan, and sunk senseless at her feet" (pp. 187–8). Similarly, the next time she sees Essex, after both have been away from London for a considerable time, she experiences "fear" and "horror" (p. 220), feels herself "deeply disordered" (p. 203), succumbs to "agitation" and "sensibility" (p. 203), and then to "[a] suffocation more painful than fainting" (p. 203). Their meeting was accidental, yet she regrets that she does not altogether lose her "erring reason" when her husband unexpectedly finds them together, and does manage to faint away in an attempt to stop them from duelling (pp. 203–4).

More interesting are the forms of self-loss that emerge once Ellinor and Essex are both widowed, and so seemingly free to marry each other. Ellinor's former husband had arranged for her continued incarceration after his death, a prospect which nearly drives her mad again. This time the appearance of Essex revives her, but knowing that she cannot simply leave with him in her own person, she sends him on ahead and then plans her own escape. Significantly, she gets away from Arlington's family by faking her own death as well as the death of a servant, after which she is carried out of the castle in the casket of her servant, and has the satisfaction of seeing the servant mourned in her place.

Having effaced her own identity altogether, she re-emerges as a cross-dressed youth to follow Essex to where he is fighting in Ireland. This is Ellinor's colonial experience, a counterpart to Matilda's time in the West Indies, and she too ends up imprisoned – trapped in an enemy camp. She does not wait for a benefactor, however, but reincarnates herself yet again by drugging the commander of the camp, dressing in his clothing, and making her way to the English. She is thus temporarily reunited with Essex, but the two separate again so that Essex can seek out Elizabeth and explain why he has spent so long in Ireland, while she proceeds separately to England. She ends up shipwrecked in Scotland for many months, initially passing once again for a young man, and then for a young woman of rank, though she never reveals her true identity.

By the time Ellinor returns to England, Essex has been imprisoned in the Tower, and at this point she succumbs for the last time to madness. Long assumed dead by all, she is taken for a ghost when she wanders into the queen's chambers and berates her for having had Essex beheaded. Ellinor persists in this "undead" state some time longer, and eventually expires in front of a portrait of Essex, the same portrait she had been admiring when their unexpected meeting led to the duel between Essex and her husband. Essex is thus not fully present but only represented, even as Ellinor herself is not fully present when she expires in front of it, and in this juxtaposition one sees the pain of Ellinor's story. When she was functioning in the world as she was expected to, she (and arguably everyone else) was – as she said of herself and Matilda – "all an illusion" (p. 157). In her periods of madness, her presence was just as illusory, and no real indicator of her identity; as Margaret Doody has noted, "her madness is a simple reflection of what exists outside herself" (1977: 559). A substantive existence does not seem possible in Ellinor's world. What Essex called the "soul" is either trapped or driven out by appearances, with the result that the world is peopled by shadows, illusions, and ghosts, and can only be described as gothic.[27]

2

The Aesthetic of the Sublime in the Work of Matthew Lewis, Charlotte Dacre, and Charles Maturin

English interest in the sublime developed over the same half-century that saw the English monarchy come under attack in the Civil War, Cromwell's republican rule, and the Exclusion Crisis that followed the Restoration. In a world that was questioning the divine right of kings to rule, the aesthetic of the sublime provided a vocabulary for thinking about political power that did not announce itself as such, and that was therefore all the more effective in thinking about – and generally reinforcing – the traditional patriarchal structures that had come under attack. John Hall translated Longinus's *On the Sublime* in 1652, Boileau's influential French translation of the same text appeared in 1674, and yet another English translation appeared in 1698. Treatises on the sublime appeared regularly throughout the eighteenth century, the best known of which are still Edmund Burke's *Enquiry into the Origins of our Ideas Concerning the Sublime and Beautiful* (1757) and Immanuel Kant's discussion of the "Aesthetic of the Sublime" in his *Critique of Judgment* (1790).[1] Gothic novels draw on these discussions of the sublime – and its counterpart, the beautiful – in their explorations of how patriarchal societies sustain threats to their existence.

As theorized by Burke and Kant, the sublime is an experience that involves a confrontation between a perceiving subject and an overwhelmingly powerful object, the confusion of boundaries between subject and object, and finally a transcendent or totalizing vision that results from the confusion or blurring of those boundaries. According to Burke, the subject disappears involuntarily into the object, while according to Kant the subject asserts his or her superiority over the object by containing the object (or at least its idea) in his or her mind. In both cases, however, what matters most is that the difference between subject and object is to some degree effaced. That effacement of difference is the essence of the sublime experience as defined by these two thinkers.

Insofar as the sublime is associated with the effacement of difference, it is associated with the erasure of the historical world in which we live. For what is that if not a world constituted by differences – differences between subject and object, between one person and another, between one place and another, between one time and another? To close any of these gaps is to move from historical to sublime experience, and sublime experience is at the heart of the gothic.

Sublime experience thus seems to be opposed to historical experience. It transcends the historical, moving one outside the spatial and temporal confines of ordinary existence. Because it moves one to a world that is outside the reach of ordinary human existence, it is generally judged to be outside the reach of ordinary human language as well. Sublime experience is generally judged to be inexpressible experience. Finally, sublime experience is – at least as it is theorized by Burke, whose model of the sublime is most directly relevant to a reading of the gothic – *experience*. It is an *interaction* between subject and object and is therefore subjective. What one person experiences as sublime another may not.[2]

So what are the likely sources of sublime experience? As transgressive, subjective and elusive as the experience itself may be, eighteenth-century theorists were explicit about what might inspire it. In Burke's eyes, the root cause of all sublime experience is "terror." He writes:

> Whatever is fitted in any sort to excite the ideas of pain, and danger, that is to say, whatever is in any sort terrible, or conversant about terrible objects, or operates in a manner analogous to terror, is a source of the *sublime*; that is, it is productive of the strongest emotion which the mind is capable of feeling. . . . But as pain is stronger in its operation than pleasure, so death is in general a much more affecting idea than pain . . . (1968: 39–40)

Anything that inspires us with the terrifying idea of pain, danger, or death is sublime. Note, however, that terror must come from the realm of ideas rather than actual physical confrontations with what those ideas represent. Where pain, danger, and implicitly death are "simply painful when their causes immediately affect us," says Burke, "they are delightful when we have an idea of [them], without actually being in such circumstances" (1968: 51). Pain, danger, and death are not sublime in themselves. Rather, ideas of them inspire the sublime, and this refinement is important.

Sublime experience leads us toward transcendent experience, but in the end does not quite get us there. Nor would we want it to. Because the transcendence associated with the sublime might also be described as self-loss, one must wonder whether it is a truly desirable experience. Much more appealing is to imagine the possibility of loss but at the same time draw back from it, and this is the experience that Burke really describes. The sublime as Burke theorizes it is not inspired by one's actual experience of pain, danger, or death, but by one's imagining of them. Sublime experience thus emerges as self-contradictory, a seeming loss of self that is in fact self-willed and reasonably well controlled.[3]

Thus we come to the heart of the question. If the pleasure of reading gothic novels inheres in the combinations of terror and pleasure that come from contemplating the breaking of boundaries, the disappearance of the differential structures of our daily lives, what exactly do those breakdowns and disappearances look like? The chapter headings of Burke's discussion of this issue provide a checklist of possibilities. Terror can be inspired by "obscurity" that keeps us from having a "clear idea" of the danger that confronts us (pp. 58–64); it can come from "power" that leaves us "annihilated" (pp. 64–70); it might stem from a "privation" that overwhelms us (p. 71), a contemplation of "infinity" that does the same (pp. 72–4), a scene of "magnificence" (pp. 78–9), even certain kinds of light, color, sound, or taste (pp. 79–87). But this is all very abstract. Turning to gothic novels, one sees that sublimity often – though not always – derives from scenes of fantastic violence. Since that violence is very often directed against women, one can only conclude that these novels understand women as the embodiment of the "difference" that sublime experience eliminates.[4] The aesthetically privileged category of the sublime experience then emerges as a way of rendering acceptable the deaths of women, which are not the only sublime experiences in gothic novels, but are certainly key sublime experiences. I will come back to this thought, but for a quick test of its validity, think back to *The Castle of Otranto*, where the appearance of the superhuman Alfonso is as much comic as it is terrifying, while Manfred's stabbing of his daughter Matilda creates what might be read as the most sublime scene in the novel. Manfred breaks down multiple structures of difference with this single act, for his penetration of his daughter is figuratively incestuous, literally murderous, and based on the confusion of one woman with another. Manfred believes Matilda to be Isabella, and in killing one woman he figuratively kills them both, as well as the more generalized figure of female "difference" that they represent.

If sublimity can be seen as an aesthetically acceptable way of killing off women, it is also a way of killing off the beauty with which they are associated.

Sublimity and beauty have generally been perceived as opposed to each other; that is certainly how Burke seems to present them. In his analysis, sublimity grows out of an encounter with anything that is vast, obscure, irregular, uncontainable, and fundamentally isolating, while beauty is perceived in all that is small, smooth, subtly deviating from straight lines, comprehensible, and social. Not only are their sources in the world different, but they inspire equally different reactions in those who experience them. The sublime provokes terror, awe, admiration, and related emotions, while beauty inspires "love," says Burke, and this fact has everything to do with the power dynamic they provoke. If "we submit to what we admire, but we love what submits to us" (1968: 113), then anyone who experiences the sublime is oppressed by it, while anyone who perceives beauty feels himself or herself empowered by the experience.

Frances Ferguson suggests a different reading of the relationship between the sublime and the beautiful, arguing that, in Edmund Burke's work at least, sublimity is a necessary rebellion against the unnoticed and almost unnoticeable tyranny of beauty. Sublimity threatens us with danger and even death by exposing us to that which is excessive and overwhelming, but at least we recognize, and even get aesthetic pleasure from, that fact. Beauty, on the other hand, wins us over as the serpent won Eve, by charming deception, rendering us as weak as the beautiful object we perceive. Ferguson bases this argument in part on her reading of Burke's discussion of the physical response to beauty:

> When we have before us such objects as excite love and complacency, the body is affected, so far as I could observe, much in the following manner. The head reclines something on one side; the eyelids are more closed than usual, and the eyes roll gently with an inclination to the object, the mouth is a little opened, and the breath drawn slowly, with now and then a low sigh: the whole body is composed, and the hands fall idly to the sides. All this is accompanied with an inward sense of melting and languor. (Burke 1968: 149, cited in Ferguson 1992: 51)

To perceive beauty is to become almost prostrate before it, and therein lies its dangerous power.

Ferguson's argument is forceful, and if we draw out its gendered implications, its relevance to gothic fiction emerges all the more clearly. In Burke's discussion, sublimity is on the whole associated with masculinity, while beauty is explicitly feminine. To argue for sublimity as the necessary answer to a tyrannical beauty is thus to argue for the necessity of male rebellion against female power. Sublimity may well respond to beauty by destroying it, but given that the sublime episodes of gothic novels are almost always followed by a return to the banalities of everyday life – the realm of beauty – one wonders whether sublimity does not at times also reinstate or produce beauty. If so, then gothic novels play out their stories in a movement between the sublime and the beautiful, and between the masculinized and feminized forms of power that they represent.

In the next part of this chapter, I will discuss the relationship between sublimity and beauty in the works of Matthew Lewis, Charlotte Dacre, and Charles Maturin. Lewis's *The Monk*, Dacre's *Zofloya, or the Moor*, and Maturin's *Melmoth the Wanderer*[5] all demonstrate the power of sublimity over beauty in one scene after another focused on the overpowering of women. They all go a step further in their exploration of the sublime, however, imagining what might happen if women were to aspire to sublimity rather than beauty. E. J. Clery has argued that actress Sarah Siddons's enormous success "as an interpreter of the passions" on stage had resulted in her being "willingly credited with sublime genius, normally the monopoly of men." Clery attributes Siddons's successful appropriation of an admittedly masculine aesthetic to the fact that people understood that she was doing it to make money, noting that "the love of gain was a 'cool' passion, which provided an acceptable, comprehensible frame for her artistic experiments" (Clery 2000: 19, 21). The sublime women of Lewis, Dacre, and Maturin are not similarly contained by "real-world" personae, and perhaps this is why their claims to such power result – in different ways and for different reasons – in disaster. That disaster also results if women do not claim sublime power for themselves, but instead simply succumb to it, means that women in these novels find themselves in an unwelcome dilemma: they are damned if they claim power and damned if they don't.

The Monk

Matthew Lewis's *The Monk* appeared in 1796, and displayed obvious debts to a range of literary sources, including the Faust story, Walpole's *Castle of Otranto*, and the early novels of Ann Radcliffe (Paulson 1983: 219). The Marquis de Sade noted its debt to eighteenth-century history as well, stating that "'twas the inevitable result of the revolutionary shocks which all of Europe had suffered" from the French Revolution (cited in Paulson 1983: 220), and Ronald Paulson has elaborated on this point, locating the novel's revolutionary energy in the "havoc" wreaked by Ambrosio on both "the Church and his own family" as well as in "the bloodthirsty mob that lynches . . . the wicked prioress" (1983: 218). While this gothic novel is like any other in needing to be understood as the product of a range of sources, then, it is also singular insofar as it made Lewis's reputation. "Monk" Lewis came to be identified with this novel that he wrote at age 19, and his novel came to be identified with a line of fiction sometimes described as "horror gothic," in contrast to the "terror gothic" of his contemporary Ann

Radcliffe. In the former, "[n]othing is left to the imagination; all is shown." In the latter, "suggestion" is the order of the day (Miles 1995: 47).[6]

The Monk earned the label "horror gothic" because of its graphic violence. The aesthetic of the sublime frames Lewis's vision of a patriarchal society dominated by a Catholic Church so corrupt as to be dehumanizing. The novel's triple-plot structure has at its center the fall of the monk, Ambrosio, through the agency of Matilda, who is revealed on the novel's final page to be an agent of Satan. Intertwined with the story of Ambrosio and Matilda are those of two other women: Agnes, whose unhappy love affair results in her severe persecution by the prioress of the convent she has been forced to join, and Antonia, whom Ambrosio rapes and kills. These three narratives together show us a world in which the excesses of sublime power can destroy the civilized world of the beautiful: witness Matilda's empowerment as she claims for herself a sublimity that displaces readings of her as simply beautiful, or Ambrosio's power over Antonia, or the prioress's power over Agnes. Yet the novel also shows us a world in which the desire to protect beauty can spark the overthrow of a seemingly sublime force. Ambrosio's pursuit of Antonia ends in his capture by the Inquisition; the prioress is destroyed by a mob enraged by her persecution of Agnes.

Any discussion of Lewis's engagement with the sublime would do well to begin with the figure of Matilda, who first appears in the novel as a figure of beauty, and by its conclusion has been transformed into sublimity incarnate. Her identity questions the distinctions that most people make between the natural and the supernatural, human and inhuman, even female and male. Matilda enters the story disguised as the gentle male noviciate Rosario, whose head is "continually muffled up in his Cowl," though "such of his features as accident discovered, appeared the most beautiful and noble" (p. 42). She plays a young boy who is feminized first of all by the fact of his physical beauty and additionally by his cowl, which recalls the veil that covers the face of Antonia when we first meet her (Kigour 1995: 147–51). The affection she inspires in Ambrosio at this stage seems quite chaste, and recalls Burke's warning that "the passion caused by beauty . . . is different from desire" (1968: 91).

Rosario's metamorphosis into Matilda marks the point at which she becomes a recognizable danger. This occurs at the moment when she confesses her love for Ambrosio, beginning a long string of flattery that ends with her threatening to kill herself if she cannot stay at the abbey, lifting a dagger to her breast in the process. Ambrosio is seduced by the sight: "Oh! that was such a breast! The Moon-beams darting full upon it, enabled the Monk to observe its dazzling whiteness. His eye dwelt with insatiable avidity upon the beauteous Orb. A sensation till then unknown filled his heart with a mixture of anxiety and delight . . ." (p. 65). One might think here of Burke, bringing his readers to an understanding of beauty by telling them to "[o]bserve that part of a beautiful woman where she is perhaps the most beautiful, about the neck and breasts; the smoothness; the softness; the easy and insensible swell; the variety of the surface, which is never for the smallest space the same; the deceitful maze, through which the unsteady eye slides giddily . . ." (1968: 115). As Frances Ferguson leads one to see, this is beauty at its most dangerous, beauty drawing those who see it into sin, as Eve drew Adam. Ambrosio's explicit desire tells us that more than just beauty is at stake in this scene, and the threat of death hovering over the whole pushes the beautiful toward the sublime. When Matilda subsequently reveals her face to Ambrosio for the first time, her positioning between beauty and sublimity becomes still more pronounced. Her face is described in terms suggestive of blazon poetry, as one reads of the "exquisite proportion of features," of the "profusion of golden hair," the "rosy lips, heavenly eyes, and majesty of countenance" (p. 81). This is the language of beauty, and yet because these features belong not only to Matilda but also to the portrait of the Madonna that hangs on Ambrosio's wall, they ally her with divinity and so with the sublime. By the time Matilda and Ambrosio become lovers – at the end of only the second chapter of the novel – Matilda's beauty has paled in light of the increasingly sublime power of her sexuality. We are later told that Ambrosio "yield[ed] to seduction almost irresistible" (p. 226), and are reminded of Burke's description of the sublime as that which "hurries us on by an irresistible force" (1968: 57).

From that point on, Matilda is indisputably a figure of sublimity rather than beauty, though the source of her power is no longer specifically her sexuality but her ability to control the supernatural world. When Ambrosio is bitten by a serpent, she deals with the devil in order to save herself from the effects of the poison she has drawn from Ambrosio's blood into her own. Ambrosio responds to her action with "awe" (p. 232), as well as with "mingled delight and terror" (p. 233), all hallmarks of the sublime, and reflects on the change in her:

> But a few days had past, since She appeared the mildest and softest of her sex, devoted to his will, and looking up to him as a superior Being. Now she assumed a sort of courage and manliness in her manners and discourse but ill calculated to please him. She spoke no longer to insinuate, but command: He found himself unable to cope with her in argument, and was unwillingly obliged to confess the superiority of her judgment. Every moment convinced him of the astonishing powers of her mind . . . (p. 231)

Significantly, the new Matilda is a masculine Matilda, and her sublime power is thus marked as masculine as well.

The final pages of the novel reverse the dynamic of its opening. Matilda appears wearing women's clothing for the first time, and is "at once elegant and splendid," arguably beautiful in her appearance, though "a wild imperious majesty" in her expression again inspires Ambrosio "with awe" (pp. 427–8). Where she was initially a woman in man's clothing, she is now at least figuratively a man in woman's clothing, and when she is soon after revealed not even to have been human, but a devil in disguise, one realizes the danger of women's power. Matilda is such a frightening creature that she cannot be female, cannot even be male, but must be relegated to the world of demons. And not even there does her full force emerge, for that world – as Lewis portrays it – undercuts the force of the sublime by its extreme literalness.

Lewis presents the supernatural not so much as a way of transcending the natural world, but of emphasizing its limits. Matilda's transformation into Satan's minion and a sublimely powerful figure does not take her out of this world but grounds her more firmly in it, giving her a power she would never otherwise have had. "I have sold distant and uncertain happiness for present and secure," she tells Ambrosio near the end of the novel. "I have preserved a life, which otherwise I had lost in torture; and I have obtained the power of procuring every bliss, which can make that life delicious! The infernal Spirits obey me as their Sovereign . . ." (p. 428).

Matilda's alliance with Satan suggests the unacceptability of her power, though the energy with which Lewis writes her character and the fact that she exits the novel in a blaze of glory suggest a subversive endorsement of her as well. She is a sublimely superhuman creature who makes the world as she wishes it to be. At the other end of the spectrum are those who are on the receiving end of that kind of power, and whose worlds are unmade as a result. Agnes, Antonia, the prioress of the convent of St. Clare, and Ambrosio himself all finally experience the sublime as a form of dehumanization.

Agnes and Antonia are very different women whose persecution at the hands of their oppressors makes them players in two of the novel's most sublimely violent scenes. Agnes is introduced part-way through the novel as the "lovely" object of Don Raymond's affections (p. 129), and her willingness to respond to him with desires of her own is the cause of all her trouble. Her downfall is foreshadowed by the fact that she is confused with the figure of the Bleeding Nun, who – in the only scenes in the novel to turn on actual ghosts – turns out to be an ancestor of Don Raymond who was murdered by her own lover. That confusion also gives Agnes's relatives time to force her into the convent of St. Clare, where Raymond eventually finds her and impregnates her. When her pregnancy is discovered and judged a threat to the convent's reputation, she is punished severely. The prioress of the Order of St. Clare pretends that Agnes has died of an illness, then incarcerates her in a cell deep beneath the convent, where she is to remain until she dies. Agnes survives this form of live burial, even giving birth to a child during this time, and is finally discovered, barely alive and altogether unrecognizable, with the moldering corpse of her baby on her breast.

The sublimity of the scene emerges in the way in which Agnes is represented at the moment when she is discovered. Her brother Lorenzo is the one to find her, and he at first does not even know who she is. He sees

> a Creature stretched upon a bed of straw, so wretched, so emaciated, so pale, that He doubted to think her Woman. She was half-naked: Her long dishevelled hair fell in disorder over her face, and almost entirely concealed it. One wasted Arm hung listlessly upon a tattered rug, which covered her convulsed and shivering limbs: The Other was wrapped round a small bundle, and held it closely to her bosom. A large Rosary lay near her: Opposite to her was a Crucifix, on which She bent her sunk eyes fixedly, and by her side stood a Basket and a small Earthen Pitcher. (p. 369)

Lying there with her dead child on her breast, Agnes is a grotesque parody of a *pietà*, an image of death in life expressive of the fundamental ambiguity that characterizes the Burkean sublime. Lorenzo is indeed "petrified with horror" at the sight of her, and yet that response quickly gives way to feelings of "disgust and pity" that make him not only "sick at heart," but physically sick as well (p. 369). The sight of Agnes inspires a response that exceeds the sublime horror described by Burke and others. Lorenzo's revulsion at the sight of his as yet unrecognized sister stems above all from the fact that she is no longer recognizable as a woman.

Agnes's dehumanization at the hands of the prioress is matched by Antonia's at the hands of Lorenzo. We first meet her in the novel's opening scene, when Don Lorenzo's insistence that she remove her veil prefigures the violence that will be done to her later. She is described as more "bewitching than beautiful" (p. 11), though descriptions of her "rosy" lips, her "fair and undulating hair," her "full and beautiful" throat, and the "perfect symmetry" of her arms certainly suffice to categorize her as "beautiful" in Burke's terms (1968: 12). Part-way through the novel, Antonia becomes the target of the lascivious Ambrosio, and her transformation into an object of sublime violence is under way.

Ambrosio's desire to possess Antonia is figured as monstrous. He accomplishes his aim only with the help of Matilda, has to kill Antonia's mother along the way, and then is forced to fake Antonia's death as well. Having given her a sleeping potion that makes her appear to be dead for three days, he waits for her to awaken in the crypt under the convent of St. Clare, where a scene of violent struggle ends with him raping her. Immediately after he has committed this crime, he regards her with only "aversion and rage," and soon after that he feels himself "repulsed from and attracted towards her," though he can "account for neither sentiment" (pp. 384, 387). The novel as a whole gives us a good frame of reference in which to understand his feelings, however, for he felt similar "disgust" as he tired of his sexual relationship with Matilda (p. 235), and "disgust" as well after he killed Antonia's mother (p. 307). Women interest Ambrosio because he can possess them, yet possession inevitably kills them either literally or figuratively, rendering them the appallingly inhuman figures pictured here. Antonia resists this objectification valiantly, running from him even after she has been raped and succumbing to it only when Ambrosio stabs her to death.

Agnes and Antonia are victimized by the prioress and Ambrosio, who in turn are forced to relinquish their terrifying powers and themselves become victims of excess. The respectable crowd attending the festival of St. Clare turns into a disrespectful mob on learning that the prioress has supposedly killed the nun Agnes as a punishment for becoming pregnant. She at once becomes "their destined Victim," and with relentless focus they torture her, kill her, and continue to beat her body after she is dead, until it is "no more than a mass of flesh, unsightly, shapeless and disgusting" (p. 356). In a scene that recalls and intensifies her own treatment of Agnes, the prioress is the victim of a horrifying violence that strips her not only of her gender but of her very humanity, and the same mob that did this to her then destroys the convent of St. Clare itself. The destruction of the convent coincides with the destruction of the community it housed. While one might applaud the fall of this corrupt Catholic community, it would be worth keeping in mind that its fall seems tied not just to its Catholicism but also to the fact that it is a society of women. Ambrosio's corruption does not lead to the fall of the society to which he belonged, yet the prioress's crimes immediately break up the sisters of St. Clare.

The novel's most severe reckoning is left for Ambrosio, whose transformation from a figure who wields sublime power into one who falls victim to it is the most pronounced in the novel. We meet him as the powerful orator whose "charm" neither man nor woman can resist (pp. 18–19), and while he holds on to the appearance of power for much of the novel, his increasing submission to Matilda marks him as not only weak but feminine. When Ambrosio refuses Matilda's offer to call up the demonic powers that will help him get to Antonia, she scornfully tells him that his mind is "feeble, puerile, and grovelling, a slave to vulgar errors, and weaker than a Woman's" (p. 268). When he overcomes this weakness and agrees to use the magic myrtle branch to gain entry to Antonia's room, his "[c]onsciousness of the guilty business on which He was employed appalled his heart, and rendered it more timid than a Woman's" (p. 299). This feminized figure cannot act with the certainty of a Matilda, and, while she is not the force that finally destroys him, it is an equally sublime being that does. The devil that snatches him from the dungeons of the Inquisition terrifies with his physical "ugliness" and with the truths that he "unveils" (pp. 433, 439). Ambrosio learns that he has committed incest as well as matricide, and is left to die. In the last paragraph of the novel, he is physically dismembered:

> The Eagles of the rock tore his flesh piecemeal, and dug out his eye-balls with their crooked beaks. A burning thirst tormented him; He heard the river's murmur as it rolled beside him, but strove in vain to drag himself towards the sound. Blind, maimed, helpless, and despairing, venting his rage in blasphemy and curses, execrating his existence, yet dreading the arrival of death destined to yield him up to greater torments, six miserable days did the Villain languish. On the Seventh a violent storm arose: The winds in fury rent up rocks and forests: The sky was now black with clouds, now sheeted with fire: The rain fell in torrents; It swelled the stream; The waves overflowed their banks; They reached the spot where Ambrosio lay, and when they abated carried with them into the river the Corse of the despairing Monk. (p. 442)

Ambrosio's escape from his crimes comes with his death, in this powerful scene that recalls and apparently reverses the biblical creation myth, as his body and the entire world order that he represented are taken apart at the end of the novel (a point also discussed in Kilgour 1995: 162). The dis-membering of Ambrosio's existence is a sublime and ironic counterpart to the re-membering of history that closed *Otranto*.

While one cannot go so far as to say that Lewis associates sublimity only with demonized, dead, or dying women, he does so often enough to make one see that the aesthetic of the sublime is for him constructed around issues of gender. The sublime power of Matilda threatens the power of patriarchy, while the prioress and Ambrosio try to uphold the patriarchy, Agnes and Antonia are victimized by it, and the mob finally disrupts it just long enough for the corruption at its heart to be exposed and purged. What we are left with is a world in which women have been restored to their rightful identification with the beautiful in the form of the chastised Agnes and Virginia de Villa-Franca (Lorenzo's future wife); the radical promises of Matilda have receded so far into the background that they have disappeared.

Zofloya, or the Moor

Published in 1806, Charlotte Dacre's *Zofloya, or the Moor* responds directly to *The Monk* in its central story of a woman demonized by her sublime longings. Where Lewis creates in Matilda a heroine who is finally identified as the devil, Dacre imagines in the character of Victoria Lauredani a woman whose partnership with a man finally revealed as Satan begins as an empowering response to her frustrated ambitions and thwarted desires, but in the end ensures only further victimization.

Victoria's story develops in relation to those of other desiring women, the first of which is her mother, Laurina. Dacre blames the family's decline on Laurina, whose seduction by the insidious Count Ardolph results in her abandoning her household. Following this event, her son runs away out of shame, her husband dies as a result of a street fight with Ardolph, and Victoria – whom Ardolph virtually imprisons when he insists that she live with an elderly aunt – emulates her mother by escaping her confinement, going to live with a lover, and indulging her own desires from that point on.

Dacre's emphasis on the influence of a corrupt mother stands out even in a genre highly attuned to the pernicious effects of "the absence or corruption of the mother" (Hoeveler 1998: 146). Her insistence on Laurina's culpability is so extreme that it feels forced. Arguing that "we are in a great measure the creatures of education, rather than of organisation" (p. 48), Dacre chides Laurina for her failure to take responsibility for teaching her children well. Over and over again, we read some version of a lament for "the unfortunate and guilty mother, who, making light of the sacred charge devolving on her, the welfare of her children, as depending on the just formation of their minds, not only neglects that sacred charge, but seals the fiat of their future destruction, by setting them in her own conduct an example of moral depravity – depriving them of the world's respect, and rendering them thereby indifferent to their own" (p. 49). When one considers that women in the eighteenth and early nineteenth centuries had traditionally been narrowly educated to become the obedient daughters, wives, and mothers of a patriarchal society that systematically oppressed them, however, her failure starts to look more complicated. Following up on the implications of Diane Long Hoeveler's argument that Dacre's novel "turns on its head" Mary Wollstonecraft's call for the improvement of women's education, one might look at Laurina's fantastically destructive failure to educate her children as an exaggerated imagining of what happens when mothers themselves are not educated. Alternatively, we might also read Laurina's failure to educate her children as a rebellion against that same narrow system of education that Wollstonecraft protested, in favor of acting on her own desires.

The centrality of women to a strong patriarchal structure is emphasized when Laurina's family falls apart so completely on her leaving it, yet Laurina herself does not benefit from her departure. In her marriage she was a beloved equal, and even the similarity between her first name, which she took with her into marriage, and her last name, which she took from her husband, suggests this likeness: she is Laurina di Lauredani. In her subsequent relationship with Ardolph, she is entirely subject to Ardolph's control, and is even physically abused by him. Perhaps, then, the real lesson of Laurina's experience is not that bad mothers hurt their children, but that rebellious wives are punished.

The other story against which Victoria's unfolds is that of Megalena Strozzi, who provides a far different model of rebellion against the patriarchy. Megalena is a property-owning and unmarried "syren" who has no trouble seducing

Victoria's brother Leonardo, whom she first encounters asleep on the ground near her home (p. 123). She is by definition masculinized by her worldly power, even as the sleeping Leonardo is notably feminized, seen by her as "beautiful and fascinating":

> his hands were clasped over his head, and on his cheek, where the hand of health had planted her brown-red rose, the pearly gems of his tears still hung – his auburn hair sported in graceful curls about his forehead and temples, agitated by the passing breeze – his vermeil lips were half open, and disclosed his polished teeth – his bosom, which he had uncovered to admit the refreshing air, remained disclosed, and contrasted by its snowy whiteness the animated hue of his complexion. (p. 120)

Megalena easily dominates him, even convincing him to attempt the murder of her former lover. Unknown to Leonardo, the object of Megalena's vengeance is Count Berenza, who has moved on to become the lover of Leonardo's sister Victoria, and when he attacks Berenza in his bed, it is his sister whom he accidentally stabs. That he stabs her with a dagger inscribed "Megalena Strozzi" only emphasizes that the real quarrel here is between two powerful women, whose relationship – in a reversal of the usual pattern – is mediated by the men in their lives (p. 135).

Laurina and Megalena are alike in acting on their desires, as well as in the suffering they experience as a result. However, given that Laurina suffers because she gets what she wants, and Megalena suffers because she doesn't, one must conclude that breaking the rules of patriarchy has no good outcome. The only alternative is to take control of it. Enter Victoria, who tries to do just this, and while, unsurprisingly, she fails, she fails sublimely.

Victoria's development from seductive beauty into a sublimely powerful figure echoes and intensifies that of Lewis's Matilda. The intensification comes from Dacre's insistence on showing readers how difficult it is for Victoria to occupy either of these roles: that of docile beauty demands a constraining discipline against which she chafes, while that of sublime power demands a rebelliousness she would rather conceal. As these descriptions suggest, she in fact always occupies both roles at once, though as the novel proceeds, first the former and then the latter dominates Dacre's representation of her.

From the beginning, Victoria is described as "beautiful and accomplished as an angel" but also "proud, haughty, and self-sufficient – of a wild, ardent, and irrepressible spirit, indifferent to reproof, careless of censure – of an implacable, revengeful, and cruel nature, and bent upon gaining the ascendancy in whatever she engaged" (p. 40).[7] Her "accomplishments" are clearly a product of the nurture that Dacre so dutifully espouses, yet everything else about her is here attributed to a "nature" that only comes to seem less desirable as the novel proceeds. She is said to be "by nature more prone to evil than to good," and her own father fears that "her heart [is] evil" (pp. 59, 49). This struggle of nurture to overcome nature might be seen as the struggle of beauty to contain the uncontainable force of the sublime, and while beauty must fail, it scores some significant victories along the way.

Victoria's early struggles against her mother, Ardolph, and the restrictions they place on her give way – once she has been shipped off to her aunt's for disciplining – to a calm containment that lets her manipulate her jailers with ease. She finds her way from there back to Venice, where, with equal ease, she manipulates Berenza into marrying her. He seeks to mold her, ensuring that she is worthy of him in mind as well as body, and never realizes that she is doing a much better job of manipulating him to get what she wants. Repressing the "stormy passions of the soul" that render her an unfit partner for the "mild, philosophic" Berenza, she assumes a character suited to his in its "melancholy, retired, and abstracted" conduct, and convinces him of a devotion she does not feel (p. 97).[8] Words of feigned love spoken during a feigned sleep convince Berenza of her attachment to him, and draw from him the statement "Thou art mine! – Yes, I now *know* that thou art mine" (p. 99). His words echo those spoken by Matilda to Ambrosio, as well as those exchanged between the Bleeding Nun and Raymond in *The Monk*, and emphasize the doomed future of their relationship. She becomes first his lover, then his wife, and finally his murderer. Victoria's metamorphosis into her husband's murderer does not happen without help, however. It is Zofloya, the Moor of the title, who shows her the way to this crime and those that follow.

Victoria's alliance with Zofloya propels her into a socially destructive mode that far exceeds any challenge to the status quo that she could have made on her own. He comes to her attention at the moment when her desires are at their most transgressive: she is frustrated in her efforts to seduce her husband's brother-in-law Henriquez, who has arrived at their home along with his fiancée Lilla. What she cannot do in daylight hours she can accomplish while sleeping, however: she dreams of marrying Henriquez thanks to Zofloya's intervention, in a scene that anticipates the deaths of her husband and sister-in-law, though it does not accurately foretell her relationship with Henriquez. The fact that Zofloya appears in Victoria's dream just when she needs help realizing her desires suggests that he is a tool of wish fulfillment (as are dreams themselves, Freud would say, a century after Dacre), or as Hoeveler suggests, "a representation of the dark and demonic forces within Victoria's own psyche" (1998: 149). These readings needs to be complicated, however. If Zofloya fulfills Victoria's wishes, so does she fulfill his. Each is what the other needs.

Victoria and Zofloya are an interesting pair. Victoria might be described as the heroine of the novel, yet in many ways she does not fit the part. Most gothic heroines resemble her rival Lilla, who is, in Hoeveler's terms, "the epitome of an emerging British domestic ideology" (1998: 151), and in mine a walking embodiment of Burkean beauty. "Pure, innocent, free even from the smallest taint of a corrupt thought was her mind; delicate, symmetrical and of fairy-like beauty, her person so small, yet of so just proportion; sweet, expressing a seraphic serenity of soul, seemed her angelic countenance, slightly suffused with the palest hue of the virgin rose. Long flaxen hair floated over her shoulders . . ." (p. 144). Victoria is also said to be beautiful in the early pages of the novel, but the references appear almost in passing, and by the time we come across the first extended description of her – a full ten chapters into the novel – she is beginning to assume the sublime appearance that will function as shorthand for both the power and the threat that she represents:

> No, her's was not the countenance of a Madona – it was not of angelic mould; yet, though there was a fierceness in it, it was not certainly a repelling, but a beautiful fierceness – dark, noble, strongly expressive, every lineament bespoke the mind which animated it. True, no mild, no gentle, no endearing virtues, were depicted there; but while you gazed upon her, you observed not the want of any charm. Her smile was fascination itself; and in her large dark eyes, which sparkled with incomparable radiance, you read the traces of a strong and resolute mind, capable of attempting any thing undismayed by consequences; and well and truly did they speak. Her figure, though above the middle height, was symmetry itself; she was as the tall and graceful antelope . . . (p. 96)

Victoria is described here more in terms of what she is not than what she is, yet even so, her height, her dark coloring, her "fierceness," and her attractive force all point to the increasingly powerful and iconoclastic figure that she will become. Within the world of the novel, the person she most resembles is not Lilla or any other woman, but Zofloya.[9]

Zofloya will finally be revealed as Satan, but for most of the novel appears in the far more conventionally threatening guise of a black Muslim man (an "infidel," as Victoria says (p. 156)). Said to be of noble birth but enslaved after the expulsion of the Moors from Spain, his "elegant person was his least recommendation" (p. 148). His person is nonetheless part of what lets us connect him with Victoria:

> to a form the most attractive and symmetrical, though of superior height . . . was added a countenance, spite of its colour, endowed with the finest possible expression. His eyes, brilliant and large, sparkled with inexpressible fire; his nose and mouth were elegantly formed, and when he smiled, the assemblage of his features displayed a beauty that delighted and surprised. (p. 153)

Like her, he is tall and dark, and, like hers, his physical appearance – including his dress – makes visible his status as an outsider. He is initially envisioned in "a habit of white and gold" that includes "a white turban, which sparkled with emeralds, and was surmounted by a waving feather of green," and he wears "the finest oriental pearl" around his bare arms and legs, "a collar of gold round his throat," as well as "gold rings of an enormous size" in his ears (p. 145). He is an orientalist fantasy that charms but also threatens in multiple ways the patriar-chal, Christian society at the heart of the novel, and Dacre's boldness in pairing this black man with the white Victoria has been noticed in critical discussion of the marginal social status that links people of color and women (Hoeveler 1998: 148–50; Craciun 1997).

To complicate our understanding of the novel still further, one might note that Dacre herself might be identified to some degree with Victoria, and so implicitly with Zofloya as well. Kim Ian Michasiw (1997: x) makes this sugges-tion, noting that an engraved miniature of the author appeared in early editions of the novel, in which her pseudonym "Rosa Matilda" identifies her with those Matildas who were the heroines of other gothic novels (most notably *The Monk*), while her dark complexion links her with Victoria in her own novel. While one does not want to speculate too much, both the fact that Dacre was Jewish, and the fact that she seems to have had her children well before she married their father, mark her as an outsider to the eighteenth-century British culture in which she lived, and Michasiw is right to suggest that Dacre embod-ies what Maggie Kilgour has described as "the artist as goth" (Kilgour, cited in Michasiw 1997: x). Victoria, Zofloya, and Dacre all figure "the artist as goth," that is, as an invading and barbaric figure whose revolutionary energy upsets the status quo.

So what does the trinity of Victoria, Zofloya, and Dacre accomplish? Consider the stages of the partnership that Dacre imagines for her two characters. Their active collaboration begins with a garden scene reminiscent of that in *The Monk*, which in turn recalls that in the Garden of Eden. Eve loses her innocence to the seductive logic of Satan, even as Ambrosio succumbs to Matilda, and Victoria yields to Zofloya. Of these three figures seduced in the garden, however, Victo-ria is the least innocent. While she resembles Eve and Ambrosio in following her own desires, she is unique in acknowledging from the start that those desires include committing murder. To make herself available to Henriquez, she accepts from Zofloya the poisons that will kill her husband, administers them herself, allows them to be tested on an elderly female relative of Lilla as well (who of course dies), and hurries the process along as much as possible. Through these events, she binds herself ever more tightly to Zofloya, who initially describes himself as "the humble tool, the slave of [her] wishes" (p. 168), soon after goes so far as to say that she "partake[s] of [him]self" (p. 181), and thereafter asserts that her heart is his (p. 183). He insists on possessing her much as Berenza had, and by the end of the novel she has assented to his claim.

The path to Zofloya is circuitous, though, and involves two more major detours. First comes the culmination of Victoria's pursuit of Henriquez. When the death of Berenza does not lead Henriquez to leave Lilla for Victoria, Zofloya helps out by kidnapping Lilla and chaining her in a cave (a version of the live burial that Lewis inflicts on Agnes). When Henriquez still shows no interest in Victoria, Zofloya offers further assistance, making Victoria look like Lilla. While this disguise lets her win Henriquez for a night, his discovery of the deception causes him to commit suicide and drives Victoria to murder Lilla in what Hoeveler rightly describes as one of the most "bizarre" scenes in gothic fiction (at one point Victoria literally tries to shake the frightened girl out of a tree, while later she inflicts multiple stab wounds on her rival and finally hurls her down an abyss). At the heart of this remarkable series of events is a searing commentary on women and desire: Victoria's pursuit of her own desire at all costs is shocking in itself, but her willingness to do it even by transforming herself into Lilla – the beautiful, blonde type of a gothic heroine – is perhaps even more disturbing. Kristen Roupenian has discussed Victoria's rage at both her need to transform herself into such a woman and her inability to do so permanently, and has argued forcefully that killing Lilla (and all she represents) is the only way to make space for women like Victoria.[10] Literature can clear ideological ground in ways one never could in one's lived experience, and so – while actual emulation of Victoria's conduct is not a desired outcome here – an informed response to her anger is. Dacre sees that female desire is generally understood as outlawed, transgressive, and impermissible and tries to imagine what it would take to change this.

What she imagines is sadistic violence, a disturbing solution rendered all the more so because it does not in the end change anything. Victoria's last days are spent in a cave with a group of banditti headed by her brother, where she sees her mother die after a long and abusive relationship with her seducer, Ardolph, and is again subjected to the jealousies of Megalena Strozzi. Caught between her brother and Zofloya (even as she had been caught between Ardolph and her then lover Berenza at the novel's outset), she finally succumbs to the latter. Zofloya has since his first appearance had a sublime aspect, emphasized in descriptions of him as "towering" (pp. 165, 226, 227), "gigantic" (p. 191), "terrible" (pp. 176, 254), and inspiring "awe" (p. 252). In a moment that draws out the gendered/eroticized power dynamic of the sublime with rare clarity, one reads that Victoria's "ravished sense . . . confessed him a being of a superior order" (p. 227). Even when he appears in his true guise as Satan, he is still "fierce, gigantic," if now also "hideous to behold," and Victoria still responds to him with "terror" as – like Ambrosio before her – she hears how the devil manipulated her, is hurled into an abyss, and is "received into the foaming waters below" (p. 254).

Dacre's strength as a writer of gothic fiction is that she can imagine a radical assault against the patriarchal structures that trap women; her limitation is that she cannot imagine that assault succeeding. Dacre's women have no future. They can neither claim the status of a patriarch, nor change the patriarchy, nor eliminate it, and Dacre is unwilling to accommodate herself within it. The only way out is through death.

Melmoth the Wanderer

Published in 1820, Charles Maturin's *Melmoth the Wanderer* is often taken as an end-point of the "high gothic" period. It engages the familiar questions about the nature of patriarchal society, again deploying the aesthetic of the sublime to suggest both what threatens patriarchy and the means of subduing that threat. That said, however, I will argue that Maturin's understanding of the sublime complicates that of Lewis and Dacre. On the one hand, he develops a story that recounts episodes of – and is meant to inspire – the kind of sublime fear that Burke tells us is absolutely opposed to beauty. On the other, however, he develops a story in which what Leslie Moore (1990) has identified as the "beautiful sublime" brings those two aesthetic categories together. Sublime fear is moderated by its explicit engagement – even melding – with beauty.

Melmoth the Wanderer is framed by the story of John Melmoth's attendance at his uncle's deathbed, during which time he becomes acquainted with a series of tales that reveal to him the character of the man for whom the novel is named. Melmoth the Wanderer has affinities with Faust and all of the Ambrosios, Matildas, and Victorias made in his image, having apparently sold his soul for 150 years of life. He also has affinities with the figure of the Wandering Jew, experiencing those years as pain rather than pleasure, and with Mephistopheles, since he spends his time tempting others to do as he has done (Baldick 1989: xvi). Every story of Melmoth the Wanderer turns on his asking his victims to save themselves from imminent danger by changing places with him. Their constant refusal to do his bidding suggests a refusal of the gothic plot into which he has drawn them. They will not substitute their lives for his. They will not live in the space between life and death that he inhabits.

All of the tales embedded in *Melmoth* turn on questions of lineage and inheritance. John Melmoth inherits property from his uncle, but is denied access to the family history by that same uncle, who tells him to burn both a portrait that hangs in a closet and a manuscript that lies in a drawer. The portrait and the manuscript represent their wandering ancestor, of course, and John persists in finding out about both, initially by turning to the women of the household to see what they can tell him. He talks first with his uncle's housekeeper, who cannot tell him what he wants to know, and then calls on Biddy Branigan, "the doctress of the neighbourhood" and "a withered Sybil" in whom one recognizes a whole tradition of female figures whose extraordinary knowledge marks them as witches or oracles (p. 10).[11] She begins to flesh out an image of Melmoth the Wanderer, who left his family in 1646 to travel on the Continent, returned years later not aged a bit, and then disappeared again. Her story is supplemented by those that John Melmoth reads and listens to over the course of the novel, and all narratives are both cut off and completed by Melmoth's appearance – and then death or disappearance – in the novel's final pages.

The stories contained within this frame narrative vary in length and complexity. First comes the tale of the Englishman Stanton, who learns of Melmoth while traveling in Spain, encounters him again in London but refuses his help to escape from the lunatic asylum to which he has been confined by a greedy relative, and when free spends the rest of his life fruitlessly trying to locate Melmoth once more. Next comes the story of Alonzo de Monçada, an illegitimate son whose resistance to monastic life involves him in a series of adventures. Embedded in his story is that of Immalee, who is separated from her family as an infant, survives on an Indian island where she is worshiped as a goddess and becomes attached to Melmoth the Wanderer, whom she encounters again when she is finally returned to Spain as a young woman. Embedded in that story are two more, that of the Guzman family, nearly torn apart by alternating bouts of poverty and wealth, and that of Ellinor and John, lovers separated by John's mother, who wanted her son to marry another for the sake of an inheritance. While all of these stories merit comment, the most significant for my purposes are those of Alonzo de Monçada and of Immalee.

Monçada tells a story that in many ways echoes that of Lewis's Agnes. Like Agnes, he was pledged by his mother to a religious life before he was born, and like Agnes, he rebels against that life when it is imposed on him, going through a series of horrific trials and finding himself presumed dead when he is not. Unlike Agnes, however, he is an illegitimate child – the eldest son, who cannot rightfully inherit his father's property – and therein lies the threat that he poses. He disrupts the line of patriarchal descent by his very existence, and so must be secreted away.

Hiding a problem does not get rid of it, however, and the effort to protect the patriarchy by hiding Alonzo renders him an even greater threat. His rebellion against the monastic life to which he is confined leads him through a series of tortures that culminates in a punishment that leaves him "half-naked, half-drowned, gasping, choking, and delirious with rage, shame, and fear" (p. 165). Aligning Monçada's highly elliptical account of his punishment for an unnamed crime with the historical testimony of a male rape victim in the nineteenth century, Margot Gayle Backus plausibly argues that he was raped as punishment for his insistent efforts to leave the monastery (1999: 118–26). While her effort to name Monçada's crime is important, however, it is just as important to note that Monçada himself does not name it. The crucial elements of the story are replaced by a series of asterisks that emblematize this "unspeakable" crime, and its very unspeakability marks it as equivalent to the violence done to Agnes – a violence that leaves her unrecognizable as a woman and so in a sense "unread-able" – in the vaults of St. Clare.[12] The bishop who hears the story of Monçada's time in the monastery responds with "horror, disgust and indignation" at its details (though what details are included we don't know), recalling Lorenzo's response to the dehumanized Agnes, and yet Monçada's fate is not Agnes's (p. 170). His audience with the bishop does not lead to his freedom.

Having failed to win permission to leave the monastery, Monçada finds help from his brother (the legitimate heir to the family fortune), who has escaped an equally oppressive existence at his parents' home, and who enlists a monk known to be a parricide to lead Alonzo out of the convent. The monk betrays Alonzo, turning him over to the Inquisition and killing his brother, while the parents of the two boys separate. Thus Alonzo's rebellion seemingly destroys his family, though – as in *The Monk* – one would do better to blame the Catholic Church, the corruption of which is signaled both by the fire that destroys the prisons of the Inquisition and by the fate of that parricidal monk.

The pages devoted to the prison's destruction recall but outdo the destruction of the convent of St. Clare in Lewis's *The Monk*. The scene is explicitly apoca-lyptic in its image of the burning building as "a wildly painted picture of the last day," in which "God appeared descending in the light that enveloped the skies," while the prisoners and their guards "stood pale and shuddering in the light below" (p. 240). In the statement that "[t]he towers of the Inquisition shrunk into cinders – that tremendous monument of the power, and crime, and gloom of the human mind, was wasting like a scroll in the fire" (p. 241), one could ask for no better evidence that the power of the Church is a fiction – a scroll or written text made by human beings, as the derivation of "fiction" from the Latin *facio* ("to make") indicates – but what a powerful fiction it is. The Inquisitors "[stand] their ground" through the disaster, and their crimes are not undone (p. 242). This is a "day of judgement" on which "fathers and sons, who perhaps had been inmates of adjacent cells for years, without being conscious of each others vicin-ity or existence" still "did not dare to recognize each other," while even those "parents and children who *did* recognize and stretch out their wasted arms to each other" know they have different fates and do not come together (pp. 240–1).

The Church maintains itself at the expense of the family, and so the one patriarchal structure destroys another.

This is a point that the mob does not understand. The monk who has betrayed Alonzo also "cut [his] father's throat" (p. 221), and that crime is punished in a scene of mob violence that echoes but actually outdoes the killing of the prioress in *The Monk*. Spectators at a religious procession blame this man for the weakening of the power of the Church, and – with a violence likened to that of tigers and bulls as it pursues its "work of blood" – kill the parricide in horrifying stages. "Bloody, defaced, blackened with earth, and battered with stones, he struggle[s] and roar[s]"; after further violence, he is reduced to "a mangled lump of flesh," who "[w]ith his tongue hanging from his lacerated mouth . . . with, one eye torn from the socket, and dangling on his bloody cheek; with a fracture in every limb, and a wound for every pore . . . still howled for 'life – life – life – mercy!' till a stone, aimed by some pitying hand, struck him down" (pp. 255–6). Even now, however, his dissolution is not complete. He falls, "trodden in one moment into sanguine and discoloured mud by a thousand feet," and in the end nothing at all is left of his body: "not . . . a joint of his little finger – a hair of his head – a slip of his skin." Like Lewis's prioress, he is reduced to "a bloody formless mass" (p. 256). The crime of killing one's father evokes the strongest punishment portrayed in the novel, in a moment of pure sublimity that imagines the effacement of anything threatening to a patriarchal structure.

Maturin calls on the aesthetic of the sublime to represent the cost of thwarting patriarchy in any form. The death of the corrupt monk represents a particularly savage form of justice that pits a mob against an official of the Church hierarchy in a virulent anti-Catholicism that equals if it does not surpass that of Lewis, and that would have had a much more immediate reference point in the life of the Irish Protestant Maturin (Baldick 1989: xiii–xvi). Maturin himself includes a footnote directing readers to see in this scene an analog to the home-grown violence of Emmet's insurrection, an abortive rebellion in 1803 against the English rule of Ireland that nonetheless resulted in the murder of Lord Kilwarden, chief justice of Ireland, who "was dragged from his carriage," had "[p]ike after pike thrust through his body, till at last he was *nailed to a door*," and died asking to be " 'put out of [his] pain' " (p. 257). That Emmet was allied with the French in this effort increases the scene's resonance further, suggesting a link to the violence of the French Revolution as well.[13]

As sublimely spectacular as all of these scenes may be, they are matched in intensity if not effect by a series of scenes that represent not actual but imagined deaths. While still in the prisons of the Inquisition, Alonzo dreams of his own death by fire, inserting himself into a procession of victims that includes a "young Jewess" (foreshadowing his later refuge with Jews) and his own brother. He describes this "haunting of yourself by your own spectre" as "a curse almost equal to your crimes visiting you in the punishment of eternity," and details one of the most gruesome death scenes in gothic fiction:

> I was chained to my chair again, – the fires were lit, the bells rang out, the litanies were sung; – my feet were scorched to a cinder, – my muscles cracked, my blood and marrow hissed, my flesh consumed like shrinking leather, – the bones of my legs hung two black withering and moveless sticks in the ascending blaze; – it ascended, caught my hair, – I was crowned with fire, – my head was a ball of molten metal, my eyes flashed and melted in their sockets; – I opened my mouth, it drank fire, – I closed it, the fire was within, – and still the bells rung on, and the crowd shouted, and the king and queen, and all the nobility and priesthood, looked on, and we burned, and burned! – I was a cinder body and soul in my dream. (p. 236)

Fire consumes him and he consumes fire in a grotesque scene that calls to mind but intensifies the horror of Ambrosio's final days. This fate is only imagined, and yet when the fire that destroys his prison leaves everyone convinced that he has died, his dream is in a sense fulfilled. He has been released by fire into a life as his own ghost.

The "undead" Alonzo finds refuge among others who were also supposed at least legally dead: Madrid's hidden community of Jews, who have officially been forced to convert to Catholicism and so are not acknowledged even to exist under the law, but who nonetheless privately retain their Jewish identity. When he watches the destruction of the parricidal monk from a window in the home of Solomon, his first protector, he is taken to be a "spectre . . . hovering in the air, to witness the sufferings of the dying wretch" (p. 259), and when he is forced to flee the skeptical Inquisitors who hunt him down, his identity as a ghostly figure is intensified.

Alonzo goes from the protection of Solomon to that of Adonijah, who lives in an underground dwelling approached through tunnels that run from Solomon's house. Adonijah lives in a way that literalizes his status as "living dead," sharing his underground dwelling with the skeletons of his wife, his daughter, and two other people, and in a heroic effort to make sure that others' lives will not be effaced as his has been, he has committed himself to staying there until he has recorded their stories. Monçada becomes his amanuensis in this project, yet has no faith that the act of writing will rescue these lives from oblivion. On the contrary, once he learns that the stories he will record turn on encounters with Melmoth the Wanderer, he is convinced that recording them will lead to his own doom as well. While a prisoner of the Inquisition, he had been repeatedly visited by Melmoth and had repeatedly reported these visits to his interrogators. He had hoped thus to indicate his resistance to Melmoth, but instead he became identified with him and an "object of . . . terror" for whom the Inquisitors could imagine no fate but death (p. 225). To record Melmoth's wanderings is therefore to him "a task of horror unspeakable" that makes him "an added link to the chain . . . drawing [him] to perdition" and "the recorder of [his] own condemnation" (pp. 270–1).

The way out of the many forms of sublime terror envisioned by the novel is through another and more complicated form of the sublime: the sublime as it responds not to that which is terrifying but that which is beautiful. There is an obvious paradox in this statement, for up to this point in my argument the beautiful has been defined – following Burke – as that which inspires social rather than sublime passion. Frances Ferguson's argument for a similarity between the two suggests that both beauty and the sublime overwhelm those who experience them, though in very different ways, and Leslie Moore has argued for still more complicated relationships between them. Her analysis of how a group of early eighteenth-century readers responded to Milton's *Paradise Lost* develops a reading of sublimity as an experience that can be channeled and shaped by a beautiful stimulus, emerging as "a kind of admiration . . . 'uncomplicated with Terror,' but . . . thoroughly mingled with the human and the sexual" (1992: 66). Her discussion focuses on readings of Adam's response to Eve. Maturin's version of something very similar appears in his portrait of a latter-day Eve named Immalee who will find her Adam – merged with Satan – in Melmoth the Wanderer.

Immalee's evolution from the confident nature goddess whom we first encounter living on an island near India into the woman who gives birth to the child of Melmoth the Wanderer recalls but also counters the life of Lewis's Matilda. Immalee is introduced as a figure of beautiful sublimity whose very existence critiques the destructive force of the terribly sublime Melmoth. The two exist as equal and opposite, one allied with divinity and the other with the demonic. They exist at the margins of their society and define its boundaries, the extremes of good and evil that cannot be surpassed.

The reader initially encounters Immalee not directly, but through stories about her. She is said to be the new goddess of the island on which she lives, who rules with a benevolence that distinguishes her from her Hindu predecessor, "the black goddess Seeva," whose "hideous idol, with its collar of human sculls, forked tongues darting from its twenty serpent mouths, and seated on a matted coil of adders, had there first received the bloody homage of the mutilated limbs and immolated infants of her worshippers" (p. 272). This "white goddess" who "demand[s] no suffering from her worshippers" effortlessly wins devotees (pp. 279, 274), and her "sanctity" is firmly established when she appears just as two lovers commit themselves to each other at the shrine associated with her (pp. 275–8). Her power stems from her gentleness and her "supernatural loveliness" (p. 273), which is worth describing at length:

The form was that of a female, but such as [the young Indians] had never before beheld, for her skin was perfectly white, (at least in their eyes, who had never seen any but the dark-red tint of the natives of the Bengalese islands). Her drapery (as well as they could see) consisted only of flowers, whose rich colours and fantastic groupings harmonized well with the peacock's feathers twined among them, and altogether composed a feathery fan of wild drapery, which, in truth, beseemed an "island goddess." Her long hair, of a colour they had never beheld before, pale auburn, flowed to her feet, and was fantastically entwined with the flowers and the feathers that formed her dress. On her head was a coronal of shells, of hue and lustre unknown except in the Indian seas – the purple and the green vied with the amethyst, and the emerald. On her white bare shoulder a loxia was perched, and round her neck was hung a string of their pearl-like eggs, so pure and pellucid, that the first sovereign in Europe might have exchanged her richest necklace of pearls for them. Her arms and feet were perfectly bare, and her step had a goddess-like rapidity and lightness, that affected the imagination of the Indians as much as the extraordinary colour of her skin and hair. (pp. 278–9)

Immalee's worshipers understand her to be "an incarnated emanation of Vishnu" (p. 273), and their assimilation of her into Indian mythology may or may not be enough to counteract what is just as easily read as her imperial power. The flowers, shells, and birds' eggs that she wears are clearly meant to portray her as a latter-day Eve, a child of nature as yet unfallen. However, one might also note that those same flowers and shells constitute the natural resources of territory colonized by Europeans (the British particularly), and that she is not so different from a character such as Belinda in Pope's *The Rape of the Lock*, who adorns herself with the spoils of empire when she sits at her dressing table (L. Brown 1993: 103–34). Whether one reads her as colonizer, native, or both, however, she is unquestionably beautiful – in fact, her white skin and auburn hair make her a Pre-Raphaelite beauty several decades ahead of her time – and it is beauty that inspires a sublime response in the lovers she startles with her presence. Notably, the two lovers react to her in different ways. The woman cowers "in an uncouth posture of fear," while the man "[sinks] his face to the earth in mute adoration" (p. 378), in a tellingly gendered response.

If Immalee's beauty makes her a sublime figure to Indians, her experiences on the island are what garner a response from the family she rejoins on her return to Spain. Her mother describes the island as "that heathen land, that region of Satan" (p. 332), and the family priest responds to her brother's desire to see her well married by saying, "There are many of our Catholic nobility who would rather see the black blood of the banished Moors, or the proscribed Jews, flow in the veins of their descendants, than that of one who . . ." (p. 337). While she does not quite inspire sublime terror in these scenes, it is clear that the place she has come from would. This fear of foreign places, foreign religions, and especially foreign men clearly manifests the various prejudices of the European ruling classes, and yet the fear of a being like Melmoth is greater still.

Immalee herself displays none of these prejudices. Her memories of the island color all of her experience in Spain, and the former inevitably seem far preferable to the latter. Sleep takes her back to the "shores of beauty and blessedness" she was forced to leave (p. 345), while in her waking hours she must be obedient to a family whose ways and beliefs she does not like. She tells Melmoth, "in the life that I now lead, dreams have become realities, and realities seem only like dreams" (p. 345), and it is in part because she identifies Melmoth with the island that she loves him so.

Imaginatively suspended between India and Spain, past and present, Immalee lives in a liminal state that further connects her to Melmoth, who is himself suspended between the living and the dead. When she is married to him – at night, in a ruined chapel, by a priest later revealed to have been already dead – one would think that she has given herself over fully to the demonic force that he embodies, and yet that does not prove to be the case. She does not entirely understand the force Melmoth embodies, but hopes all along to persuade him to her Christian faith, and so she continues, caught between the demonic and the divine. Even after her marriage has been revealed, after her child has been born and died, after she has turned down Melmoth's offer to save her from lifelong imprisonment in the Inquisition, she does not let him go. As she dies and her family priest commits her soul to heaven, she asks, "Will he be there?" (p. 533).

Immalee recalls both Lewis's Matilda and Dacre's Victoria in her suspension between the natural and supernatural worlds. And while Maturin's vision of her as the embodiment of a "beautiful sublime" initially makes her seem more socially acceptable than either of her predecessors, she is finally just as dangerous as they are. She is worshiped by foreigners, but feared by those at home who anticipate the damage she might do to their society, and, like Matilda, like Victoria, is written out of a narrative that cannot find a place for her.

3

Rethinking the Sublime
in the Novels of Ann Radcliffe

That John Keats could make a wry comment about "what fine mother Radcliff [*sic*] names" he had used in his poem "Eve of St. Mark" vividly conveys just how influential Radcliffe's version of the gothic was.[1] Writing in a tradition that was already fairly well established, she developed it so fully that her name became almost synonymous with the form. Eugenia DeLamotte notes that Radcliffe's contemporaries "recognized her as, if not the fountainhead, at least the opener of the floodgates for those tales with which, according to the *Critical Review* in 1796, the press had been inundated since 'Mrs. Radcliffe's justly admired and successful romances'" (1990: 11).[2] Robert Kiely has commented as well on the fact that Radcliffe's "gently euphemistic prose, her fainting heroines, and explainable ghosts were reproduced by other writers so quickly and on such a large scale that they were clichés before they had time to become conventions" (1972: 65). The task for the critic, then, is to determine just what she contributed to the form that made everyone so eager to imitate her.

Robert Miles has argued for Ann Radcliffe's "consolidation of the plot of the female Gothic" in *The Romance of the Forest* (1995: 101), and in this chapter I move to a similar conclusion by different analytical means. Radcliffe's centrality in shaping what Ellen Moers first called the "female gothic" is clear. Moers defined this sub-genre of the gothic as one in which "woman is examined with a woman's eye, woman as girl, as sister, as mother, as self," and, more precisely, in which women "give *visual* form to the fear of self" (1985: 109, 107), i.e. in which they produce images that in some way represent themselves. Juliann Fleenor reads female gothic as a form focused on a "conflict with the all-powerful devouring mother," an argument that is consistent with Moers's insofar as that "mother" may be "a double, a twin perhaps, to the woman herself" (1983: 16), and argues that this relationship can be worked out in any number of ways. Radcliffe's novels clearly place mother–daughter relationships at their center, exploring the workings of this relationship in a patriarchal society. The strength of this exploration is in its devising an aesthetic that insists on rather than obscures difference, as a way of allowing the daughter, whose story is always at the center of the novel, to separate from her mother and take her place in that larger society.[3] Radcliffe accomplishes this by moderating her engagement with – and at key points revising – then current thinking about the sublime.

Radcliffe's engagement with the tradition of writing about the sublime is complex. Even as she famously invokes the supernatural in her works only to explain it away in the end, so she gestures toward the sublime of writers like Walpole and Lewis only to set it aside. She does not endorse either their vision of sublimity as an experience based on the violent effacement of differences, or their reliance on its disruptive power to negotiate the social problems represented in their novels. Instead, she redefines sublimity as an aesthetic that multiplies differences, and that therefore empowers rather than effaces women.[4] And, while she sees a value in sublime experience, she does not see it as a viable way of addressing the social problems with which her novels also deal. Those she insists on engaging through social mechanisms.

A Sicilian Romance and *The Italian*

A Sicilian Romance was written early in Radcliffe's career, while *The Italian* is acknowledged to be the masterful accomplishment of a mature writer.[5] The plots of both develop through a calculated resistance to the patriarchal plots of the Burkean sublime, as they explore the ways in which the lives available to women are really no better than living deaths. These deaths are not the sublime events we saw in Walpole, Lewis, and Maturin, but are instead the seemingly routine erasures of women from the public sphere that mark the experiences of so many women in Radcliffe's novels. Life as a wife and life as a nun are the options most often presented to those women whose desires conflict with the desires of people in power, and, consistently, those options are figured as equivalent to death.[6] Indeed, when the women in question will not accept either of these options, physical death almost always awaits them right around the corner.

The importance of resisting these options is Radcliffe's subject in these novels. In *A Sicilian Romance*, she explores them from multiple perspectives. In the background are the stories of Louisa de Bernini, who marries the Count Mazzini only after the man she really loves has been killed, and of her dear friend Madame de Menon, whose brother is the man killed and whose husband is the killer. When we first hear these stories, Louisa has been presumed dead for many years, and Madame de Menon has essentially taken her place, having served all that time as the tutor of the two daughters Louisa left behind: Emilia and Julia. The stories of these two young women become entwined with that of a third – Cornelia, whose brother Julia loves – and while they initially threaten simply to repeat what has gone before, they finally recover and find a way past the seemingly limited options available to them.

The stories of Emilia and Cornelia do not result from the sorts of persecution that will characterize Julia's experiences, and that fact alone suggests that the ordinary options for women serve only to limit their lives. Emilia has only a minor role in the narrative, spending all of her time in her father's castle, not because she has been forcibly confined there, but because – not yet being desired in marriage, or destined for a convent – she has no other place to go. Cornelia's story is more involved, for she is a noble but poor woman who loves the equally noble but equally poor Angelo, and their lack of resources initially prevents their marriage. Cornelia conceals her passion for Angelo, but will not marry another, agreeing to take the veil instead. She is to be spared this fate when her father discovers her love for Angelo and agrees to the marriage, but at that very moment stories of Angelo's death cut off the possibility of their marriage and result in her deciding once again on the convent. When Angelo – who has not died – discovers what has happened, he becomes a priest and passes his life in the same religious establishment to which Cornelia belongs. They see each other only once, then lead separate lives, and Cornelia dies soon after Julia meets her.

Cornelia's story combines a perhaps incredible level of coincidence with a more considered commentary on the ways in which women's choices in life lead consistently to loss – of their lovers, of themselves, of their lives. Julia's story makes much clearer the powers that operate to put women in this position. Her father destines her to be the wife of the ambitious and tyrannical Duke de Luovo, and while she replies that "to obey [him] would be worse than death" (p. 55), he is so insistent that she is forced to flee her home to escape this fate. She takes shelter for a time in her maid's home town, but gives that up for the seemingly greater safety of the abbey of St. Augustin. There she faces the choice of either marrying de Luovo or becoming a nun, both of which are represented as equally dreadful: "From a marriage with the duke . . . her heart recoiled in horror, and to be immured for life within the walls of a convent, was a fate little less dreadful" (p. 142). She nonetheless resolves on the latter until she discovers her beloved

Count de Vereza – whom she had presumed dead – to be still living. At that point she escapes the convent and after still more life-threatening adventures finds herself unexpectedly in the Castle of Mazzini with a woman whom she discovers to be her mother. Once again refusing the death offered to her – this time a very literal death – she is able, with the help of Vereza, to free both herself and her mother from their prison.

Notably, Julia's escapes from her tyrannical father hinge on the help of several people: she initially attempts to escape her father's castle with the help of her brother, Ferdinand, and her lover, Hippolitus, but they are betrayed by a servant; she succeeds on a second attempt, aided by her maid and her maid's lover; she then finds her way to the abbey with the help of her former tutor, Madame de Menon; finally, when the abbey ceases to be a safe haven, it is Madame de Menon and her brother Ferdinand who arrange her flight. That servants and tutors should help her is perhaps explained as an alliance among people who are relatively disempowered. That her lover should also try to help her one can put down to self-interest. That her brother should oppose his father by supporting first her and later her mother suggests a rewriting of the rules of patriarchy – though by no means an abandonment of its structure – to accommodate and render visible the women who make it possible.

Radcliffe's central emphasis in this – and in all of her novels – is on rewriting what Burke and his peers would have defined as sublime experience to show that it is at best a temporary escape from, and at worst actively perpetuates, the oppressive politics of a patriarchal society. Sublime experience isolates, overwhelms, and eventually effaces those individuals who succumb to it, and so is not something Radcliffe can endorse. Her characters end up in the public sphere, in communication with other people and able to act on their own behalf. And it is her capacity to endow her female characters, in particular, with agency in the public sphere that renders Radcliffe's novels so successfully feminist.

Radcliffe's genius is to accomplish this goal in part through what Alison Milbank (1993) has identified as an important feminist revision of the Burkean sublime. Milbank points out that theorists of the sublime from Longinus on had associated sublime experience with "the masculine public arena of privileged equals, in which the orator 'transports' his hearers to new appreciations of their shared discourse" (1993: xii), while Burke contributed to this aesthetic his identification of it as a psychological experience rooted in terror (1993: x). She then argues that Radcliffe picks up Burke's interest in the sublime as an aesthetic that overwhelms those who experience it, but follows poets like James Thomson in locating the source of the sublime in nature, thus "open[ing] up the concept of the sublime as a democratic experience, since all people can respond to the beauties of creation" (1993: xiii). Following Samuel Monk, an influential critic of the early twentieth century, Milbank argues that this form of the sublime and its association with "the chivalric, the Gothic and the Ossianic takes the place, for women deprived of Greek and Latin, of classical education" and allows them to "establish . . . a rival cultural genealogy" (1993: xiv).

The natural sublime in itself is thus seen as open to appropriation by women, and Milbank's reading anatomizes its specific workings, showing how the passivity that leaves women – or anyone – open to sublime experience will in fact lead to useful knowledge. Her example is that of Madame de Menon in *A Sicilian Romance*, who follows "a view so various and sublime, that she pause[s] in thrilling and delightful wonder" until it leads her to the figure of her supposedly lost pupil, Julia (p. 104, cited in Milbank 1993: xvii). Similarly, Milbank argues that, in Radcliffe's later novels, "protagonists' acknowledgment of the sublime power of forces in nature and history beyond their control is followed by literary or musical creation, as an Emily St Aubert 'transposes' her immediate sensations into 'composition' of a more objective and universal character," with the result that "[p]rivate feelings can become public, and female experience is enabled to reach out to claim representative human status" (1993: xix). Thus "the Burkean sublime has become both a means of dramatizing human, and particularly female, subjection, and a catalyst to its overcoming" (1993: xix).

Milbank's reading of Radcliffe's rendering of the Burkean sublime is compelling, and leads one to ask a question that Milbank herself does not quite ask, namely, whether in Radcliffe's novels sublime experience does not become self-subverting. Such would seem to be the case, for scenes of sublimity in her novels seem regularly to lead women away from their initially transcendent experience and into the world that in so many ways wants to exclude them, a world whose realities Radcliffe insists they understand and respond to constructively. A still fuller response would acknowledge that Radcliffe's response to the sublime subverts at least Burke's version of the sublime in a variety of ways. At times she deliberately exposes and/or resists the oppressive dynamic on which a sublime moment is built. At others she contents herself with insisting on the importance of moving into and then right back out of that Burkean moment. At still others she goes so far as to restructure those moments, to try to shape a sublime experience that does not erase but instead acknowledges and even generates difference.

If sublime experience in Radcliffe leads one inevitably and ironically back into the world, the most important form of that experience occurs not as a result of human interaction with nature, the supernatural, or even the divine. Instead, it occurs in mother–daughter relationships, which – as I noted earlier – have long been recognized as central to the genre of female gothic. Critics have had much to say about Radcliffe's engagement with this subject, and here again, Alison Milbank's discussion is particularly helpful. Her introduction to her edition of the novel (Milbank 1993) reads Radcliffe's portrayal of mother–daughter relationships in light of what recent criticism has identified as a pre-Oedipal sublime.[7] This way of understanding mother–daughter relationships clearly relies on the analytical framework provided by psychoanalysis, in which the pre-Oedipal phase of development is that phase in which the child has not yet separated from its mother, and directs us to see the struggle of the gothic as the struggle of the daughter to separate from the mother. Claire Kahane first articulated this way of reading gothic, arguing that the mother was often literally represented by the gothic castle or house in which the heroine is trapped, and Milbank builds on Kahane's work, arguing that "[t]he sublime here is the location of the repressed and unrepresented mother, and it tempts the heroine to return to a complete identification with this buried experience" (1993: xxi). Where this complete identification would in turn result in repression of the heroine, however, Milbank argues that Radcliffe does not play out this dynamic, but instead insists on recovery of the mother as the necessary first step in the heroine's emergence as a distinct individual. Thus Milbank argues that, in *A Sicilian Romance*, for example, Julia's discovery of her mother in the dungeons under the family castle results not in Julia's being subsumed by her mother in a moment of sublime self-loss, but in her coming to understand herself "as the product of the union of male and female – of a truly sexual union – and . . . that the mother is also a lover" (1993: xxv). Julia's discovery of her mother results in her understanding of the complexity of her mother's identity, in other words, and in her understanding of herself as separate from her mother.

If one follows Milbank in understanding the sublimity of this moment to inhere in the potential merging of mother and daughter, then it is clear that one must read this scene as one in which sublime experience is avoided – or at least quickly set aside – as social reality comes to the fore. There is one more theoretical paradigm that may be helpful, however, and that is one generated by critical efforts to define a "female sublime." In an essay that Milbank also cites, Patricia Yaeger identifies the "female sublime" as a rhetorical mode, "a vocabulary of ecstasy and empowerment, a new way of reading feminine experience" (1989: 192). Barbara Claire Freeman argues quite differently that

> the female sublime is neither a rhetorical mode nor an aesthetic category but a domain of experience that resists categorization, in which the subject enters into relation with an otherness – social, aesthetic, political, ethical, erotic – that is excessive and unrepresentable. The feminine sublime is not a discursive strategy, technique, or literary style the female writer invents, but rather a crisis in relation to language and representation that a certain subject undergoes. (1995: 2)

Most interesting for my reading of Radcliffe are not the ways in which these two theorists oppose each other, but the ways in which they are in dialog. Yaeger is interested in women's writing as a way of reinventing existing notions of the sublime and so is Freeman, who says at one point that her "central question is not, what is the feminine sublime? but rather, how does it signify?" (1995: 10) For all of their differences, both Yaeger and Freeman finally point to a female sublime that posits not a relationship in which the self masters the overpowering other, but a relationship "that permits both a saving maintenance of ego-boundaries and an exploration of the pleasures of intersubjectivity" (Yaeger 1989: 205), that "involves taking up a position of respect in response to an incalculable otherness" (Freeman 1995: 11). Both are interested in forms of the sublime that acknowledge forces of overwhelming excess in the world around us, forms of "otherness" with which one can forge a connection, but to which one need not submit and which one need not conquer.[8] And this is Radcliffe's interest too.

With this line of thought in mind, one can see that Julia's discovery of her mother at the end of *A Sicilian Romance* is a discovery of someone whom she rightly identifies as other than herself but also somehow essential to definition of that self. Julia's first sight of her mother simply shows her "the pale and emaciated figure of a woman, seated, with half-closed eyes, in a kind of elbow-chair," whose "mild dignity . . . excited in [her] an involuntary veneration" (p. 174). The two do not yet know each other, but the mother's "wild surprise" at her unexpected visitor gives way in a moment to recognition of her daughter, and she immediately "faint[s] away" (p. 174). Julia in turn feels "astonishment," followed by a "multitude of strange imperfect ideas" that leave her "lost in perplexity" (p. 174). She starts to get her bearings when she looks in her mother's face and sees not the original of her own features, but rather "the resemblance of Emilia!" (p. 174). A scene that begins with the hallmarks of the Burkean sublime – literal loss of sense on one side, veneration and astonishment on the other – opens out into sublimity of another sort. Julia does not see in her mother a mirror-image with which she can fully identify, but the image of her sister, who mediates and so complicates the moment of identification. Identification of her mother and so of herself proceeds not through the merging of one into the other, but rather through the opening out of their identities into those of others. This process of identification is completed when the marchioness awakens and asks about her husband, at which point "Julia [throws] herself at the feet of her mother, and embracing her knees in an energy of joy, answer[s] only in sobs" (p. 174). The moment is sublime in its understanding of the multiple ties that go into the definition of a single individual, and it is this form of sublimity that Radcliffe explores once more in *The Italian* (1797), another novel in which the heroine's discovery of a mother she had thought dead helps bring her trials to a successful close.

The Italian explores the placement of women in patriarchy in a way that recalls but elaborates *A Sicilian Romance*, again scrutinizing the social structures that conspire to render women invisible, and again recognizing the Burkean sublime as the aesthetic that serves to mask these structures. Even as the Burkean sublime is undercut, however, Radcliffe works to redefine sublimity in a way that acknowledges and complicates our understanding of female subjectivity, rather than effacing it, and again it is the heroine's relationship to her mother that facilitates that exploration.

The heroine of *The Italian* is Ellena di Rosalba, who – like Julia in *A Sicilian Romance* – is from the start fairly secluded from society. Where Julia was locked away in a castle with her sister and tutor, so Ellena lives with an elderly aunt. And where Julia's attraction to the Count Vereza can be seen as the cause of subsequent efforts to confine her, so Ellena's involvement with her suitor, Vivaldi, precipitates all of her problems. At the request of Vivaldi's mother, Ellena is abducted from the home of her recently deceased aunt and taken to a remote convent, where she is given a choice between becoming a nun or agreeing to an arranged marriage. She refuses both options, saying that she is "prepared to meet whatever suffering [the abbess] shall inflict upon [her]" instead (p. 84). The only other "evil" that Ellena can imagine being inflicted on her is permanent confinement from the world, though an experienced reader of gothic will know that death is yet another alternative. Having articulated these scenarios, the novel plays them out one after the other.

Volume I devotes considerable time to Ellena's imprisonment in the convent of San Stefano. Notably, she is "not . . . shocked by a discovery of the designs formed against her, since, from the moment of her arrival at San Stefano, she had expected something terribly severe, and had prepared her mind to meet it with fortitude" (p. 84). This all too comprehensible misery is countered, however, by what any reader of Burke would describe as the sublime pleasure she takes in contemplating the setting in which she finds herself. Ellena's walk through an unguarded door at the convent of San Stefano into a room with a view of the surrounding landscape invokes but also critiques Burke's thought with a rhetoric as subtle as it is incisive. In this "turret . . . suspended, as in air, above the vast precipices of granite, that formed part of the mountain" on which the convent is situated, Ellena looks out "with a dreadful pleasure" that directs one to read her experience through Burkean lenses (p. 90). "The consciousness of her prison" is said to disappear as "her eyes ranged over the wide and freely-sublime scene without" (p. 90):

> Here, gazing upon the stupendous imagery around her, looking, as it were, beyond the awful veil which obscures the features of the Deity, and conceals Him from the eyes of his creatures, dwelling as with a present God in the midst of his sublime works; with a mind thus elevated, how insignificant would appear to her the transactions, and the sufferings of this world! How poor the boasted power of man, when the fall of a single cliff from these mountains would with ease destroy thousands of his race assembled on the plains below! How would it avail them,

that they were accoutred for battle, armed with all the instruments of destruction that human invention ever fashioned? Thus man, the giant who now held her in captivity, would shrink to the diminutiveness of a fairy; and she would experience, that his utmost force was unable to enchain her soul, or compel her to fear him, while he was destitute of virtue. (pp. 90–1)

This much-discussed passage fascinates not simply because it envisions Ellena escaping the confines of the physical world to dwell with the Deity in sublime unity, but because it implicitly opposes this form of sublimity to that which would be created by the spectacle of a cliff falling on thousands of men. Ellena's vision of sublimity as union with the divine contrasts with her vision of the sublimity caused by confrontation and destruction. Further, even while one might feel that her repeated mentions of "men" and "man" are meant to invoke all humanity, it is hard not to read those words as detailing a more specifically gendered dynamic, in which her male and male-identified oppressors – "accoutred for battle" as they are – will themselves be oppressed.

In a couple of ways, then, this passage offers a vision of sublime experience that recalls but revises sublime scenes as they have emerged in Walpole and Lewis, yet Radcliffe herself cannot finally endorse even this revised form of sublime experience as a lastingly viable way for her heroines to cope with the world. She stresses that Ellena's sense of union with God is illusory, that Ellena dwells only *"as it were*, beyond the awful veil," and only *"as* with a present God" (italics mine). Ellena can retreat to this turret from time to time, but it offers no real escape from her problems. Indeed, it is available to her only so long as she is resident in the convent, and when her refusal to take the veil means that she will be immured and left to die in the labyrinth of secret spaces beneath the convent, she must flee. Notably, that crisis coincides with the very human intrusion of Vivaldi onto that sublime landscape: "perched on a point of the cliff below" her window, Vivaldi outlines a plan for her escape, and it is in this reclaiming of the sublime by the human that the solution to Ellena's problems emerges (p. 124).

Ellena's refusal to become a nun sits alongside her repeated refusals to marry against her will. She never even considers the partner chosen for her by Vivaldi's mother, and puts off Vivaldi – to whom she is in fact pledged – as long as she can. Ellena's wariness of marriage stems from her desire to preserve a sense of her own self-worth once married, and while it is clear how a marriage made under duress would erode that sense, what is less obvious is the way in which all romantic relationships seem to threaten the self as well. Relevant here is Terry Castle's discussion of Radcliffean gothic as a genre characterized by what she calls the "spectralization of the other." Talking specifically about *The Mysteries of Udolpho*, Castle traces the way in which lovers reduce their beloveds to ghostly images that "can be appropriated, held close, and cherished forever in the ecstatic confines of the imagination" (1995: 136), and her argument clearly pertains to Radcliffe's other novels as well. In the first chapter of *The Italian*, Vivaldi takes leave of Ellena physically, but with "[t]he beauty of her countenance haunting his imagination, and the touching accents of her voice still vibrating on his heart" (p. 7). Similarly, Ellena associates Vivaldi with her deceased aunt, and "her love for the one was so intimately connected with her affection for the other, that each seemed strengthened and exalted by the union" (p. 57). And the beloved who has been reduced to this ghostly status arguably does become "a source of sublime and life-sustaining emotion" (Castle 1995: 136).

Even as these actions take place, however, Radcliffe seems to recognize that the cost of this ghostly imaging is the loss of the other, at least in a physical sense. To take the other into one's mind is to deny her or him an independent existence, as Castle sees. It is in some sense also to kill off that other, at least figuratively. This sublime and life-sustaining experience would seem to involve as much figurative violence as any of the sublime experiences considered to this point, and this is surely yet another reason why Radcliffean gothic stands back from any full-fledged endorsement of either Burkean sublimity or the structure of human relationships that it supports. Ellena and Vivaldi will marry by the end of the novel, but not before their connection to each other has been significantly redefined.

Before I talk about just how that redefinition takes place, however, there is one last invocation and resistance of the Burkean sublime in this novel that merits discussion, and that is Ellena's confinement and near murder at the hands of the priest Schedoni. That Schedoni balks at the murder is important, for he mistakes a miniature around Ellena's neck for a picture of himself, and believes that he is about to kill his own daughter. The scenario here is nearly that of *The Castle of Otranto*, but this time the supposed father puts the dagger down. He does not kill Ellena, but instead conducts her away from his home, and sets about reuniting her with Vivaldi. The novel in this way again avoids the sublime erasure of difference that novels like *The Monk* allow.

In turning away from this form of the sublime, Radcliffe would seem to turn away not only from its threat to the self, but also from the promise of revelation that accompanies that threat. Where Walpole and Lewis link sublime experiences with the revelations that bring their stories to a close, Radcliffe seeks another way by which the truth can emerge. In part, she turns to storytelling as the vehicle for truth-telling, and, unlike Walpole and Lewis – who make sure that everyone involved knows the truth about everything that pertains to them – Radcliffe allows her characters access to the truth only when it will serve some practical purpose. She has Schedoni commit suicide at the end of the novel, and while his death perhaps recalls the Burkean sublime, combining the violence of self-murder with the revelation of much that has to this point been mysterious in the novel, it is finally not sublime but ironic. In spite of all that he is able to tell his rapt auditors about the sins of his life, Schedoni dies without ever discovering that Ellena was his stepdaughter and not his daughter. Radcliffe denies him the holistic vision accorded to Manfred and Ambrosio, refusing to privilege the insight of this corrupt man.

More importantly, however, Radcliffe repeats the move that she made at the close of *A Sicilian Romance*, reuniting Ellena with the mother she has long presumed dead, and in the process reinventing the sublime. The seeds of this reunion are planted early in the novel, when Ellena – imprisoned in the convent of San Stefano – hears "[a]mong the voices of the choir . . . one whose expression immediately fixed her attention," one that "seemed to speak a loftier sentiment of devotion than the others, and to be modulated by the melancholy of an heart, that had long since taken leave of this world" (p. 86). Listening to this voice, Ellena "felt that she understood all the feelings of the breast from which it flowed" (p. 86), and she worries later that she has offended this woman whose "regard . . . was not only delightful, but seemed necessary to her heart" (p. 88). This woman is a nun named Olivia, and one is hardly surprised to discover, near the end of the novel, that Olivia is Ellena's mother. Susan C. Greenfield identifies this moment as one that takes Ellena back to the pre-Oedipal moment of unity with the mother (2002: 67–9), and that has in turn – as I have discussed – been identified as a form of the sublime. As in *A Sicilian Romance*, the assertion of this bond between mother and child results not in the absorption of one by the other, but in a connection that paves the way for separation. Once Olivia reveals that not the vicious Schedoni but instead the virtuous Count di Bruno was Ellena's father, and that she herself is Ellena's mother, Ellena's marriage to Vivaldi can go forward.

Radcliffe understands that sublimity must be redefined as a generative rather than a destructive principle. She understands as well the ironic truth that what it must generate are structures of difference, though she wants to change – rather than simply replicate – those that already exist. Thus, in the final chapter of *The Italian*, Radcliffe generates a vision of a world marked by differences that seem to multiply as one reads, and that by the end do not quite make sense. The scene opens with a fairy-tale vision in which nobles and peasants celebrate together, but Ellena is still "the queen" (p. 413). Similarly, "[t]he style of the gardens" is said to be "that of England, and of the present day, rather than of Italy; except 'Where a long alley peeping on the main,' exhibit[s] such a gigantic loftiness of shade, and grandeur of perspective, as characterize the Italian taste" (p. 412). So far we see only a careful articulation of sameness and difference, but things change when the servant Paulo rejoices that people "[m]ay fly in the sea, or swim in the sky, or tumble over head and heels into the moon," only to be corrected by "[a] grave personage" who comments, "You mean swim in the sea, and fly in the sky, I suppose . . . but as for tumbling over head and heels into the moon! I don't know what you mean by that!" (pp. 414–15). This final exchange moves us into a world shaped by an excess of joy, a world that opens out into a complex and highly articulated – or differentiated – structure. It is a world that we do not quite recognize, and in that is her great success. In confronting that differentiated structure, and in acknowledging our own difference from it, we understand that these differences are what allow us to live our lives intact and empowered.

The Romance of the Forest and *The Mysteries of Udolpho*

Radcliffe's *A Sicilian Romance* and *The Italian* turn away from the Burkean sublime, with its insistence on the effacement of the individual, suggesting instead that sublimity should be redefined as an essentially generative experience. This is seen primarily in the mother–daughter relationships that emerge in these novels, and that propel both mothers and daughters into recognition of their own complicated subjectivities. The novels Radcliffe wrote between these two – *The Romance of the Forest* and *The Mysteries of Udolpho* – complicate this vision by focusing particularly on the heroines' progress in the world once their mothers are really and truly dead.[9] In *The Romance of the Forest*, Adeline's mother dies while she is yet an infant, and although evidence of Adeline's maternal heritage is important to establishing her identity at the end of the novel, the way in which the connection is established differs significantly from what we have seen in *A Sicilian Romance* or *The Italian*. In an even more notable shift in focus, Emily's mother passes away by the end of the first chapter of *Udolpho*, and any complications associated with her memory are fairly easily resolved. What changes when mothers drop out of the picture like this? Does Radcliffe turn away even from her own revisions of sublimity as the key to self-realization? If she does, what is gained and what is lost by this move?

The Romance of the Forest flirts with the Burkean sublime on many occasions, exploiting the thrills it can create while making unusually clear the patriarchal politics on which it is founded. Towards the end of the novel, Adeline ventures into the Alps with the La Luc family, and the "sublimity of the scenery" signals its capacity to take viewers beyond this world (p. 265). La Luc comments in utterly predictable language that such scenes "lift the soul to their Great Author," allowing one to "contemplate with a feeling almost too vast for humanity the sublimity of his nature in the grandeur of his works" (p. 265), yet when Adeline looks at the same landscape, she offers the far more idiosyncratic observation that "[i]t seems . . . as if we were walking over the ruins of the world, and were the only persons who had survived the wreck" (p. 265). She understands what La

Luc does not, that sublimity as it is usually understood grows out of the oppression of people and places, and indeed, her prior experiences with what Burke would have called the sublime make this dynamic all too clear.[10]

The novel opens with a "scene" that even one of its principal players recognizes as something "like a vision, or one of those improbable fictions that sometimes are exhibited in a romance" (p. 8). What has happened is this. Pierre La Motte, the player in question and "a gentleman, descended from an ancient house of France" (p. 2), has been forced to leave Paris for exile in the south of France as a way of escaping his gambling debts. When he loses his way just outside Paris, he seeks help from the inhabitants of a "small and ancient house, which stood alone on the heath" (p. 3), where he finds himself taken prisoner and fully expects to be robbed or even killed. What happens instead is that he is confronted with a beautiful young girl who will turn out to be our heroine, the above-mentioned Adeline, and told by a man whom Adeline believes to be her father: "if you wish to save your life, swear that you will convey this girl where I may never see her more" (p. 5). When the pair exit the house, they also exit the fairy-tale narrative it seems to represent. From that point on, the novel moves slowly to strip away such enchantment and expose the often brutal patriarchal politics behind it, concluding its action in a public courtroom where Adeline gains both recognition and power. That a courtroom should prove the antidote to the gothic terrors of the house on the heath is ironic, for both are clearly run on patriarchal principles. Radcliffe's interest all along seems to be less in dismantling patriarchy than exposing its workings and exploring the roles open to women within it. To this end the novel imagines not one, not two, but three different patriarchal societies in seventeenth-century Europe: the Forest of Fontangville, Leloncourt, and finally the city of Paris.

Adeline, Pierre La Motte, and his wife end their flight from their various oppressors in the Forest of Fontangville. Far from providing a pastoral alternative to the difficult lives they have all left behind, it does just the opposite, and they find themselves living in a nightmarish world that not only replicates but intensifies the world they knew. They make their home in the gothic ruins of the abbey of St. Clair, in an environment that might have been conjured by Burke. The remains of the chapel inspire in La Motte "a sensation of sublimity rising into terror – a suspension of mingled astonishment and awe!" (p. 15). "Terrors, which she neither endeavoured to examine, or combat," overcome Madame La Motte at the very prospect of staying in this place overnight (p. 17). The fears inspired by the abbey start to seem more justified when the family learns that it was the property of "a nobleman, who now resided with his family on a remote estate," and that it "was reported, that some person was, soon after it came to the present possessor, brought secretly to the abbey and confined" (p. 30). Not long after this, La Motte lifts the lid of a well-hidden chest only to discover "the remains of a human skeleton" (p. 54). Adeline then has dreams about a man dying in a hidden room of the abbey, and finally she discovers – through a door hidden behind the arras in her room – both a bloodstained dagger and a mysterious man-uscript. Her secret readings of the manuscript fill her with horror, yet its frag-mented narrative does not reveal what happened to its author. To discover that she will need to leave the cocooned world of the forest, and one major obstacle prevents her from doing so: the Marquis de Montalt.

The Marquis de Montalt has considerable power over La Motte, both because he owns the building in which the latter is living, and because he has recently been robbed by La Motte, whom he can therefore have imprisoned at any moment. When the marquis inevitably blackmails La Motte, Adeline is his price for silence, and he gets what he wants, at least for a time. With La Motte's help, as well as that of his servants, he manages to kidnap her and bring her to a home that is the decadent counterpart to the decaying abbey of St. Clair. Adeline is "astonished" by the silk hangings, and frescoes "representing scenes from Ovid," but recognizes the danger she is in, and prevaricates well enough to keep the marquis at a distance (p. 156). She escapes both him and his dubious offers of marriage by jumping out of a window (following in the footsteps of Richardson's *Pamela*, who at one point escapes persecution in just the same way), and while she is eventually returned to La Motte, who once again agrees to turn her over to the marquis, she escapes a second time and is then able to leave the forest once and for all.

From a forest that is the preserve of the decaying and decadent nobility (the very nobility who would be guillotined by the thousands in the years just after this novel was published), Adeline escapes to the village of Leloncourt. This is the birthplace of La Motte's servant Peter, and, once there, she is taken in by the family of Arnand La Luc, the village pastor. La Luc's own home is said to be "delightful," while "the philanthropy which, flowing from the heart of the pastor," was diffused through the whole village, and united the inhabitants in the sweet and firm bonds of social compact, was divine" (p. 277). The words "social compact" indicate that we are to read this as a society modeled on the principles articulated by Locke and especially Rousseau,[11] and it is a community in which hierarchies of both class and gender seem less pronounced than they are else-where in the novel. That said, however, there are limits to this egalitarian vision. La Luc may be a benevolent man, but he looks startlingly like La Motte insofar as he is "descended from an ancient family of France, whose decayed fortunes occasioned them to seek a retreat in Switzerland" (p. 245), and it is not the col-lective efforts of the villagers, but his own "philanthropy" – described as "divine," no less – that creates the social harmony we are meant to admire. He is a senti-mentalized version of Filmer's noble patriarch, but a patriarch still, and his is a world in which women's roles continue to be carefully circumscribed. La Luc's sister is mildly satirized for her devotion to herbal medicines, while his daughter, Clara, is chastised for playing the lute rather than attending to her social duties (Johnson 1995: 88–9). Claudia Johnson has taught us to see this treatment of women as part of a more widespread tendency in the 1790s to render women "equivocal beings," out of place in the worlds of reason and of sentiment, both of which at this point are male domains, and her insight sits well alongside Carol Pateman's understanding (Pateman 1988) that a world defined by a social contract rather than literal patriarchal lines of rule is nonetheless a "world without women" (the phrase is David Noble's).

Alternative to both these settings is the city of Paris, where the novel's mysteries are finally resolved. The royal court, the prison, and the court of law are the locations of the activity that takes place there, and ironically these institutions – none of which leaves much space for women – are precisely where Adeline comes into her own. Caught up in the machinations of Montalt – who has managed to have La Luc's son condemned to death at the same time as he is bringing La Motte to trial for robbing him – she travels to Paris to testify on behalf of the latter. As the trial goes forward and the truth of the dealings between La Motte and Montalt are revealed, she also learns that Montalt is her uncle, that he killed her father to gain possession of the abbey of St. Clair, and that he wished to hold on to it by killing her as well. It should come as no surprise that the property originally belonged not to Adeline's father, but to her mother – who died shortly after her birth – and that the marquis is yet another patriarchal authority whose power is built on the oppression of women. More surprising is Adeline's accession to all that he has lost.

By the conclusion of the trial, Adeline has been transformed from a penniless, helpless young woman beholden to La Motte, La Luc, their sons, and even the servant Peter into a wealthy young woman able to help every one of those people in return. She might be said to have taken on the role of patriarch herself,[12] as she moves into the place occupied first by her biological father and then by the marquis. That she does this by reclaiming the legacy of her mother, however, suggests alternatively that matrilineal descent is what is truly empowering here, though it surfaces only for this brief moment before Adeline marries and literally leaves behind (though she does not absolutely give up) that maternal legacy.

The Mysteries of Udolpho explores from another perspective the placement of – and possibilities for – women in patriarchal society. The novel exploits with great skill the power of the Burkean sublime to engross its readers, but at the same time insists – as does Radcliffe's other work – that this form of sublimity intensifies and obscures rather than resolves the problems that interest her most. The novel turns on Emily St. Aubert's efforts to ensure her own survival following the deaths of first her mother and then her father. Forced to live with her aunt, Madame Cheron, and the man her aunt has recently married, Montoni, she must not let herself be overwhelmed – literally or metaphorically – by the variously awe-inspiring and terrifying scenes she encounters.

The pleasures of the Burkean sublime are, as usual, generated largely by the spectacular landscapes in which Emily finds herself at various points in the novel, and especially the mountainous terrain in which Udolpho stands. The terrors are just as expectedly generated by Montoni, whose name marks him as a human counterpart to the mountains, and again suggests that this form of sublimity is gendered male.[13] As terrifying as Montoni himself is everything associated with him – his henchmen, Udolpho itself, and the original owner of the castle, Signora Laurentini. Laurentini is particularly worth our attention, for it is in part through her character – especially as it exists in relation to Emily – that Radcliffe explores the possibilities and limits of female independence.

Laurentini is associated with terror for much of the novel, but the reason for this association shifts significantly over time. Emily articulates the nature of this shift towards the end of the novel, when she realizes that "Signora Laurentini . . . instead of having been murdered by Montoni, was, as it now seemed, herself guilty of some dreadful crime" (p. 650). Instead of having been victimized by a patriarchal society, Laurentini finds a way to make that society her victim, and in the swing from one extreme to the other there is a transition that echoes the story of Lewis's Rosario, the submissive noviciate who evolved into the devilish Matilda. Where Lewis portrays a resourceful woman as the devil incarnate, however, Radcliffe sees her in a far more complex way – as utterly human, and damaging not only to the society around her, but also to herself.

Laurentini is introduced into the novel indirectly, when the servant Annette tells Emily about the woman who originally owned the castle of Udolpho, and one day mysteriously disappeared. Since Laurentini's disappearance resulted in Montoni's inheriting the castle that dominates so much of the novel, one is quickly led to wonder whether he murdered her for the sake of her property, a conjecture that seems all the more warranted as we watch him imprison both Madame Cheron and Emily for the very same reason. Annette finishes her account of Laurentini's disappearance by saying that Laurentini "has been seen . . . walking the woods and about the castle in the night" (p. 238), and while Emily scoffs at this story, she nonetheless finds herself frightened by the thought of this "strange history" and its relation to "her own strange situation" (p. 240). In this frame of mind, Emily remembers seeing a picture "concealed by a veil of black silk" that according to Annette had "something very dreadful belonging to it" (p. 233) and she "resolve[s] to examine it," becoming increasingly "agitated" as she ponders "its connection with the late lady of the castle" (p. 248). By the time Emily actually lifts the veil – only to discover that it is "no picture" – she "drop[s] senseless to the floor" (p. 248). We do not learn at this point what exactly Emily has seen behind the veil, but as the novel progresses, she associates that terrifying sight with that of a dead body that she stumbles across. The movement from the story of Laurentini to the mystery behind the black veil to the actual body "deformed by death" (p. 348) suggests a reprise of that form of the sublime that we saw in Lewis or Maturin – a sublimity predicated on the erasure of the recognizably human and its transformation into something terrifying – yet the novel famously pulls back from this scenario in its closing pages. There the figure is revealed to be not Laurentini or anyone else, but a wax figure of a decaying corpse – a *memento mori* that is meant to inspire penitence. By then this anticlimax is almost expected, because Laurentini has appeared – alive, if not quite well – in a very different context.[14]

While we might be glad to turn away from this vision of Laurentini and the sublime thrills inspired by the sight of victimized women, it is disturbing to recognize that Laurentini does participate in the process that produces such horrors, and even more disturbing to see that she perpetuates as well as suffers from it. She figures largely in the novel's final few chapters, when she is revealed to have seduced the Marquis de Villeroi and conspired to murder his wife, who is also – and not coincidentally – Emily's aunt. Notably, her crimes led to no reward, but instead "left her to the horrors of unavailing pity and remorse, which would probably have empoisoned all the years she had promised herself with the Marquis de Villeroi" had he not had been still more remorseful and so abandoned her (p. 659). She is a threat to patriarchy, and deals an effective blow to the marquis' family, but she is not in the end a threat on the order of Lewis's Matilda. Undermined by her own transgression, she spends the rest of her life in a convent, shrouded in the identity of the mad Sister Agnes, and so self-tortured that she becomes almost literally a shadow of her former self. She becomes a ghostly presence, haunting the environs of her convent with music of "uncommon sweetness" whose source no one can identify (p. 525), and by the end of the novel really is a kind of *memento mori*. She is a victimizer who became a victim of her own crime, and a warning – more touching than terrifying – of the price of passion.

Emily is like Laurentini in her possession of substantial property, even in her love of a man who appears less than virtuous,[15] but entirely unlike her in her ability to command her feelings. Emily is schooled in this command by her father, who from the beginning of the novel warns her to avoid "ill-governed sensibility", which can leave us "victims of our feelings, unless we can in some degree command them" (p. 80). It is this capacity for self-control that renders her successful in the world, a worthy inheritor of her father's property.

The novel plays quite consciously with Radcliffe's established pattern of empowering women through the recognition of maternal ties. Contrary to what Radcliffe's earlier novels might lead one to expect, Emily's mother never reappears as an important figure in the novel after her death in its first chapter. The novel plays with readers' expectations on this subject, to be sure, through its recurrent focus on the miniature of a woman – not Emily's mother – which she sees her father kiss; through its insistence on Emily's resemblance to the late Marchioness de Villeroi, murdered mistress of the Chateau-le-Blanc, where Emily finds shelter after escaping Montoni and the castle of Udolpho; through Laurentini's mistaken identification of Emily with the marchioness. All of these details lead one to think that the marchioness must have been Emily's mother, yet this is not the case. Emily is not propelled into happiness by the recovery of a lost maternal connection. Rather, even her link to the woman figured in all these scenes – and there is one – insists yet again on the importance of paternity.[16] For the marchioness was Emily's aunt, and the sister of Emily's father.

Emily's tie to her father is asserted in various ways, the most important of which he articulates on his deathbed, when he asks of her three things: that she destroy without looking at them a packet of mysterious papers that presumably tell the story of the murdered marchioness; that "whatever may be [her] future circumstances," she never sell La Vallée; and that "whenever she might marry" she "make it an article in the contract, that the chateau should always be hers" (p. 78); and finally – as mentioned above – that she protect herself from "the dangers of sensibility," not shutting off her feelings, but not succumbing to them either. These pieces of advice constitute St. Aubert's efforts to protect his daughter, and together point to his clear understanding of what it takes for a woman to protect herself in late eighteenth-century society. He seeks to guarantee her material and her moral well-being in a world in which both are vulnerable to attack, and seems mindful of the fact that these two things are linked. Mary Poovey has argued that the phenomenon of sensibility encouraged sympathetic responses for others primarily because they "advanced one's own welfare and gratified the desire for approval" (1979: 307). Sensibility aided and abetted capitalist greed, in other words, and if Emily can protect herself from one, she can protect herself from the other. His desired legacy to her is thus an independence – a personal integrity or wholeness – that ensures she will not lose herself or her property to another. That legacy is almost instantly challenged, however, when Emily is forced to leave La Vallée for the home of her aunt, Madame Cheron, whom her father has made her guardian, and from that point on, her life turns into a series of threats that she must fend off.

Emily's paternal legacy shows an unexpected fragility almost at once. Immediately after she has left La Vallée, she learns that the debt-ridden estate has been leased to tenants without her knowledge. It appears she might lose her father's property before she has even had a chance to inhabit it, and her situation gets worse when Madame Cheron marries Montoni, who moves them still farther from home, first to Venice, and then to the castle of Udolpho, where she and her aunt are virtually imprisoned. Montoni's interest in both women turns entirely on the fact that they either have or can help him attain property that will rescue him from a desperate financial situation, and to their credit, he does not get what he wants from either one. Emily is initially valuable to Montoni because of her potential to marry well, and she sees at once that he "[seeks] to aggrandise himself in his disposal of her" (p. 145), steadfastly refusing to do as he wishes. Indeed, it is her refusal to wed the Count Morano that is the immediate cause of the group's move from Venice to the isolated castle of Udolpho, where Montoni can better terrify her into acting as he wishes. Similarly, when Montoni insists that property she has inherited from her aunt is his by legal right, she has the temerity to disagree, saying: "the law, in the present instance, gives me the estates in question, and my own hand shall never betray my right" (p. 381). Emily's resistance is all the more significant given its context: Madame Cheron's death was the indirect result of her refusal to sign over the property in the first place, after she learned too late that this is what Montoni had really wanted in marrying her. Emily finally does agree to give up her inherited property in exchange for a promise of freedom that, unsurprisingly, turns out to be false. Thus when she escapes from Udolpho and finds her way to her next shelter – the Chateau-le-Blanc, with the Villefort family – she appears farther than ever from her father and the life he had wished for her.

Emily begins to recover her losses – material and otherwise – from the time of her arrival at Chateau-le-Blanc. During the stay in this region, she learns that Montoni has died mysteriously in prison, and her aunt's properties are restored to her. At the same time that she hears this news, she also learns that the tenants at La Vallée are coming to the end of their lease, so that she can return to her father's home. Finally, she inherits part of Laurentini's property as well, and with it a new understanding of her family's history, and of her father in particular (whose infidelity to her mother had been falsely suggested by the mysterious papers he had Emily destroy, and the miniature over which he wept).[17]

Having survived more threats than her father could have imagined possible, Emily has one more hurdle to navigate. She has long been courted by Valancourt, and while her father seemingly approved him as a mate, while her aunt even endorsed their engagement (though only because she wanted the social connection with his family), their marriage is delayed until the end of the novel. Their connection is initially severed by Montoni, but later denied by Emily as well, when she learns that Valancourt spent time in the gaming houses of Paris – and even found himself in debtor's prison – while she was at Udolpho. Such behavior grows from a sensibility more motivated by passion and greed than it ought to be, and only when he convinces Emily that he has repented as well as reformed – that he is more like her father than like Montoni – does she agree to marry him.

The novel concludes with a series of negotiations that make clear Emily's allegiances. She sells the estate she inherited from her aunt, gives away the legacy that she inherited from Laurentini, and buys back her father's boyhood home of Epourville, which financial exigencies had forced him to sell. She rids herself of property that has come to her through women, in other words, even as she consolidates that which is associated with her father, and when it comes to choosing a place to live, she of course returns to La Vallée.

Even more strongly than *The Romance of the Forest*, then, *The Mysteries of Udolpho* suggests that the way for a woman to escape the gothic nightmare of patriarchal society is – ironically – through identification with the patriarch. Laurentini errs when she tries to act in defiance of a society that does not serve her interests, playing neither a properly female nor a properly male role. Emily defies convention insofar as she insists that women can effectively oppose those men who would victimize them, but uses her independence to preserve rather than disrupt the patriarchal line on which that society is founded.

4

From the Sublime to the Uncanny
Godwin and Wollstonecraft

The novels of Ann Radcliffe state explicitly that we are haunted by ghosts of our own making. In fact, gothic novels have always known this, though their explanations for these hauntings have not always had the rational quality that Radcliffe offers. Emily's fear of finding Laurentini's body under the black veil does not quite correspond to Manfred's fear on actually encountering the ghost of Alfonso, or to Raymond's terror at the repeated visits of the Bleeding Nun. While these experiences are not fully analogous, however, all three effectively amount to the same thing: a forced reckoning with a long-buried piece of family history. One might borrow a phrase from Maturin and describe these frightening encounters with one's past as "self-hauntings." One might also look forward from the gothic to Sigmund Freud and his concept of the "uncanny" to explain what is happening in situations like these.

Freud's essay "The Uncanny" opens with a fairly simple definition of uncanny experience as "undoubtedly related to what is frightening – to what arouses dread and horror" (1955[1919]: 219). While Harold Bloom (1982) and others have argued forcefully that Freud's concept of the uncanny is essentially a version of sublime experience, it is important to note that Freud himself distinguishes between them.[1] He contrasts his study of the uncanny with the majority of "comprehensive treatises on aesthetics, which in general prefer to concern themselves with what is beautiful, attractive and sublime – that is with feelings of a positive nature – with the circumstances and the objects that call them forth, rather than with the opposite feelings of repulsion and distress" (1955: 219). While one might pause at Freud's conflation of beauty with sublimity, as well as at his unqualified association of both with "positive" feelings rather than the more complicated dynamics demonstrated in earlier chapters – indeed, for Bloom this second point alone provides good reason to be "very wary" of taking Freud literally (Bloom 1982: 101) – the distinction is nonetheless instructive. The uncanny resembles the sublime insofar as it is an aesthetic that is based on the psychology of fear, yet that fear is untempered by the twinge of pleasure that Edmund Burke associated with the sublime. Lars Engle notes the uncanny's motivation by internal rather than external forces, and explores how uncanny experiences unsettle our sense of ourselves, destabilizing our sense of our own identity, and trapping us in "paralysis and alienation" (1989: 114). Uncanny experiences do not resolve in the way sublime experiences do, but instead leave us profoundly estranged from ourselves and "no longer knowing how to live in the world" (1989: 114).

Freud goes on to define the uncanny primarily as "that class of the frightening which leads back to something long known to us, once very familiar" (1955: 220). He identifies that "something" as one of two things: either it pertains to supposedly past stages of cultural development ("when primitive beliefs which have been surmounted seem once more to be confirmed"), or it pertains to past stages of individual psychological development ("when infantile complexes which have been repressed" are "once more revived by some impression") (1955: 249). Freud gives many examples of both of these forms of the uncanny, arguing that the former is most common, and that most of us will experience the uncanny when something occurs to confirm our belief in a spirit world, or fate, or some such thing. It is the latter, however, that seems to interest him the most.

"The Uncanny" devotes a good deal of space to an analysis of E. T. A. Hoffman's story "The Sandman." Freud's interest in the story focuses on the central character of Nathanael and his relations with a series of father-figures: his own father, a lawyer and family friend named Coppelius, an optician named Giuseppe Coppola (who seems to be none other than Coppelius in another guise), and a professor named Spalanzani. Nathanael's father and Spalanzani are both benevolent figures, but Coppelius/Coppola is not. The young Nathanael is terrified by Coppelius, whom he identifies as the mythical "sandman" famed for tearing out children's eyes, and whom he blames for his father's death. As a college student, he is equally terrified by the optician Coppola, whose appearance on the scene coincides with other disruptions in his life: his turning away from his fiancée, Clara; his falling in love with Spalanzani's daughter, Olympia;

his eventual madness when he discovers that Olympia is an automaton, constructed by Spalanzani, with help from Coppola, who has supplied – and in a dramatic scene, tears out – the eyes. Home from college and recovered from his madness, Nathanael is on the verge of marrying Clara when he catches sight of a figure we assume to be Coppelius/Coppola returned one last time, and kills himself.

Freud looks at what we might call Nathanael's "haunting" by Coppola; he looks as well at the consistent association between Coppola and eyes, and – working from the premise that "anxiety about one's eyes, the fear of going blind, is often enough a substitute for the dread of being castrated" (1955: 231) – explains the story as being about the son's fear of castration at the hands of his father (or the father's substitute). He rightly sees the son as eerily confronted by a father-figure whose appearance repeatedly truncates his relationships with women and so threatens his virility, and this piece of his argument might be further developed if we connect it with what he has to say about "doubles" as a source of the uncanny.

Freud follows Otto Rank in his thinking on the double, reading it as "an insurance against destruction of the ego" and "preservation against extinction" (1955: 235). Freud does not link these remarks to what he has said about fathers and sons, and yet he might have. For do sons not protect against "extinction" of the family name? Is the father not replicated in the son christened "Junior"? The son will finally be the father's heir rather than his double, but only after the Oedipal conflict is resolved, and the son has realized that he cannot literally take the father's place in his mother's bed. Until then, the father–son relationship is one of uncanny doubling, and the structure of patriarchy is not perpetuated but threatened by it.

In Hoffman's story, of course, the conflict is not resolved. Nathanael does not engage in incestuous sex with his mother, but he behaves just as destructively when he falls in love with the automaton Olympia, whom Freud reads as a "materialization of [his] feminine attitude towards his father in his infancy," and an object of "narcissistic" love (1955: 232). Even Nathanael finds Olympia oddly still and silent until he turns his attention on her, at which points he finds her considerably enlivened. His obsession with her – or with himself, Freud would say – keeps him from Clara and eventually drives him to suicide.

Freud's reading of the Hoffman story offers one very strong explanation of uncanny experience: that it consists of encounters between people or events that are fundamentally alike. Uncanny experiences confront us with mirror-images of ourselves or our culture that terrify us because we do not understand them, and that threaten us insofar as they threaten to undermine the version of reality with which we live every day. The son needs to differentiate himself from the father.

The lover must separate from the beloved. What is happening now must be seen as distinct from what happened before. Should these differences not be asserted, one will be caught in a stasis – Engle's "paralysis," or, better yet, a pattern of recurrence – in which one is haunted by the constant repetition of the same scenario. Neil Hertz (1985: 97–121) has gone so far as to say that it is this compulsion to repeat the past that is at the heart of the uncanny, and, insofar as repetition of events is again a perpetuation of likenesses, I agree. The uncanny keeps one from moving forward. It thwarts the hierarchical structure of patriarchy and the "progress" associated with the rational world of enlightenment.

Freud's stated reading of the uncanny is not the only one the essay offers, however. He clears the way for that reading only by setting aside another by E. Jentsch, who also used Hoffman's story of the Sandman to make a case for the workings of the uncanny. Jentsch argued that "intellectual uncertainty" resulted in uncanny effects, and located such uncertainty in the figure of Olympia, whose status as human or automaton is unclear for so much of the story (Freud 1955: 221, 227). Freud summarizes the Hoffman story in such a way that both Jentsch's thinking and the figure of Olympia herself seem "irrelevant" to the theory of the uncanny he has developed (1955: 230), and yet they are not. In arguments that at times complement and at times displace Freud's, feminist critics have argued that women are crucial figures for the uncanny in both Hoffman's story and Freud's essay as a whole. While Freud ignores the figure of Olympia, he is fascinated by what he sees as the uncanny fact that, while on vacation in a provincial Italian town, he was repeatedly drawn to a street populated by prostitutes, and later in the essay he volunteers that many people have found female genitals – which lead to the original "home" of all human beings – to be uncanny as well (1955: 245). Even when he acknowledges the uncanny nature of these encounters with women, however, he still blunts their full force.

Freud systematically ignores or downplays the uncanny power of women as he makes his argument for the uncanny as an encounter of like with like.[2] Robin Lydenberg summarizes feminist critiques that show how Freud's attention to "maternal genitals" prevents his having to face more threatening images of women as either "the pre-oedipal phallic mother, who threatens castration" or "the mother as envied source of plenitude and procreation" (1997: 1078). She cites Sarah Kofman's still more extreme observation that the Hoffman story eliminates mothers altogether, imagining "procreation as an all-male enterprise" (1997: 1078). All of these readings take Freud as their reference point, making the argument that women are uncannily "other." One can discuss women and the uncanny in yet another way by considering their relation not to Freud but to each other. Consider the Hoffman story one last time, and this time focus on two women who are clearly doubles for each other: the eerily lifeless pastiche of parts that is Olympia and the altogether lively and self-possessed figure of Clara.

One might say that Freud is right not to talk about the connection between these two figures, for while they are related through the structure of the story, they do not ever see or interact with each other, and do not experience each other as uncanny. That said, Hoffman's story clearly asks us to think about the connection between them, and resolves any uneasiness others may feel at their doubling by allowing only one to be on stage (as it were) at a time. When Nathanael becomes obsessed with Olympia, Clara drops out of the picture (though she is present in the letters she sends), yet once Olympia has been torn apart Clara is back in Nathanael's life. Further, Nathanael commits suicide not only because he has seen a figure in the distance whom we assume to be Coppelius (this is Freud's reading), but because he has seen Clara right in front of him and confused her with Olympia. The narrator tells us that, when Nathanael looks through his perspective to try to identify the "strange little gray bush" that may be Coppelius, "Clara stood in front of the glass" (p. 213). In this moment Clara stands for Coppelius, and when the now hysterical Nathanael begins shouting "Spin round, wooden doll," we realize that she stands for Olympia too. What is happening here? Why does the figure of Clara merge with that of Olympia, and why is Olympia terrifying?

An answer is suggested by the last paragraph of the story, which informs us that, years later, "Clara had been seen sitting hand in hand with a pleasant gentleman, while two bright boys were playing at her feet" (p. 214). This vision of "domestic happiness" suggests that what was terrifying about Olympia was her inability to mother children, and so to extend the patriarchal line (it is significant that Clara has two boys). To say this is to say in another way that she is a figure who threatens not only Nathanael's virility but the possibility of reproducing patriarchy more generally, and to modify Freud only slightly in placing the fear of at least figurative castration at the center of the essay.

William Godwin, Mary Wollstonecraft, and the Uncanny

Where Ann Radcliffe taught women to empower themselves within patriarchy, William Godwin and his fellow radical Mary Wollstonecraft seriously considered the possibility of moving beyond patriarchal politics altogether. Both developed their thinking on these matters in political treatises that exposed British society as a mechanism for the production of gothic lives, and both explored the difficulty of escaping those lives in novels structured around disturbing and often uncanny patterns of repetition. Godwin's *Enquiry Concerning Political Justice* (1793) systematically indicts the evils propagated by government and advocates the development of a society founded on principles of rational anarchy. His novel *Caleb Williams* (1794) plays out the ideas of *Political Justice* in fictional form, but

complicates them significantly in its consideration of how the irrational workings of the human psyche can disrupt this vision. Similarly, Mary Wollstonecraft's
Vindication of the Rights of Woman (1792) argues that women's social subordination to men results above all from the way they are educated, and advocates
change. Yet at the time of her death she was writing a novel called *Maria: The
Wrongs of Woman* (1792), which imagines the fate of one particular woman who
knows from experience that "the world was a vast prison, and women born
slaves," and yet keeps propelling herself back into the prison.[3]

Godwin

William Godwin's *Political Justice* anatomizes at length the ways in which government oppresses its citizens, arguing for a reasoned progress toward a world
in which government has dissolved and individuals regulate their own conduct.
Writing after the French Revolution had seen its revolutionaries turn into
terrorists who sent thousands to the guillotine, and at a moment when England
was censoring its own citizens heavily in response, he knew full well that his
political vision needed defending against those who assumed that the kind
of change he was advocating could only come about through the violence of
revolution. He tackles this objection directly in his final chapter:

> No idea has excited greater horror in the minds of a multitude of persons than
> that of the mischiefs that will ensue from the dissemination of what they call lev-
> elling principles. They believe "that these principles will inevitably ferment in the
> minds of the vulgar, and that the attempt to carry them into execution will be
> attended with every species of calamity". They represent to themselves "the un-
> informed and uncivilized part of mankind, as let loose from restraint, and hurried
> into every kind of excess. Knowledge and taste, the improvements of intellect, the
> discoveries of sages, the beauties of poetry and art, are trampled under foot and
> extinguished by barbarians. It is another inundation of Goths and Vandals, with
> this bitter aggravation, that the viper that stings us to death was fostered in our
> own bosom". (p. 778)

Godwin understands that revolution is almost inevitably seen as a literally gothic
invasion or sublime disruption, and seeks to quell those fears by arguing that
efforts to suppress change would involve equal barbarism: "Tyrannical and
sanguinary must be the measures employed for this purpose," he writes (p. 782).
As Maggie Kilgour has argued, Godwin aims to avoid "the extremes of repression . . . and revolution," seeing one as generative of the other, and advocates
instead "a *media via* of gradual illumination" through processes of "investigation"
(1995: 53). As Kilgour also demonstrates, he thus tries to avoid the gothic
scenario both framed and rejected by Edmund Burke (in his *Enquiry into the
Origins of the Sublime* and *Reflections on the Revolution in France* respectively), and

to map out a way forward that proceeds through discussion, rational inquiry, and the telling of truth. And then he writes *Caleb Williams*.

Whether *Caleb Williams* should be classified as a gothic novel is a question worth asking. If the hallmarks of gothic fiction so far have been its grounding in patriarchal fictions and its engagement with the aesthetic of the sublime, Godwin's novel clearly gets points for the first, but less obviously for the second. Godwin delineates the patriarchal structures of British society in more specific detail than any writer discussed so far, though he modifies the gender analysis we have examined to explore issues of class. Setting the story in contemporary England rather than in a remote time and place, showing himself to be more interested in the corruption of the law than the corruption of the church, Godwin brings the gothic home, using it – as it has always been used – to depict the suffering of innocent victims. Emily Melville dies as a result of her cruel mistreatment by her uncle Tyrrel; the Hawkinses die as a result of Falkland's lies; Williams is relentlessly persecuted by Falkland. In every case, the social systems that should protect people victimize them instead, and so we would seem to be more than half-way to a gothic plot. But where is the revolution, the "inundation of Goths"? How can a novel be gothic without them?

Godwin turns away from the aesthetic of the sublime as we have seen it thus far, going a little farther down the path laid out by Anne Radcliffe. Where she conjures a supernatural world in which we can almost believe only then to explain it away, his constant references to such gothic creatures as demons and devils allude to the genre even as he makes clear from the start that his usages are all metaphorical.[4] He thus reminds his readers of the gothic even as he forces them to recognize it as a vehicle for social criticism, and he goes farther still when he strips away even metaphorical allusions to gothic in favor of focusing directly on "things as they are."

To say that Godwin rejects the sublime altogether would be wrong, however. Even a casual reader of *Caleb Williams* cannot fail to take in that the novel is tightly structured around the relationship between Caleb and Falkland, each of whom threatens to overwhelm the other in turn. The interaction between these two characters participates in the subject–object dynamic of the sublime, in other words, but might be still more effectively described in terms of the related concept of the uncanny.[5] For, as critics have long been aware, the two men are really doubles for each other, and their relationship is defined above all by the tense equilibrium at its heart.[6]

Caleb Williams and social class

Subtitled "Things As They Are," Godwin's novel scrutinizes class structure in late eighteenth-century British society. He interests himself not in royalty or aristocracy, but rather in those classes which constituted a much larger proportion of the population: the "squirearchy," that class of men whose power went hand in hand with their inherited property, and the laboring class. Lamenting the rigidity of this hierarchy, decrying the abuses it allows, he explores but does not embrace alternative political models, or even allow that there might be a political solution to the problems he portrays (though he does in *Political Justice*).

The squirearchy is represented by three men: Ferdinando Falkland, his neighbor Barnabas Tyrrel, and his half-brother Forester. Each of them owns land and enjoys the privileges of a landowner: they function as justices of the peace within their own communities, control the people in their communities indirectly because they have enough money to employ them (and to persecute them if they fail to please), and control still more directly the people who work for them in their own households. Beyond these similarities, however, these men differ from each other in significant ways.

Falkland is not an aristocrat but behaves like one. As a young man he read "the heroic poets of Italy," from whom "he imbibed the love of chivalry and romance" (p. 12). While "[h]e had too much good sense to regret the time of Charlemagne and Arthur," he nonetheless "believed that nothing was so well calculated to make men delicate, gallant, and humane, as a temper perpetually alive to the sentiments of birth and honour" (p. 12), and his "Ode to the Genius of Chivalry" wins him admiration. He is concerned above all for his own reputation, and perhaps for the reputation of his class as well. At the height of Tyrrel's persecution of the Hawkinses, he lectures Tyrrel on the privileges of rank:

> "It is very true . . . that there is a distinction of ranks. I believe that distinction is a good thing, and necessary to the peace of mankind. But, however necessary it may be, we must acknowledge that it puts some hardship on the lower orders of society. It makes one's heart ache to think, that one man is born to the inheritance of every superfluity, while the whole share of another, without any demerit of his, is drudgery and starving; and that all this is indispensable. We that are rich, Mr Tyrrel, must do every thing in our power to lighten the yoke of these unfortunate people. We must not use the advantage that accident has given us with an unmerciful hand. Poor wretches! they are pressed almost beyond bearing as it is; and, if we unfeelingly give another turn to the machine, they will be crushed into atoms."
> (p. 80)

Falkland's sense of "noblesse oblige" has a counterpart in his sense of what is owed to him. He expects an almost feudal loyalty from those who work for him, and the violation of that bond is what motivates his persecution of Caleb.

Where Falkland fancies himself an Italianate aristocrat, Tyrrel "might have passed for the true model of an English squire" (p. 19). He has little talent for letters, but is a superb sportsman whose "form might have been selected by a painter as a model for that hero of antiquity, [Milo], whose prowess consisted in felling an ox with his fist, and devouring him at a meal" (p. 19). He is a "rural Antaeus" whose power literally comes from his association with his land (Antaeus was a champion wrestler who won so long as his feet touched the ground, and was defeated by Hercules, who had the wit to lift him), and he understands this (p. 20). He knows that his social power is based in his economic power, and is not afraid to assert it.

Mr. Forester is Falkland's "elder brother by the mother's side" (p. 144) and the most liberal of the three. Caleb first knows him as a man who made it "his principle to do every thing that his thoughts suggested, without caring for the forms of the world," though he sees that Forester is "at the same time . . . deeply impressed with the venerableness of old institutions" (p. 147). He initially befriends Caleb because he sees "no reason why a peasant, with certain advantages of education and opportunity, might not be as eligible a companion as a lord" (p. 147), but later cannot see past circumstantial evidence to imagine that Caleb might not be guilty of crimes against Falkland. Where Falkland puts his faith in antiquated codes of honor and Tyrrel trusts to money, Forester trusts the law.

From one perspective, the main action of the novel consists in these men's efforts to preserve their own authority and that of their class. Falkland and Tyrrel are the major forces in this effort, and it is ironic that they are in competition with each other. Tyrrel feels his authority waning in the face of Falkland's magnanimous behavior, especially to his niece Emily Melville, and Emily's death as a result of Tyrrel's persecution leads Falkland to publicly pronounce him a social exile. Falkland is in turn humiliated when Tyrrel not only forces his way back into the company from which he has been expelled, but assaults him. That these events lead Falkland to kill Tyrrel and then allow the Hawkinses to hang for his crime is an indictment of him, his class, and the legal system that supports him.

Even as the novel interrogates the class structure that it finally preserves, it explores at least one alternative. Caleb's time with Raymond and his band of thieves initially has the appearance of a Robin Hood episode. Raymond insists that he and his men belong to the "profession of justice," that they "who are thieves without a licence, are at open war with another set of men who are thieves according to law" (p. 224). He sees himself as one among a society of equals and urges Caleb to join them. Caleb perceives much good in this society: its members are "generally full of cheerfulness and merriment," can "expatiate freely," "form plans and execute them," act on their own "inclinations," and not feel obliged "tacitly to approve that from which they suffered most" (p. 226). Yet he also views them as a group of people who have "cast off all control from established principle," who have as "their constant object to elude the vigilance of the community," and who have been sufficiently wounded by that society to have become brutal themselves, "habituated to consider wounds and bludgeons and stabbing as the obvious mode of surmounting every difficulty" (pp. 226–7). They are social outcasts who ignore "the first interests of human society" and so their own interests as well (p. 235).

The Caleb who turns his back on this society of thieves is also the Godwin of *Political Justice*, turning away from revolution as a solution to social problems. In a remarkable description of this community, Caleb perceives it as a source of untapped social energy, arguing:

> Energy is perhaps of all qualities the most valuable; and a just political system would possess the means of extracting from it, thus circumstanced, its beneficial qualities, instead of consigning it, as now, to indiscriminate destruction. We act like the chemist who should reject the finest ore, and employ none but what was sufficiently debased to fit it immediately for the vilest uses. But the energy of these men, such as I beheld it, was in the highest degree misapplied, unassisted by liberal and enlightened views, and directed only to the most narrow and contemptible purposes. (p. 227)

Caleb's thoughts on social engineering advocate harnessing what in other novels has appeared as the sublimely explosive power that will ensure social change. He imagines a society that is inclusive but also selective – it will extract the "beneficial qualities" of energy and leave the rest behind – and in this reveals a conservative drive for limited change that puts him squarely in the company of other gothic novelists.

While Caleb laments the thieves' decision to position themselves outside mainstream society, he tries to fight Falkland's persecution of him by doing exactly the same thing. He disguises himself as one socially marginal person after another: an Irish beggar (pp. 242, 247), a farmer (p. 262), a Jew (p. 263), and a "twisted and deformed" young man (p. 276). So far is he from being truly in control of these efforts, however, that Falkland – with the help of the vengeful Gines, whose treatment of Caleb led to his own expulsion from Raymond's society of thieves – can keep him not just at, but moving along the margins of society simply by making sure that people regularly discover his identity. As Kilgour has argued, Caleb's story at this point demonstrates above all "how the individual becomes an outcast from society" (p. 68), and Caleb eventually refuses this positioning, putting himself right back at the center of things when he takes Falkland to court. In the first version of the novel's ending, he cannot change anything and ends up losing his mind. In the second, he does make himself heard only to recant his own actions. "Things as they are" are just fine, it would seem.

Caleb, Falkland, and the uncanny

What accounts for Caleb's fate? Why in the novel's original ending does he not only fail to win a fair hearing of his case against Falkland but also go mad? Why in the published ending does he back away from his success and judge himself no longer a victim but a murderer deserving of death? And why does the gothic scenario he has been fighting intensify in both cases?

The best answers to these questions move beyond analysis of class privilege and the social placement of individual characters to consider how relationships between individuals can disrupt class structure altogether. While Caleb is introduced to us as Falkland's secretary, this hierarchy is quickly destabilized as Caleb sets about discovering whether or not Falkland murdered Tyrrel. For a time Caleb actually has the upper hand in the relationship, spying on Falkland, and repeatedly manipulating him into what he hopes will be revealing situations as he seeks the answer to his question. Falkland in turn resents this treatment, asking at one point whether his "passions" are "to be wound and unwound by an insolent domestic" (p. 123), and reasserts his authority as master. This tug of war sets a pattern, as power shifts from one to the other and back again. "[W]e were each of us a plague to the other," says Caleb (p. 128), and while Falkland's admission of his guilt seems to create a sense of equilibrium as Caleb becomes his "confidant" (p. 142), this situation doesn't last. The two men shadow each other to the end of the novel, each seeking to make peace with an "other" that is better seen as an aspect of himself.

Insofar as they double each other, Caleb and Falkland have an uncanny connection that is figured in Caleb's insistence on speaking a truth that Falkland thought he had thoroughly repressed. The uncanny here announces its proximity to the sublime as Caleb describes his efforts to determine Falkland's guilt or innocence. His curiosity is unbounded, and Falkland's efforts to check him arouse only "a kind of tingling sensation" that is "not altogether unallied to enjoyment" and that becomes increasingly "irresistible" (p. 113). Caleb responds affectively to Falkland as to a sublime stimulus. As he gets closer to the truth, he feels at one time "a magnetical sympathy" with his "patron" (p. 117) and at another "as if [his] animal system had undergone a total revolution" (p. 125). Of this last occasion, he goes on to say:

> My blood boiled within me. I was conscious to a kind of rapture for which I could not account. I was solemn, yet full of rapid emotion, burning with indignation and energy. In the very tempest and hurricane of the passions, I seemed to enjoy the most soul-ravishing calm. I cannot better express the then state of my mind than by saying, I was never so perfectly alive as at that moment. (p. 135)

As many critics have noticed, Caleb's tie to Falkland here has a passionate – even erotic – intensity that Falkland himself has resisted.[7] What follows is almost anti-climactic, as Falkland catches him trying to break into the chest which he believes contains evidence of Falkland's guilt, and then later confesses to Caleb that he is indeed the murderer.

The novel's second half essentially repeats the action of the first, for as soon as Caleb has forced Falkland's secret out into the open, it is buried for a second time. As Kilgour also discusses (1995: 65), this time it is Falkland who spies on Caleb, refusing to let Caleb leave his service, pursuing him relentlessly when he does, and doing all he can to make sure that Caleb does not speak – or at least does not speak credibly – what he knows. The uncanny quality of the con-nection between the men intensifies through this series of actions, as Falkland tells Caleb:

> You little suspect the extent of my power. At this moment you are enclosed with the snares of my vengeance unseen by you, and, at the instant that you flatter your-self you are already beyond their reach, they will close upon you. You might as well think of escaping from the power of the omnipresent God, as from mine! (p. 150)

Falkland's reach is tremendous. Before Caleb has even fled Falkland's service, he meets with Forester at an inn, the two talk – though Caleb knows that Falkland would not wish it – and then "[w]ithout the smallest notice, and as if he had dropped upon us from the clouds, Mr. Falkland burst[s] into the room" (p. 155). Once Caleb has left Falkland's employ, he is pursued from place to place, dis-covered in spite of disguise after disguise, and Caleb assumes throughout that Falkland is the one chasing him, asking at one point: "Did his power reach through all space, and his eye penetrate every concealment?" (p. 249) Caleb is wrong to think that Falkland is the cause of his being arrested over and over, but right to think that Falkland has him under constant surveillance. Toward the end of the novel, Falkland tells Caleb: "I had my eye upon you in all your wander-ings. You have taken no material step through their whole course with which I have not been acquainted" (p. 291).

When Caleb spies on Falkland, he ensures that Falkland will come to see him as an uncanny presence in his life, forever rising up to tell stories that should not be spoken, and when Falkland spies on Caleb he does the same, ensuring that Caleb will come to see his master as a sign of everything that he has tried to leave behind in his life. Each regards the other with a paranoia that transforms into a negative what would in other circumstances be a great strength: their capacity for strong feeling, or sensibility.[8]

Falkland's sensibility is evident from the moment he is introduced into the narrative. He is "a man of small stature, with an extreme delicacy of form and appearance" in whom "every muscle and petty line of his countenance seemed to be in an inconceivable degree pregnant with meaning" (p. 7). One might follow Claudia Johnson's lead and read Falkland as one of those men of the 1790s who have redefined sensibility as a masculine rather than feminine capacity. Alternatively, one might read him as simply feminized by the specific adjectives Godwin uses to describe him: "pregnant" and "delicate." The association of pregnancy with femininity needs no explanation. The association of delicacy with femininity is less obvious. Ann Jessie Van Sant points out that the term "*delicacy*, before use of the term *sensibility* was widespread, brought several ideas into close association: sensuous delight, superiority of class, fragility or weakness of constitution, tenderness of feeling, and fastidiousness." She notes further that Samuel Johnson identified delicacy as a quality of "feminine beauty" (1993: 3).

Falkland's well-developed sensibility is written on his body, then, and evidences itself in his conduct as well. He "fe[els] for" Emily Melville's "unprovided and destitute situation" (p. 44), even as his "compassion" is "excited in favor of Hawkins" (p. 68), and, when forced to oversee the trial of a young man who has inadvertently killed a man, the evidence presented "sm[ites] upon the heart of Mr. Falkland," who "at one time start[s] with astonishment, and at another shift[s] his posture like a man who is unable longer to endure the sensations that press upon him" until he "new str[ings] his nerves" to hear more (pp. 134–5). As long as his strong sensibilities are directed outwardly – as long as they let him sympathize with others – they are admirable. They become self-destructive when they no longer facilitate such connections. When Falkland murders Tyrrel and lets others hang for his crime, he feels for himself above all others, and in that selfishness is the real problem. His sensibility increasingly manifests itself as disease, as he suffers from fits of melancholy and near madness, isolating himself from the world even as he keeps a watchful eye on all around him.

If Falkland is a man of feeling whose sensibility finally betrays him, Caleb's situation is not much different. While he initially appears to be a child of enlightenment who is devoted to "mechanical pursuits" and "desirous of tracing the variety of effects which might be produced from given causes" (p. 6), it quickly becomes clear that he is dominated as much by his feelings as Falkland ever was. The passionate pursuit of Falkland described above, the "magnetical sympathy" he feels for him, his "rapture" on believing he has learned the truth of Falkland's story all attest to this. Just as the socially useful capacity for sensibility has metamorphosed in Falkland's case into a damaging selfishness, however, so in Caleb's it metamorphoses into an equally damaging insistence on forcing Falkland into a relationship that he does not want. "This confidence," Falkland tells Caleb, "is of your seeking, not of mine" (p. 141), and Caleb realizes almost at once that, in learning Falkland's "secret," he has "made [himself] a prisoner" (p. 144).

Caleb and Falkland imprison each other, and the toll of their actions shows on their bodies. At Falkland's penultimate appearance in the novel,

> he appeared like nothing that had ever been visible in human shape. His visage was haggard, emaciated, and fleshless. His complexion was a dun and tarnished red, the colour uniform through every region of the face, and suggested the idea of its being burnt and parched by the eternal fire that burned within him. His eyes were red, quick, wandering, full of suspicion and rage. His hair was neglected, ragged and floating. His whole figure was thin, to a degree that suggested the idea rather of a skeleton than a person actually alive. Life seemed hardly to be the capable inhabitant of so woe-begone and ghost-like a figure. (pp. 290–1)

When we see him for the last time he has "the appearance of a corpse" (p. 329). Caleb's body is less dramatically marked, but in the novel's original ending he loses his mind. Both men register their diseased sensibilities in their appearance and conduct, as their very bodies become gothic prisons.[9]

Both Falkland and Caleb may find themselves prisoners of their own misguided sensibilities, but their stories do find voice in Caleb's narrative, which he writes both to console himself and in the hope that "posterity may . . . render [him] a justice which [his] contemporaries refuse" (p. 5). In the novel's published conclusion he finds justice even before posterity has a chance to weigh in, though he recants it the moment it is granted him. In the novel's original conclusion, however, the case for narrative as a means of redressing past wrongs emerges all the more strongly.

In his final ramblings, as written in that original conclusion, Caleb feels himself falling apart: "If I could once again be thoroughly myself, I should tell such tales!" (p. 346) He has dreams that he does not understand, that blend uneasily into his waking moments, and he decides that "it is all one at last . . . there was nothing in life worth making such a bustle about . . . when people are dead, you know, one cannot bring them to life again! – dead folks tell no tales – ghosts do not walk these days" (p. 346). These statements disavow the accomplishments of his own narrative and of gothic novels generally, for, with their help, dead folks do tell tales, and ghosts do walk. Only by telling these stories is there a hope that the injustices done to them will be recognized and rectified.

Mary Wollstonecraft

Mary Wollstonecraft has an important and complicated place in the tradition of gothic writers. Her *Vindication of the Rights of Woman* makes clear that she not only disliked but found dangerous the kind of fiction that they wrote. On the other hand, her unfinished novel *Maria* clearly grows out of and develops their work, demonstrating the gothic quality of all women's lives (not just the lives of the upper class) in all kinds of circumstances (not just in that precarious interval between losing a parent and gaining a husband). In the world of "things as they are," she argues, women are trapped by the social institutions that shape their lives from start to finish. They are trapped by the mere fact of being women, and while she would not reduce women to their bodies, she finally does use the image of the female body as itself a prison to suggest how deep the problem runs.

Vindication of the Rights of Woman critiques British society with the aim of elucidating and suggesting correctives for women's place within it. Appalled by a culture in which custom and law conspire together to ensure women's subordination, Wollstonecraft insists that women's reason should be cultivated through education, and that in this way they will be able to assume their rightful place as equals to men. Her argument resembles Godwin's in its reliance on reason to effect social change, and in its assertion that "all will *be* right" though it is not yet so (p. 95).

Throughout the *Vindication*, Wollstonecraft consistently portrays women's lives in terms that call to mind the images of imprisonment used and interrogated by the gothic tradition. She critiques forcefully writers whose thoughts on women's education she reads as particularly detrimental to women's development as rational beings, and important for my argument is her contention that one particular "feminine weakness of character, often produced by a confined education, is a romantic twist of the mind, which has been very properly termed *sentimental*" (p. 305). It is worth quoting at length her description of how this "weakness" emerges:

> Women subjected by ignorance to their sensations, and only taught to look for happiness in love, refine on sensual feelings, and adopt metaphysical notions respecting that passion, which lead them shamefully to neglect the duties of life, and frequently in the midst of these sublime refinements they plump into actual vice.
>
> These are the women who are amused by the reveries of the stupid novelists, who, knowing little of human nature, work up stale tales, and describe meretricious scenes, all retained in a sentimental jargon, which equally tend to corrupt the taste, and draw the heart aside from its daily duties. I do not mention the understanding, because never having been exercised, its slumbering energies rest inactive, like the lurking particles of fire which are supposed universally to pervade matter.
>
> Females, in fact, denied all political privileges, and not allowed, as married women, excepting in criminal cases, a civil existence, have their attention naturally drawn from the interest of the whole community to that of the minute parts . . .
>
> But, confined to trifling employments, they naturally imbibe opinions which the only kind of reading calculated to interest an innocent frivolous mind inspires. Unable to grasp anything great, is it surprising they find the reading of history a very dry task, and disquisitions addressed to the understanding intolerably tedious,

and almost unintelligible? Thus are they necessarily dependent on the novelist for amusement. (p. 306)

Her anger is clearly directed at all of those novels of sensibility – among which I would include gothic novels as a subset – that aim above all to engage the feelings of their readers. Should there be any doubt at all, one need only look ahead to Jane Austen's *Northanger Abbey*, written probably in 1798 though not published for another twenty years. I will have more to say about *Northanger Abbey* later, but its seemingly specific responses to this passage merit mention now.

Austen's story turns on the adventures of Catherine Morland, who gets into trouble from immersing herself in gothic novels and using them as a lens onto the everyday world around her. While Catherine eventually learns that the melodrama of gothic does not translate directly into the world of lived experience, she – and we – also come to see that the world of lived experience is in fact just a little more gothic than most people would like to admit. The plot of Austen's novel thus demonstrates her awareness of the dangers to which Wollstonecraft points, even as it complicates this view by showing that simply dismissing novels of this sort is overly hasty. These sentiments are also articulated directly within the narrative itself, in two passages.

When Catherine and her friend Isabella "shut themselves up, to read novels together," the novel's narrator defends them:

I will not adopt that ungenerous and impolitic custom so common with novel writers, of degrading by contemptuous censure the very performances, to the number of which they are themselves adding – joining with their greatest enemies in bestowing the harshest epithets on such works, and scarcely ever permitting them to be read by their own heroine, who, if she accidentally take up a novel, is sure to turn over its insipid pages with disgust. (pp. 33–4)[10]

With "genius, wit, and taste" to recommend them, novels are works "in which the greatest powers of the mind are displayed, in which the most thorough knowledge of human nature, the happiest delineation of its varieties, the liveliest effusions of wit and humour are conveyed to the world in the best chosen language" (p. 34). And, much later, Catherine herself will say to another female friend – Eleanor Tilney – that she reads novels like those of Anne Radcliffe in preference to almost all else. "I can read poetry and plays, and things of that sort, and [do] not dislike travels," she says. But "history, real solemn history, I cannot be interested in . . . I read it a little as a duty, but it tells me nothing that does not either vex or weary me. The quarrels of popes and kings, with wars or pestilences, in every page; the men all so good for nothing, and hardly any women at all – it is very tiresome" (p. 97).

Austen's response to Wollstonecraft is firm and persuasive. Novels can tell important truths, and truth-telling genres like history have been particularly unjust to women. Wollstonecraft herself clearly had some hope for the power of fiction, because, near what proved to be the end of her life, she took up the issues of the *Vindication* yet again. She began writing a novel, and not just any novel, but a sentimental novel with obvious ties to the gothic tradition.

Maria, or the Wrongs of Woman

The posthumous publication of Wollstonecraft's *Maria* by her husband William Godwin after her death in childbirth marks the novel itself as something of an uncanny production,[11] and the story it tells is built around an uncanny and unsettling pattern of repetition. Its protagonist is haunted by a cycle of loss and desire from which she is finally unable to extricate herself. Wollstonecraft's unfinished novel imagines Maria as a woman who escapes a home ruled by a tyrannical father only to find herself married to the still more brutish George Venables. Venables has married her for her money more than anything else, and while he will sanction virtually any conduct within their marriage, he will not let her leave it. Indeed, when she finally takes their daughter and leaves him, he has her followed, drugged, and locked up in a madhouse, while the child is kidnapped and sent to a wet nurse, where it dies. In the madhouse, she finds two unexpected avenues of support, one in her servant Jemima, and another in a fellow prisoner named Henry Darnford, who eventually becomes her lover. The story as we have it ends with the three of them escaping the madhouse, and Maria going to court to defend herself against her first husband. Beyond that there are only possibilities for an ending, most but not all of which are tragic.

The novel's story of a woman held captive for her money rivals anything found in Radcliffe, and the gothicism of that earlier fiction is even intensified in Wollstonecraft's story of "things as they are." As Maggie Kilgour has also noticed, that intensification is announced in Wollstonecraft's opening paragraph:

> Abodes of horror have frequently been described, and castles, filled with spectres and chimeras, conjured up by the magic spell of genius to harrow the soul, and absorb the wondering mind. But, formed of such stuff as dreams are made of, what were they to the mansion of despair, in one corner of which Maria sat, endeavouring to recal her scattered thoughts! (p. 75)

These lines juxtapose imagined dangers with reality, and tell us – as Kilgour succinctly puts it – that "reality is worse than fiction or, rather, that for women reality *is* gothic" (1995: 82).

Criticism has discussed the novel's gothicism from a variety of perspectives, focusing on the tyrannical government and husband who persecute Maria so relentlessly, on the ideological forces that teach Maria to romanticize the very men who betray her over and over, on Maria's thwarted efforts to escape her literal prison by means of her imagination and, especially, her writing.[12] My own argument will build on all of these to talk about the novel's depiction of uncanny relationships as yet another mark of its engagement with gothic.

Maria's early days at the madhouse are peculiarly haunted. In a general way, her past life returns to trouble her: "The retreating shadows of former sorrows rushed back in a gloomy train, and seemed to be pictured on the walls of her prison, magnified by the state of mind in which they were viewed" (p. 75). More specifically, though, it is the far happier memory of her daughter that she cannot escape.

> Her infant's image was continually floating on Maria's sight, and the first smile of intelligence remembered, as none but a mother, an unhappy mother, can conceive. She heard her speaking half cooing, and felt the little twinkling fingers on her burning bosom – a bosom bursting with the nutriment for which this cherished child might now be pining in vain. (p. 75)

Maria is at this point uncertain about her daughter's fate. "To think that she was blotted out of existence was agony . . . yet to suppose her turned adrift on an unknown sea, was scarcely less afflicting" (p. 76), and it is precisely this suspension between unknowns that accounts for her daughter's "floating" image in her mind.

Even as Maria's memory of her daughter marks a loss, however, it also reminds Maria that she is a mother. In Maggie Kilgour's words, it "restores her to herself" (1995: 93), and her identity as a mother is part of what helps her move at least imaginatively beyond her confinement. With no way to "escape from sorrow" and "the events of her past life pressing on her," Maria decides to write the story of her life, in the hope that it will "instruct her daughter, and shield her from the misery, the tyranny, her mother knew not how to avoid" (p. 82). Maria's narrative is not only written for her daughter, however, but in some way also compensates for her loss. Thus when Maria learns of her daughter's death, she immediately turns away from the narrative as well, giving it to the man who Maggie Kilgour has suggested might be read as a substitute for her daughter (1995: 89) – and the man who emerges as a second and much more dangerously uncanny presence in Maria's life – Henry Darnford.

An understanding of Maria's relationships with men generally will be very helpful in coming to terms with Darnford's role in her life. Mary Poovey's seminal discussion of Maria's reliance on sensibility to navigate male–female relationships makes clear the dangers of that reliance (Poovey 1984). On the one hand, sensibility sufficiently frees Maria from the restriction of social conventions that she feels able to give away her possessions (as when she gives a mattress to her nurse's sister Peggy), and does not feel a need for marriage to sanction romance. On the other, she is repeatedly drawn into and betrayed by exactly the sort of sentimental narratives against which Wollstonecraft wrote in the *Vindication*. Daniel O'Quinn furthers this last point when he argues that the same novels that lead women to see their lives through fictional lenses lead men to behave wantonly in real life. Thus a cycle is set up in which "women's desire is inculcated by novels in a manner that enables men to practice seduction. In other words, men's acts of seduction exist in a parasitic relation to the delusory effects of women's confinement to novels" (1997: 766). Both Poovey and O'Quinn discuss the fact that, as a young woman, Maria heard the story of her uncle losing the woman he loved to his best friend and became not a cynic but a "romantic," who supplemented what she heard with what she read to "form an ideal picture of life" (p. 128). She falls in love with and marries George Venables in part because she has projected on to him all the qualities she wishes him to have, misreading at every stage the meaning of his conduct. Even after her miserable marriage has led to her confinement in the madhouse, she continues this pattern.

Fellow inmate Henry Darnford has also been imprisoned by relatives who want his money, and, as many critics have noted, when he starts sending her books to read, she is seduced not just by the texts themselves, but by his notes in the margins. "[W]ritten with force and taste," not to mention "a degree of generous warmth, when alluding to the enslaved state of the labouring majority, perfectly in unison with Maria's own thinking," they pique Maria's interest in their author (pp. 85–6). The texts these comments annotate would give any good reader of Wollstonecraft pause, for they include Dryden, Milton, and Rousseau, all of whom come in for severe criticism in the *Vindication* for their attitude toward women. Maria's conduct is governed by no such good sense, however, and by degrees, "fancy, treacherous fancy, beg[ins] to sketch a character, congenial with her own, from these shadowy outlines" (pp. 85–6). According to the dynamic outlined above, she is playing her part, casting Darnford as the hero in the imagined romance of her own life.

Maria's fanciful "sketching" of Darnford quickly metamorphoses into a desire to see him, and while she manages not only to see him but eventually to become his lover, critics have long noted that she continues to project on to him her own fantasy of what he should be. O'Quinn's discussion of these "projections" is especially helpful here, moving systematically through a series of passages that make clear how tiny glimpses of Darnford give "an outline to the imagination to sketch the individual in the form she wishe[s] to recognize" (p. 89, cited in O'Quinn 1997: 774).[13] Indisputable as these arguments are, however, the possibility exists that more than sentimental novels might account for her tendency to shape her life according to fiction. Darnford may be her "dream lover" (Kilgour 1995: 89), but when he first arrives on the scene he is also an eerily familiar stranger, and while her active imagination may in the end betray her, it seems to be motivated in part by the aim of controlling his uncanny presence.

Waking one morning after "dream[ing] of her child," Maria goes to the window at the time she knows Darnford generally takes a walk, but has missed him. When she does the same thing the next morning, all she sees is "the back of a man, certainly he, with his two attendants, as he turned into a side-path which led to the house" (p. 89). From this little bit of detail comes a "confused recollection of having seen somebody who resembled him" (p. 89), and when on yet another day she finally sees his face, "it conveyed no distinct idea to her mind where she had seen it before" (p. 90). Even when the sound of his voice convinces her that "she had certainly, in a moment of distress, heard the same accents," she is still unable to recognize him (p. 90). The figure of Darnford knits itself together piece by piece – rather like the human equivalent of Alfonso's ghost in *The Castle of Otranto* – and when they finally meet there is a moment of recognition. Darnford greets Maria with the words "This is extraordinary! – again to meet you, and in such circumstances!" (p. 93) Beyond a reference to "the co-incidence of events which brought them once more together," however, we are not told exactly how they know each other or who Darnford is (p. 93). Godwin later identifies him as the person who protects Maria from her husband's pursuit, and while he may well be, he is also the person who – according to all the projected endings for the novel – will treat her just as badly as all the other men in her life have done. He is indeed an uncanny figure, whose appearance marks the return of that oppressive male presence.

In a series of projected endings to the novel, Wollstonecraft suggests that Darnford divorces, or leaves, or abandons Maria, and in the most fully developed of these an abandoned and pregnant Maria swallows laudanum, thinking back on the daughter she believes to have been murdered, and envisioning that child "mourning for the babe of which she was the tomb" (p. 202). This vision of the woman's body as carrying not a fetus but a corpse is shocking, and makes clear how women can be drawn into or made complicit in their own fate in a patriarchal world. Betrayed by their sensibilities, betrayed by the bodies that manifest those sensibilities, their bodies can become emblems of the imprisonment they not only suffer themselves but also inflict on those who rely on them.

While the gothic romance of Maria's life constitutes the bulk of the story that Wollstonecraft has to tell, she does gesture toward an alternative in her account of Maria's relationship with her attendant Jemima. Jemima's presence in the novel expands yet again our sense of the possibilities of gothic narrative, drawing into their sphere the lives of women who are lower-class and even criminal. As Maria quietly works to enlist Jemima's help in her efforts to escape the madhouse, she begins to develop a sympathetic relationship with this woman whose story turns out to be much like her own. Jemima's story is the all too common narrative familiar to us from sources such as Defoe's *Moll Flanders* or Hogarth's *Harlot's Progress*: she is employed as a servant, becomes pregnant by her master, is forced out of her employment by her mistress, and from then on leads an ever more difficult life, aborting her child, stealing and prostituting herself to survive, then starting the whole cycle over again when she gets a job as a laundrywoman.[14] She is in the end happy to leave the madhouse with Maria, hoping to forge a life outside the brutally oppressive circumstances she has known thus far. And in the conclusion of that projected ending for the novel on which I focused above, the suicidal Maria is drawn back into life by the appearance of Jemima and the daughter she thought she had lost. Sympathetic bonds between females – as opposed to those we have seen throughout the novel between women and men – may let women survive (Poovey 1984; Johnson 1995; Greenfield 2002).

5

Uncanny Monsters in the Work of Mary Shelley, John Polidori, and James Malcolm Rymer

One of the more seductive details in the history of gothic fiction is that Mary Wollstonecraft and William Godwin were the parents of Mary Shelley. It is almost irresistible to see this line of biological descent replicated in the line of literary descent that traces the passage of ideas from the writings of the parents to the writing of the child. As others have noted, *Frankenstein*'s reflections on the trauma of birth seem to reflect on Shelley's and her mother's experiences with pregnancy (Wollstonecraft died giving birth to Shelley; see Moers 1985), and the novel is dedicated – as well as indebted – to Godwin. If one is going to think about genealogies, however, they need to be more complicated than this one. Shelley's novel draws on many literary and cultural sources – religious controversy, scientific debate, romantic poetry, and more – to push gothic fiction into new territory. *Frankenstein*'s central antagonism between Victor and his creation suspends us in an uncanny whose force derives from the multiple uncertainties with which it confronts us. The boundaries between culture and nature, human and inhuman, parent and child, male and female all seem threatened by Victor and his creation.

The gothic novels discussed thus far generally adhere to a highly predictable structure, tracing the protagonist's movement from sheltered innocence through fearful entrapment to grateful liberation. Events turn on the righting of a wrong that offends the clearly cultural order as well as the seemingly natural one. Walpole's Theodore deserves the throne of Otranto not only because of his heroic behavior, but because he is the biological heir to it. Similarly, Radcliffe's Ellena can marry Vivaldi not just because they love each other, but because she is nobly born. By ensuring that apparently radical actions finally reaffirm a social order based on "blood," these novels raise important social questions only to evade them. Godwin breaks this pattern with his questioning of class structure, even as Wollstonecraft refuses to accept that one's gender will determine one's social place. Shelley looks still more self-consciously at the link between nature and culture, thinking more radically than any gothic writer so far about what it might mean for a body to be produced culturally rather than naturally. Victor Frankenstein's monster is the first in what Judith Halberstam has identified as a long line of gothic monsters, whose very bodies register – and in some sense "tell" – the gothic story in which they appear, "condensing various racial and sexual threats to nation, capitalism, and the bourgeoisie in one body" (Halberstam 1995: 3).

Halberstam's *Skin Shows* argues that "the emergence of the monster within Gothic fiction marks a peculiarly modern emphasis upon the horror of particular kinds of bodies," and while she notes that "there are connections to be made between [late eighteenth-century] stories of mad monks, haunted castles, and wicked foreigners" and the stories of monsters that are her subject, she cautions against taking those connections "too far" (1995: 3). She is right to caution against reading the Ambrosios of early gothic too easily into figures such as Dracula which emerged a century later, and she is just as right to note that there was a transitional period, "from the late eighteenth century to the nineteenth century," when "the terrain of Gothic horror shifted from the fear of corrupted aristocracy or clergy, represented by the haunted castle or abbey, to the fear embodied by monstrous bodies" (1995: 16).

Eighteenth- and early nineteenth-century interest in monstrosity was fed from a range of different sources. Achievements in that most rational field of science were leading people into surprisingly irrational and even gothic-looking territories. Marie-Hélène Huet discusses the rise of "teratology," a "science of monsters" that developed in the late eighteenth and early nineteenth centuries and "attempted to classify all monstrosities," focusing on what we would now call biological life forms (1993: 108). At the same time, beginning in the early eighteenth century, work in the mechanical sciences had led to the development of automata so sophisticated they seemed to challenge what it meant to be human; Jacques de Vaucanson's creations of the 1730s – including a mechanical flute player and a "defecating duck" – are perhaps the most famous of such marvels (Kenner 1968). All of this was happening as Britain's increased contact with foreign peoples – as it acquired colonies and engaged in trade around the globe – raised debates about their civility, savagery, or even humanity. Halberstam comments on the fact that the increased reach of the British empire had resulted in greater efforts to "define an essential English character" (1995: 16). In a closely related point, she also notes that that the decline in aristocratic power corresponded with a rise in the power of the bourgeoisie, so that "the blood of nobility now became the blood of the native," both of which "were identified in contradistinction to so-called 'impure' races such as Jews and Gypsies" (1995:16).

The word "monster" comes from the Latin *monstrum* – "something marvelous; orig[inally] a divine portent or warning," according to the *Oxford English Dictionary* – and its root lies in the verb *moneo*, "to warn." Monsters do indeed tend to function as warnings or admonitions of one sort of another. They function as uncanny doubles of our societies, reflecting back to us images of everything that we have cast out as undesirable or threatening to the status quo, and forcing us to face that which we would prefer to leave hidden. Exactly what is threatening changes from one society to another, and from one historical moment to another. Halberstam argues for gothic monsters as creatures that can generate multiple meanings, stating that "[t]he monster functions as monster . . . when it is able to condense as many fear-producing traits as possible onto one body" (1995: 21). Yet in discussing nineteenth-century monsters in particular she also insists on their association with parasitism, "a non-reproductive sexuality" that "exhausts and wastes and exists prior to and outside of the marriage contract" (1995: 16–17). This vision of nineteenth-century monsters as at once infinitely productive and non-reproductive interests me enormously, because it goes to the heart of how gothic monstrosity interacts with the inevitably patriarchal social structures in which it exists. Gothic monsters have great generative capacity, but they do not re-generate patriarchy. In this way they are the direct heirs of such early gothic villains as Manfred and Ambrosio, both of whom not only fail to perpetuate their family lines but actually turn those lines back on themselves in acts of figurative and literal incest, respectively.

Frankenstein

Mary Shelley's *Frankenstein* can be read as a novel about patriarchy, exposing the instability of the father–son lines that seem so essential to its continuity, and interrogating its fantasy of a world without women. Even as patriarchal authority was being shored up by advances in science that identified the father rather than the mother as the parent responsible for a child's biological inheritance (Huet 1993),

Shelley's novel suggests that lines of succession are not so easily determined. The novel is structured around three concentric stories of weak or failed father–son relationships: the framing story of Walton, who takes up "a sea-faring life" in spite of his "father's dying injunction" not to (p. 6);[1] the story of Victor Frankenstein, whose creation of the monster results in the deaths of all who are close to him and guarantees that he will not be the son whom his father had thought "might carry his virtues and his name down to posterity" (p. 18); and the story of the monster, who devotes himself to murdering Victor, belying Victor's early hope that "no father could claim the gratitude of his child so completely as I should deserve theirs [i.e. that of the new species he would create]" (p. 36).[2]

The weakness of these father–son relations emerges all the more clearly because of the nearly complete absence of mothers in the story. Putting transformative pressure on the gothic convention that dictates a motherless heroine, Shelley eliminates not one, not two, but three mothers from her narrative. Elizabeth Lavenza loses hers and is adopted into Victor's family; Victor's mother dies just before he is to go to school in Ingolstadt; Victor's creature has no mother, but is the work of Victor alone. In fact, Victor's great achievement is to take on not only the role of the father, but of the mother as well. As many critics have noted, his creation of new life without the involvement of a woman challenges women's procreative power. Insofar as Victor succeeds in creating life without the help of a woman, his challenge is successful, yet he finds his creation repulsive and spends much of the novel trying to kill it. How are we to read this ambivalence? What does it mean to take women out of the procreative process?

Existing criticism of the novel has much to say on these issues. Sandra Gilbert and Susan Gubar note that Victor is feminized in the creation of the monster, and that his labor is represented in terms that invoke what women experience when going through the labor of birth (1979: 232). Anne K. Mellor sees Victor as "stealing the female's control over reproduction" and so "eliminat[ing] the female's primary biological function and source of cultural power" (1988: 220). Alan Bewell's discussion of the novel's debt to contemporary ideas about pregnancy speaks to both readings, showing us how Victor's procreative power is tied to eighteenth-century belief in "the power of a pregnant woman's imagination and desires to mark or deform a developing fetus" (1988: 109). Key here, he goes on, was "the notion that a woman's imagination functioned mimetically," so that "Monsters and monstrous marks . . . represent the destructive intervention of female imagination and desire in the transference and reproduction of the human image" (1988: 109, 112). Bewell sees in this disastrous process of creation Mary Shelley's critique not of women's creative power, but of "the prevailing idea of the poet" – articulated by her husband, Percy Bysshe Shelley – "as an isolated genius whose fixation on the ideal necessarily leads him into conflict with nature and society" (1988: 119). Huet argues along similar lines, reading Shelley's novel as "the last and perhaps most explicit image of an old myth" that was at last waning, "a two-thousand-year-old tradition closely tying the birth of monstrous children to their mother's deranged imagination" (1988: 162), and seeing in this focus on monstrous female creativity an erasure of legitimate male procreativity as well. Finally, Bronfen (1992) shifts the angle of vision when she reads Victor's act as an effort to eliminate not just women, but death, with which they are consistently associated. Whichever interpretive path one takes, however, the novel clearly condemns his action.

Victor himself judges his creature a mistake the second it comes to life, perhaps recognizing on some level that his error lay at least partly in his manipulation of the patriarchal dynamic. One can easily read this manipulation in Oedipal terms that continue the reading begun above. In his struggle with his father, Victor creates his monster through a "penetration" of mother nature that the novel strongly urges one to read as at least figuratively incestuous.[3] This reading is reinforced when he dreams of embracing his fiancée, Elizabeth, only to have her metamorphose into his dead mother. At this point, however, Victor's Oedipal yearnings – because they are not resolved but played out – begin to tear apart the structure of patriarchy. Instead of perpetuating the family line, he goes back to its source, back to the mother. Further, in this creation of a creature out of the bits and pieces of dead bodies, one can see a piecing together of a patriarchal history that is bigger than that of a single family, an action that recalls the piecing together of Walpole's Alfonso, but in a way that threatens rather than reinstates the patriarchal line of descent. Victor's creature is not a patriarch, but a pastiche of precursors whose legacy he actually distorts.

Victor's creature thus emerges as an ironic mirror of the patriarch, a double whose creation grows out of the collapse of the patriarchal family (or at least this one patriarchal family), and whose systematic killing of Victor's family members simply furthers – or makes visible – that process. Neither Victor nor the monster fully appreciates this fact, however. The monster's earnest efforts to assimilate himself into human society make clear that he sees the patriarchal family as both functional and desirable, and his failure to gain acceptance there does not diminish his longing for it. When he asks Victor to make him a mate, he expresses a wish to re-create his own life in the image of the very social structure that has excluded him. Victor sees a little more clearly that the family he makes might not function in the way he wants it to, but understands this not as a problem with its patriarchal structure but simply as a problem with women. He worries first of all that his male and female creatures might loathe each other, and further, that the as yet uncreated female "might become ten thousand times more malignant than her mate" (p. 138). A female monster might destroy the balance of power that exists in patriarchal culture, and even aid in the far more catastrophic undermining of human society as a whole. Were the pair to want children, Victor worries that "a race of devils would be propagated upon the earth, who might make the very existence of the species of man a condition precarious and full of terror," while he himself would be seen as a "pest, whose selfishness had not hesitated to buy its own peace at the price perhaps of the existence of the whole human race" (p. 138).

Mary Shelley's monsters threaten to invert the order of patriarchy, to create a world in which female power is invested with a potency that has been suppressed in everyday life. Victor's fear of that power is great, though it should pale beside the fact that his initial creation of the monster proved the patriarchal dream of a world without women to be untenable. Women's power might be dangerous, but it seems to be equally dangerous to do away with or usurp that power.

Shelley's monster is limited by the fact that he cannot reproduce himself. He can undo the line of patriarchal succession that produced him, but that is all. Far more dangerous would be a monster who could produce an alternative to that line of succession all on his own, and, to his credit, the monster tries. He recognizes the power of sensibility – and of sympathetic feeling – to create community and tries to cultivate it. His efforts are worth charting.

Monstrous Sensibility

The reading I have developed so far suggests that the monster functions as a double for patriarchy generally, and for Victor Frankenstein specifically, a physical reminder of the destructive energy at the heart of the patriarchal family.[4] At the same time, however, the monster yearns to be seen as an individual subject in his own right, and his autobiographical narrative maps his efforts to achieve it. He is an unlikely man of feeling whose sensibility allows him to establish an independent subjectivity and whose capacity for sympathetic connections leads him to seek membership in a human community. His failure to manage the latter leads David Marshall to read the novel as "a parable about the failure of sympathy" (1988: 195).

From the time he first opens his eyes, the monster comes to know the world through his senses.[5] "A strange multiplicity of sensations seized me," he tells Victor, "and I saw, felt, heard, and smelt, at the same time" (pp. 79–80). His mind is a blank slate – John Locke's *tabula rasa* – on which sensations are inscribed, and over time he learns to "distinguish between the operation of [his] various senses," to act on the knowledge they give him, and to experience more complicated sensations such as pleasure and pain (p. 80). These complex sensations in turn give way to complex feelings such as "reverence" and "love" (p. 85), and in watching old Mr. DeLacey comfort his granddaughter Agatha, the monster feels "sensations of a peculiar and overpowering nature . . . a mixture of pain and pleasure, such as [he] had never before experienced, either from hunger or cold, warmth or food." He finally turns away from the scene, "unable to bear these emotions" (p. 85).

During the time he spends watching the DeLacey family, the monster receives an education in the use and meaning of emotions. He sees that Felix and Agatha "appeared to weep," and asks, "What did their tears imply? Did they really express pain?" He is "deeply affected" by their unhappiness from the start, though it is only through time and "perpetual attention" that he is able to understand the motivation for – and meaning of – what he has observed (p. 87). Over time his affective responses come to mimic theirs: "when they were unhappy, I felt depressed; when they rejoiced, I sympathized in their joys" (p. 89). He starts to understand that affective responses can create bonds between people, and this knowledge is reinforced when he reads the novel that of all others epitomizes the cult of sensibility: Goethe's *Sorrows of Young Werther*. He writes, "The gentle and domestic manners it described, combined with lofty sentiments and feelings, which had for their object something out of self, accorded well with my experience among my protectors, and with the wants which were for ever alive in my own bosom" (p. 103).

If the monster is Lockean in his way of learning, he is Burkean in his understanding of the relationship between affective relationships and aesthetics. Burke understands beauty as an aesthetic that promotes love and brings people together in community, and, much as the monster wishes to belong to a community, he knows full well that he lacks the beauty that would provide his entrée. This eight-foot giant has "features" that Victor "had selected . . . as beautiful" when he made him, yet Victor himself can see that he failed in his attempt:

> His yellow skin scarcely covered the work of muscles and arteries beneath; his hair was of a lustrous black, and flowing; his teeth of a pearly whiteness; but these luxuriances only formed a more horrid contrast with his watery eyes, that seemed almost of the same colour as the dun white sockets in which they were set, his shrivelled complexion, and straight black lips. (p. 39)

The monster sees this too, the first time he sees an image of himself. In a scene that recalls first Narcissus and then Milton's Eve admiring their own beauty in pools of water, the monster writes:

> I had admired the perfect forms of my cottagers – their grace, beauty, and delicate complexions: but how was I terrified, when I viewed myself in a transparent pool! I started back, unable to believe that it was indeed I who was reflected in the mirror; and when I became fully convinced that I was in reality the monster that I am, I was filled with the bitterest sensations of despondence and mortification. (p. 90)

Burke suggests that the opposite of beauty is not sublimity but "ugliness," and, as Denise Gigante has argued, ugliness is what both the monster and the reader are taught to see here.

Gigante's discussion of the monster's ugliness merits summary here. Where eighteenth-century aesthetic theory had defined ugliness primarily in negative terms, saying what it is not, Gigante develops language to say what it *is*. She draws first on Burke's comments that the ugly is the "opposite" of beauty insofar as it presents us with creatures which are not seamlessly unified and lovely, but full of "cracks and fissures" like those on Frankenstein's creation, whose "visceral reality . . . leaks through to destroy all fantasy" (2000: 569–70). Focusing particularly on the monster's "dull yellow eye," she notes that it forces one to focus on the physical reality of the body above all else, "block[ing] out our access to the 'soul,' to the infinite abyss of the 'person,' thus turning it into a soulless monster" (2000: 571). Kant's analysis of ugliness as something that "disgusts" viewers lets her claim further that ugliness is that which simply "stops us in our tracks as something we can't even imagine" (2000: 577–8). It comes very close to the sublime, but denies us what Gigante describes as the "elevat[ion] from terror to a comprehension of greatness" that she reads as characteristic of the Burkean sublime (2000: 575), even as it is more radically uncontainable than the "limit-lessness" of the Kantian sublime (2000: 577–8). It is not overwhelming so much as it is simply "other" or alien to our experience.

It is as the monster learns from repeated experience that he "cannot inspire love" (p. 119), Burke's corollary of beauty, that he comes to an understanding of his own "ugliness" and its potential power. He deliberately decides that he "will cause fear," Burke's corollary of sublimity, instead, and so he does (p. 119). Gigante might debate whether he can succeed in this effort, given her reading of him as not so much terrifying as incomprehensible. There is no question, however, that – endowed with the capacity for strong feelings but not allowed to use them in the benevolent ways he wishes – the monster instead embarks on a career of killing motivated above all by hatred. In his rage he is the equal of Dacre's Victoria, and his passion – like hers – is "detrimental" to him (p. 119).

Shelley's monster is a creature of frightening and fantastic possibility. On the one hand he stands as a warning of the dangers of trying to make a world without women, and on the other he seems to embody the possibilities of a world in which social structures reflect cultural rather than biological ties. The possibility of what Gilles Deleuze and Félix Guattari (1987) have called "affiliative" rather than "filiative" ties has strong appeal. The question is how to realize them, and at the same time that this creature was trying unsuccessfully to do so, another was having only slightly better luck: the vampire.

Vampires

"From 1730 to 1735, all we hear about are vampires."[6] So say Deleuze and Guattari (1987: 237), and they are not only right, but arguably understating the case. "[V]ampire epidemics" reportedly plagued eastern Europe from the 1670s through the 1770s, with the most intense activity being reported in the first half of the eighteenth century (Frayling 1991: 19). There were even then various efforts to rationalize the notably irrational vampire phenomenon: were they corpses that had been buried prematurely? corpses that were "[u]nnaturally well-preserved"? victims of plague or rabies? the offshoot of a form of religious heresy or "community superstition"? Christopher Frayling offers all of these explanations as possibilities (1991: 25). As for why these stories came to general attention in Europe when then did, Paul Barber offers a historical analysis: after the Peace of Passarowitz was signed in 1718, Austria gained control of and in fact occupied parts of Serbia and Walachia, places where belief in vampirism was well established. In time, Barber argues, "the occupying forces, which remained there until 1739, began to notice, and file reports on, a peculiar local practice: that of exhuming bodies and 'killing' them" (1994: 5). This practice was aimed at exterminating those believed to be vampires, of course, and as news of this phenomenon trickled into society at large, interest in the subject of vampires grew. By the 1750s, everyone who was anyone had written about the vampire craze; even such major figures as Rousseau and Voltaire felt obliged to enter into the discussion (though only to critique it – see Frayling 1991: 30–1). The vampires that so interested people at this time were not the elegant creations familiar to us from Anne Rice's "Vampire Chronicles" or Bram Stoker's *Dracula*, but rather were creatures of folklore – peasants and bourgeois turned revenants – who tore open their victims with little finesse to get the blood they needed. Middle- and upper-class vampires did not make their appearance until John Polidori published *The Vampyre* in 1819, but – having waited so long to make their entrance – they have never since stepped off the stage.

By the time Polidori wrote his short narrative, the potency of the vampire as a metaphor for the predatory nature of social institutions such as the government, the church, and the bourgeoisie had long been recognized; the very title of a 1732 article from the *Gentleman's Magazine* – "Political Vampires" – makes clear how easy it was to use vampirism as a metaphor for "blood-sucking" of all sorts (Frayling 1991: 27). Polidori's accomplishment was first of all to extend the metaphor into a narrative, and to then complicate it by suggesting that vampires might be seen not simply as creatures who drain the life out of everything, but as creatures who reimagine the world as they do so. Polidori's story was initially attributed to his by then estranged employer, Lord Byron, and while the tale is indeed his own, Nina Auerbach notes that it bears a "symbiotic" relation to a fragment of a vampire story that Byron had begun at the same weekend gathering that prompted Mary Shelley to write *Frankenstein* (1995: 15). The fictional story of the vampire Lord Ruthven and his friendship with the young Aubrey testifies to the complicated personal and literary relationship between Byron and Polidori, then, and inaugurates what Auerbach identifies as the story at the heart of vampire narratives for the first half of the nineteenth century: a story of friendship between men. That this relationship also becomes the source of the story's most frightening moments suggests further the difficulty of maintaining these relationships in a society that needs male–female relationships to reproduce itself.

Auerbach's argument that early vampire stories are about male friendship lets one read Polidori's narrative as at least a partial fulfillment of the narrative that Frankenstein's monster wanted to see written. The sympathetic social connection that he sought with Frankenstein and others is for a time realized in Polidori's story of the vampire Lord Ruthven and his friend Aubrey, who are presented as counterparts of each other. Ruthven is "a nobleman, more remarkable for his singularities, than his rank," with a face whose "form and outline" are said to be "beautiful," in spite of its "deadly hue," and a "dead grey eye" whose look is said to inspire people with "awe" (p. 3).[7] Aubrey is a "handsome, frank, and rich" gentleman who was orphaned as a child and has grown up "cultivat[ing] more his imagination than his judgment." He believes that "the dreams of poets [are] the realities of life," and is "startled" when he learns that "except in the tallow and wax candles, that flickered not from the presence of a ghost, but from want of snuffing," this is not the case (p. 4). Taking consolation for the loss of his fantasy world in the admiration of the women who flock to him, he is ready to "relinquish his dreams" when he meets Lord Ruthven.

Ruthven presents to him – as to everyone – an unreadable façade, and "the very impossibility of forming an idea of the character" of this man leads to Aubrey "form[ing] this object into the hero of a romance, and determin[ing] to observe the offspring of his fancy, rather than the person before him" (p. 5). We have seen this dynamic before, in Maria's responses first to Venables and then Darnford, and know that it can only lead to disillusionment. That disillusionment begins when the two arrange to travel together, and Aubrey has a chance to observe Ruthven's conduct. He is generous, but gives his money to those driven by "lust" or "iniquity" rather than by need; those whom he helps inevitably come to a bad end; and he himself gambles and leads others to ruin in the process. A letter from his guardians further attesting that the effects of Ruthven's "licentious habits" are magnified by his "irresistible powers of seduction" confirms Aubrey's sense that his companion is "evil," and when he catches Ruthven seducing their landlady's daughter, they part (p. 7).

Eve Kosofsky Sedgwick (1985) has shown us how women can mediate relationships between men and so make homosocial relationships possible, but here this dynamic is complicated. The landlady's daughter initially seems to block rather than enable the connection between Ruthven and Aubrey, for it is her appearance in the story that prompts the initial breakdown of the friendship. As it turns out, however, the problem is not that she appears in the story, but that her role has not yet been fulfilled. The letter that gives Aubrey the details of Ruthven's conduct focuses less on what Ruthven has done than on how he has affected the women he seduced, telling us "that he had required, to enhance his gratification, that his victim, the partner of his guilt, should be hurled from the pinnacle of unsullied virtue, down to the lowest abyss of infamy and degradation" (p. 7). In this language one hears echoed the fates of those earlier sexual reprobates, Ambrosio and Victoria, and one realizes that Ruthven's friendship with Aubrey is mediated not so much by women as by the consumption of women. Their deaths literally keep him alive and connected to his friend. And so Ruthven eventually ruins the landlady's daughter (who simply disappears), and her parents as well, though only after Aubrey has left the scene.

The friendship between the two men breaks down when the heterosexual violence lurking behind it is exposed, and Aubrey travels on his own to Greece, where he in turn becomes attached to the beautiful Ianthe. While Aubrey still does not understand the behavior of men like Ruthven, the supposedly innocent Ianthe does, and she tells the skeptical Aubrey about vampires, only to be killed by one herself shortly after. Ianthe's killer inevitably turns out to be Ruthven, and while Aubrey apprehends this only in the midst of a "violent fever" that leads him to discredit the identification, he is nonetheless horrified to awaken from his illness to none other than Ruthven himself, who has come to care for him. A friendship that thrives only with the killing of women can hardly appeal, and yet the two reconcile sufficiently that they again travel together on Aubrey's recovery. This time they separate only when Ruthven is seemingly fatally shot, an event Aubrey promises to keep secret for a year and a day.

The relationship between Ruthven and Aubrey falls apart completely when Ruthven turns up alive and well in a London drawing room some time later. Aubrey is plunged into a hysteria that is rendered all the worse when he can do nothing to prevent Ruthven's marriage to his sister, which takes place near the story's end. Why he can do nothing is an interesting question. Could he not simply break his promise to Ruthven and expose him for what he is? To be sure, Ruthven threatens him with the negative consequences of such an action, saying to him: "Remember your oath, and know, if not my bride to day, your sister is dishonoured. Women are frail!" (p. 22). Dishonor is surely a less dire fate than death, however, and so one still wonders at his silence. Nina Auerbach points to Aubrey's unwillingness to break his vow as a sign of the primacy of the relationship between the two men (1995: 14), and while she may be right to do so, by this time the relationship between the men is so destructive that one wonders what is gained by sustaining it.

Aubrey will not break his vow, but he does try to stop the wedding, and when he fails to do so, ensures his own destruction as well. We read that "his rage, not finding vent, had broken a blood vessel," that "the effusion of blood produced symptoms of the near approach of death," and that after midnight – after his vow has expired, and he has told his story – he dies (pp. 22–3). While the final line of the story tells us that "Aubrey's sister had glutted the thirst of a Vampyre!" (p. 23), the person whom we actually see die from loss of blood is Aubrey himself. Auerbach has suggested that "Ruthven drinks Aubrey vicariously through his women" (1995: 17), and the story's conflation of brother and sister as the vampire's final victims emphasizes this point.

Vampire stories reached a mid-century climax with James Malcolm Rymer's serialized story of *Varney the Vampire, or, The Feast of Blood*.[8] Published between 1845 and 1847, this "penny dreadful" offers a vision of vampires that turns Polidori's on its head. Where Polidori's vampire systematically undermines the patriarchal and heterosexual world in which he participates, Rymer's novel shows us vampires whose "undead" existence is a punishment for crimes they committed against that same world, and who seek nothing so much as reintegration with it. Auerbach has demonstrated *Varney*'s interest in a "kinship" that is dangerous in its assertion of close ties between those who are vampires and those who are not: Varney becomes increasingly human as his story unfolds, even as the humans become increasingly vampiric in their violently self-serving conduct. My own analysis builds on this work to consider why – even though the boundaries between vampires and humans blur so thoroughly – the former never quite disappear into the latter.

One of the most astonishing things about Varney is that for a considerable portion of the novel readers cannot be sure whether or not he is really a vampire. The first scene of the novel shows him attacking the beautiful Flora Bannerworth in a manner that conforms to what even the members of the Bannerworth family understand about vampires, and while they initially relegate their knowledge to the realm of superstition, circumstantial evidence fairly quickly persuades them to belief in the flesh and blood reality of the species. Only their friend and protector Dr. Chillingworth resists seeing Flora's attacker as a vampire, not simply because he is a scientist committed to a more rational view of things (though we are allowed to think so for several hundred pages), but because he himself restored Varney to life many years earlier, after Varney was hanged for robbery. While, on his reanimation, Varney first screamed and opened his eyes, Chillingworth recollects that it was only when Varney "suddenly sprang up and laid hold of me, at the same time exclaiming, – 'Death, death, where is the treasure'," that he "fled from the room and the house, taking my way home as fast as I possibly could" (p. 330). In his flight, Chillingworth recalls Victor Frankenstein fleeing his newly animated creature, and, like Victor, he so fears pursuit by the man he has revived that he leaves his home in London, and does not encounter Varney again until Varney's assault on the Bannerworth family begins in earnest. Having heard this story, the Bannerworth family ceases to think of Varney as a vampire, though others do not, and yet even this version of events is not complete. Chillingworth did to all appearances restore the hanged corpse to life, but as it turns out, moon-light would have done the same, for Varney is a vampire after all, and has been for hundreds of years; the text states at different points that he has been a vampire since the time of Edward III (in power 1327–77), and through the reign of Henry IV (in power 1399–1413), to the restoration of Charles II (1660). So why all the confusion?

These twinned stories of Varney's reincarnation emphasize the novel's tendency to blur the distinction between humans and vampires, yet they also demonstrate the reason the distinction emerged in the first place. Varney's initial incarnation as a vampire occurs as punishment for the crime of killing a member of his family – his wife, in one version of the story, and his son in another (pp. 771, 856) – while his subsequent revival from hanging occurs after he has been hanged for robbery (as noted above). Varney may be virtually human, but he does not resemble just any human. Rather, he is indistinguishable from those who commit crimes against property and the patriarchy it supports. Such crimes were what made him a vampire in the first place, and the novel emphasizes this fact through its inclusion of a scene in which Varney himself is present at what the novel describes as the "resuscitation" of another vampire (p. 751).

The scene is predictably set in a graveyard, and Varney makes one of a group of five gathered to revive a member of their "fraternity," a society based on an uncanny social contract if ever there was one (p. 752). That the man they are to usher into the world of the "undead" is identified as part of their community even before he has risen from the grave again blurs the distinction between vampires and humans, and the ceremony by which he is revived drives the point home. "Where lies the vampyre? Who was he?" asks Varney. "A man of good repute," is the reply. "What made him one of us?" asks Varney again. "He dipped his hands in blood," Varney is told. "There was a poor boy, a brother's only child, 'twas left an orphan. He slew the boy, and he is one of us" (p. 753). The "man of good repute" killed his nephew not with a weapon, but with "unkindness . . . harsh words, blows, and revilings," and it turns out that this is not his only crime (p. 754). When the newly arisen vampire comes out of the grave to make his way in the world, he attacks a nightwatchman, who sees in the creature a likeness to one Mr. Brooks, who "went to the city every day . . . for the purpose of granting audi-ences to ladies and gentlemen who might be labouring under any little pecuniary difficulties, and accommodating them. Kind Mr. Brooks. He only took one hundred pounds per cent" (p. 756). The "respectable" Mr. Brooks was a money-lender, and if "[t]here were people who called him a bloodsucker while he lived . . . now he was one practically" (p. 756). He has been exhumed by his fellow vampires, told "who and what he is," and left to "do [his] work in the world until [his] doom shall be accomplished" (p. 755).

But what exactly is a vampire's "work"? The newly arisen vampire described above is instructed as follows: "Pursue your victims in the mansion and in the cottage. Be a terror and a desolation, go you where you may, and if the hand of death strike you down, the cold beams of the moon shall restore you to new life" (p. 755). This language suggests that vampires exist to wreak havoc among rich and poor alike, but that their efforts are to be focused on the home. Given that Varney and Mr. Brooks were both identified as vampires for crimes against their own families first of all, one sees that their punishment is endlessly to repeat their crimes. They must forever prey on the young women whose blood keeps them alive, and while we do not see how Mr. Brooks accomplishes this, Varney most often gains access to such women by posing as a respectable member of the upper classes. To do so he has to supply himself with money, of course, and to do that, he turns to robbery. Thus the cycle continues, and in such creatures one starts to see the outlines of Bram Stoker's *Dracula*, who will become the paradigm of the vampire for decades to come. *Dracula* will present a more complicated picture of an aristocratic man whose obsession with acquiring women and property seem on the one hand to mark him as a patriarch *par excellence*, while on the other his foreignness and propensity for non-reproductive sex will mark him as everything that will destroy patriarchy in England. Still, the resemblance is there.

If Varney stands behind the late nineteenth-century figure of Dracula, he also stands behind Anne Rice's very different late twentieth-century vampires, whose first-person narratives attest to the trials and tribulations of immortal life. Rymer tells his story at least partly from Varney's perspective, showing us a creature who wearies increasingly of his existence in the realm of the "undead." Varney is killed more than once in the novel, but moonlight always revives him, even as the blood of young women sustains him once he has been revived, and he becomes increasingly troubled by the fact that for him to live, others must die. While those who die are generally not the women whose blood he takes, but those who know that he is a vampire and seek to kill him, Varney suggests at one point that this linking of life and death could be at least temporarily broken by "the voluntary consent of one that is young, beautiful, and a virgin" (p. 686). The vampire lore here is a little unclear, but the action of the novel as a whole – much of it dominated by Varney's efforts to marry and enter into mainstream society – suggests that he can escape his status as humanity's uncanny "other" only by an action that would reverse the effects of his former crimes and reconstitute the family he has destroyed. In that effort he does not succeed.

Varney can neither forget the fact that he is a vampire nor live with it, though he tries. A failed attempt to commit suicide by drowning himself convinces him to "shake off all human sympathies," and, like Frankenstein's monster before him, to "be the bane of all that is good and great and beautiful" (p. 787). Arriving at the home of those who rescued him from the sea, he tells himself "I am that which I am" (p. 789) and his very presence inspires those who see him with an "awe" that suggests his sublime power (p. 780). In a replay of the attack on Flora Bannerworth with which the novel opened, he now attacks his host's daughter Clara. Where Flora eventually became Varney's friend and protector, however, Clara dies from the shock of the attack, and after death becomes a vampire herself, thanks to Varney's efforts to revive her. Clara is the only female vampire we see, the only vampire whose fate is not determined by crimes she committed during her life, and the only vampire we see killed as well (a mob puts a stake through her heart). Looking at her now twice-killed body, Varney mourns the effects of his "work" and buries her so that she may rest in peace (p. 844). He cannot remain the "dread and desolation" he pledged to be (p. 787), and when the priest Mr. Bevin offers to become his friend, echoing the Bannerworths in his insistence that vampires are made by God and so have a place in the world (p. 846), one sees another way in which he might be reintegrated into the society he longs to join. Varney himself turns his back on this possibility, knowing from experience that he will be chased away at some point, and the novel ends with a report of Varney's second and seemingly successful suicide attempt as he leaps into Mount Vesuvius. His death recalls but revises those of Lewis's Ambrosio and Dacre's Victoria, for his fate is not punishment so much as relief. Thus it is ironic that he takes with him a witness who is to publish an account of his death that will ensure his immortality: "You will say that you accompanied Varney the Vampyre to the crater of Mount Vesuvius, and that, tired and disgusted with a life of horror, he flung himself in to prevent the possibility of a reanimation of his remains" (p. 868).

Varney is to the end of the narrative humanity's uncanny "other," and if the deep source of that "otherness" lies in his crimes against his family, his physical appearance guarantees that all who meet him register his difference from them. His great height would make him unusual among humans in any case, but it is his pallor that consistently causes people to wonder about who he really is. When he is on the boat from which he will make his first suicide attempt, we read that "many a curious glance was cast at him, for although he had humanised and modernised his apparel to a great extent, he could not get rid of the strange, unworld-like . . . look of his face. He was very pale too, and jaded looking . . ." (p. 873). Newspaper reports of his death at Mount Vesuvius tell how he began his journey up the mountain from a hotel in Naples, where he was described as "a most peculiar looking man, and considered by the persons of the establishment about the ugliest guest they had ever had within the walls of their place" (p. 868). He is the "ugly Englishman" to his Italian guide and to the German newspaper that reports his death, and while his ugliness marks his otherness – as it did with Frankenstein's monster – his appearance is an effect rather than a cause of his crimes. Rymer's story is thus a morality tale in which the wrongs of an individual are literalized in his monstrous body so that they can be seen and punished. In writing such a tale, he reverses the radical perspective of Mary Shelley, whose monstrous creation commits crimes only after he has been unjustly excluded from the society he wishes to join.

6

Confronting the Uncanny
in the Brontës

The novels of the Brontë sisters continue but also complicate the gothic realism that entered the tradition with Godwin and Wollstonecraft, asking whether sensibility can yet provide escape from narratives of social terror. While critics have discussed all of the novels written by Anne, Emily, and Charlotte Brontë under the rubric of the gothic,[1] my focus will be on the two that are probably the best known: Emily Brontë's *Wuthering Heights* and Charlotte Brontë's *Jane Eyre*. Acute sensibilities alert the central characters in these novels to the uncanny realities of their lives, and offer solutions to the forms of estrangement or alienation signalled by the uncanny.

These novels engage the uncanny in ways that expand the discussion to this point, and so a brief return to Freud's essay on the subject will be helpful. Early in his essay, Freud analyzes the uncanny in terms of its etymology. He makes much of the fact that the German word for uncanny is *unheimlich*, which literally means "unhomely," and he notes as well that the *unheimlich* is opposed to but also generated by – and occasionally even identified with – the *heimlich* or "homely." The next step in this line of thought is one that Freud did not take, but that Maria Tatar does, when she notices that uncanny experiences must therefore have to do with "home." Tatar offers this analysis as a step in her reading of gothic novels, which she understands as explorations of this estrangement from home,[2] and the Brontës take us farther than any novelists we have read thus far in exploring the ways in which familiar domestic spaces are "haunted" by uncanny presences. Given that one might (following Claire Kahane) read these domestic spaces as figures for the people who inhabit them, it also makes sense that the Brontës' consideration of the often eerily double-edged nature of life at home is paralleled by their consideration of individual identities and the doubling of "self" that we have seen so often.

The Brontës' transformation of "home" into the *unheimlich* begins with their transformation of generic conventions. While the fantastic idiom of gothic and the realistic idiom of domestic fiction might at first glance seem opposed, literary criticism has become increasingly interested in the connections between the two. Hélène Moglen has argued that "from its inception, the novel has been structured not by one but by two mutually defining traditions: the fantastic and the realistic" (2001: 1), and Simon Avery has argued that "it is at the interface between these two types of writing – the gothic on the one hand and the realist on the other – that the most disturbing and innovative effects of the Brontë novels occur" (1998: 121). Nancy Armstrong offers a still more precise terminology when she identifies the Brontës' work as domestic fiction with a distinctly gothic edge, and while one can debate whether novels like *Wuthering Heights* and *Jane Eyre* domesticate the gothic or gothicize the domestic, the conjunction of the terms "gothic" and "domestic" is useful.

Armstrong's influential study, *Desire and Domestic Fiction* (1987), demonstrates that eighteenth- and nineteenth-century domestic novels did not simply describe but actually contributed to the constitution of middle-class womanhood. She sees the Brontës putting pressure on a tradition of domestic fiction that was already well established by the time they wrote, no longer "aspir[ing] to respectability" but instead "playing out a fierce struggle to socialize desires whose origin and vicissitudes comprised one's true identity as well as his or her possibilities for growth" (1987: 198). Armstrong comments on the sisters' understanding that "[t]o make the language of social behavior reveal the ordinary self at its truest and deepest, the Brontës had to dismantle that language" (1987: 192), noting that they "have come to be known for a literary language that allows emotion to overpower convention and become a value in its own right, blotting out all features of political person, place, and event" (1987: 197). If she is impatient with the fact that "their language of the self" intermingles "Gothic claptrap" with "sacred – often Miltonic – figures" (1987: 197), she is also right to see it as worthy of comment. Both Emily and Charlotte Brontë indulged in a certain amount of "Gothic claptrap" to signal not only their engagement with, but also their interrogation of, the gothic tradition that they so significantly revised.[3]

Wuthering Heights

Published in 1847, Emily Brontë's *Wuthering Heights* tells the by now legendary story of Catherine and Heathcliff, whose impassioned relationship defines their lives and persists beyond their deaths. Early critics noticed and responded negatively to the novel's gothicism, prompting a response from Charlotte Brontë in her 1850 preface to the novel.[4] Acknowledging that "over much of *Wuthering Heights* there broods 'a horror of great darkness'," Charlotte explains this quality in two different ways. She begins by saying that her sister wrote what she knew, "being herself a native and nursling of the moors," then goes on to make the contradictory claim that "the writer who possesses the creative gift owns something of which he is not always the master, something that at times strangely wills and works for itself." In this two-sided story of the novel's creation, Charlotte pinpoints the novel's gothically doubled structure. It is at once a narrative of local knowledge and a tale of possession, a story that

> was hewn in a wild workshop, with simple tools, out of homely materials. The statuary found a granite block on a solitary moor: gazing thereon, he saw how from the crag might be elicited the head, savage, swart, sinister; a form moulded with at least one element of grandeur – power. He wrought with a rude chisel, and from no model but the vision of his meditations. With time and labour, the crag took human shape; and there it stands colossal, dark, and frowning, half statue, half rock; in the former sense, terrible and goblin-like; in the latter, almost beautiful, for its colouring is of mellow grey, and moorland moss clothes it; and heath, with its blooming bells and balmy fragrance, grows faithfully close to the giant's foot. (p. liv)

These "homely" materials that the artist begins with end up as a creation that is "half statue, half rock," "goblin-like," and "almost beautiful." The novel emerges as a pattern of uncanny doubles, one piece mirroring but also subverting another so that our sense of the whole is powerfully uncertain.

Charlotte Brontë's suggestion that the novel is built on a pattern of doubling gestures towards the central relationship of Heathcliff and Catherine, and is played out in that relationship. Insofar as it is a "colossal, dark, and frowning" piece of work, it calls to mind the character of Heathcliff, who on his introduction to the Earnshaw household is said to be "as dark almost as if it came from the devil" and a "gipsy brat," though he is "a gift of God" as well (pp. 36–7), while as an adult he appears to his tenant Lockwood as a "dark skinned gypsy" but also a "gentleman" (p. 5). Heathcliff is an uneasily bifurcated character who does not quite fit into the place in which he finds himself. When Lockwood notes that "[t]he apartment and furniture" in the sitting room of Wuthering Heights "would have been nothing extraordinary as belonging to a homely, northern farmer with a stubborn countenance," we realize what the problem is (p. 5). Heathcliff is "unhomely," or as Freud would have it, *unheimlich*. He is an uncanny presence in the house from the start, and remains so even when he has become its master.[5]

If Heathcliff is an uncanny presence, one must ask exactly what makes him so. What familiar but forgotten reality does he make us see? What uneasiness does he represent? Even the short descriptions quoted above indicate his association with forces that in the world of gothic fiction disrupt civilized society, whether those be understood in terms of race (he is dark, like Ambrosio, Schedoni, and so many others), ethnicity (he is a Gypsy, like the fortune-teller in *The Monk*), or Christian mythology (he is a devil, like Matilda and Zofloya). This "fatherless child" threatens the fabric of the patriarchal society that has excluded him, even as he threatens more specifically the patriarchal structure of the Earnshaw family (p. 38). Named for a male child who has died, Heathcliff reincarnates the dead and threatens to displace the living, appearing to Earnshaw's son Hindley as a "usurper of his parent's affections, and his privileges" (p. 38), and even nudging ahead of Cathy in her father's affections.[6] His uncanny power results less from the occasionally overt violence of his conduct, however, than from the consistently and quietly unsettling force of his presence. He does not so much tear things apart as show us how fragile they were to begin with.

If Heathcliff is an uncanny element who enters the family from outside, Catherine Earnshaw is his counterpart on the inside. Thinking back to Charlotte Brontë's description of the novel as "terrible" on the one hand and "almost beautiful" on the other, it is easy to see Cathy as the "almost beautiful" part of the equation. "[M]ischievous and wayward," she is a "wild wick slip" who nonetheless has "the bonniest eye, and sweetest smile, and lightest foot in the parish" (pp. 38, 42). In Margaret Homans's words, she is "an outlaw" in patriarchal society (1986: 73), and is described in the novel as "very thick" with Heathcliff from almost the first moment he enters the household (p. 38).

While we know that Heathcliff and Cathy are virtually inseparable from the time they are children, it is only when they do separate that we see the intensity of their relationship. What prises them apart is the appearance of Edgar Linton as a rival to Heathcliff for Cathy's affections, and it is because Edgar stands between them through to the end of Catherine's life that their relationship becomes the uncanny nightmare that it does. That Cathy actually puts Edgar there when she agrees to marry him makes the story all the more interesting, for in so doing she casts herself in what would seem to be an all too familiar gothic scenario.

The scene that Cathy engineers seems to place a beautiful young woman between the physically dark, morally dubious figure of Heathcliff and the physically fair, morally good figure of Edgar, and finally to pair her with the latter. The clarity of the pattern belies the complexity of the tale, however, for Cathy is not threatened by one man and saved by the other in the manner of most gothic heroines. The only threat Heathcliff poses is to her social acceptability, and while Edgar can make her "the greatest woman of the neighborhood" (p. 78), she does not need him to make her socially legitimate. Indeed, one might just as plausibly reverse the perspective of the preceding argument. Maybe Edgar should be seen as the real threat, using marriage to draw Cathy into the lovely but limiting world of Thrushcross Grange, equivalent to a "heaven" in which she has no place (pp. 80–1). From this point of view, Heathcliff emerges as the would-be rescuer who could keep her from such a place, the satanic figure who rebels against the stultifying perfection of Edgar's world. Both readings tell us something useful about the novel, even as they are limited by their failure to account for Cathy's agency in shaping these relationships in the first place. She desires both men, albeit for different reasons, and assumes that she can have what she wants.

Cathy sees herself as so fundamentally connected to Heathcliff as to be identified with him, and does not believe that her marriage to Edgar will in any way weaken that primary tie. When Nelly suggests otherwise, she insists: "Nelly, I *am* Heathcliff – he's always, always in my mind – not as a pleasure, any more than I am a pleasure to myself – but as my own being – so, don't talk of our separation again – it is impracticable" (pp. 82–3). In collapsing the difference between her identity and Heathcliff's, she moves what has been a relationship of uncanny doubles in the direction of what I have earlier read as the sublime, yet I wonder if it is not the very sublimity of their relationship – with its attendant self-loss – that keeps Catherine from embracing Heathcliff wholly.[7] Even as she emphasizes her likeness to Heathcliff, she is eloquent on the subject of her difference from Linton, saying again to Nelly: "Whatever our souls are made of, [Heathcliff's] and mine are the same, and Linton's is as different as a moonbeam from lightning, or frost from fire" (p. 80). Given that we live in a world in which our differences from others are also our independence and autonomy, is it perhaps possible that Catherine marries Edgar to hold on to those things?

If she does, she is successful in her attempt, but at a terrible cost. Her belief that she can marry Edgar and maintain a relationship with Heathcliff too is initially undermined by the fact that Heathcliff leaves for three years immediately after hearing of the planned marriage, and is again challenged when he makes her life intolerable on his return. With Heathcliff's arrival at Thrushcross Grange, he and Edgar resume their rivalry for possession of Cathy. Both men defy her wishes as they try to shape their relationship with her (Heathcliff courts Isabella Linton in spite of Cathy's warning him off, while Edgar insists that she see Heathcliff no longer), and yet Cathy is not malleable. If she cannot control them, she can at least control herself, and she does. "Well, if I cannot keep Heathcliff for my friend – if Edgar will be mean and jealous, I'll try to break their hearts by breaking my own," she states (p. 116), and she does exactly that, starving herself to the point of delirium and eventually death.

Cathy's deathbed visit from Heathcliff complicates the easy unity with him that she so confidently asserted before her marriage. They are quite physical with each other, but not easily so. At one point they are together in what Nelly Dean describes as "a strange and fearful picture," Cathy holding Heathcliff down by his hair while he embraces her hard enough to bruise her (pp. 160–1). This image conveys precisely how compulsive and damaging their relationship has been, and Cathy imagines leaving all of this difficulty behind her in death: "the thing that irks me most is this shattered prison, after all. I'm tired, tired of being enclosed here. I'm wearying to escape into that glorious world, and to be always there; not seeing it dimly through tears, and yearning for it through the walls of an aching heart; but really with it, and in it" (pp. 161–2).

Like Caleb Williams, like Maria, Cathy feels imprisoned by her body, and if she moves one step beyond them in imagining death as an escape into a sublime future, we must pause on the fact that death is her way out. Death will resolve the problems of her life and especially of her relationship with Heathcliff, though only because in death she will replace the difficult man in front of her with one she has remade to suit herself. "That is not *my* Heathcliff," she says when he does not please her. "I shall love mine yet; and take him with me – he's in my soul" (p. 161).[8] While Cathy's death is to an extent something she herself wills, then, it also signals the limits of her control over herself and others, and is the ironic opposite of the sublime experience she had imagined.

If Cathy's death is a way out of her troubling relationships with both Heathcliff and her husband, Heathcliff's death is his way of re-establishing his connection with her. The novel's opening and closing chapters feature scenes of Heathcliff not simply mourning for but striving to be reunited with the long-dead Cathy. Early in the novel, Lockwood spends a night at the Heights only to have his sleep interrupted by the ghost of Catherine Linton begging for entry to the house. On hearing this, Heathcliff responds by sending him out of the room and then opening the window himself to beg his "heart's darling" to come to him "at last!" (p. 28). Near the novel's close, Heathcliff tells Nelly Dean that he feels "a strange change approaching," though he is then only "in its shadow" (p. 323). That change seems to involve the shutting down of his physical body: "I hardly remember to eat, and drink," he says, and later adds, "I have to remind myself to breathe – almost to remind my heart to beat!" (p. 323) He is haunted by his Catherine, and views everything around him as "a dreadful collection of memoranda that she did exist, and that I have lost her!" (p. 324) He has not lost her permanently, though. Catherine's is the shadow in which he lives, and his wasting away seems designed to bring him ever closer to her. His smiling dead body is discovered near the window at which Catherine's ghost had appeared earlier, and the ghosts of both are said to have been seen walking together.

The gothic aspects of Cathy's life are first intensified and then apparently undone in the life of her daughter. Catherine Linton's story repeats that of her mother, but with significant variation. In contrast to her mother's at least seeming ability to shape her own life, the young Catherine does not have even the illusion of such control. Initially caught between Edgar Linton and Heathcliff, she is a pawn in their ongoing rivalry. Edgar struggles to confine her to the grounds of their estate, Heathcliff struggles equally hard to lure her onto his, and her own desire to move freely in the world results – ironically – in her being drawn against her will from one to the other. Further, Catherine is also caught between her cousins Linton and Hareton, parallels to Edgar and Heathcliff, forced to marry one while fending off the other. She is literally imprisoned at Wuthering Heights, and only when she ceases to insist on isolating herself from the others who live there – and specifically, when she forms a connection with Hareton – does she find a way to change the situation. Her engagement to Hareton brings the novel to a remarkable close, recalling but revising her mother's relationship with Heathcliff. Catherine and Hareton both become identified with the first Cathy (Hareton has her eyes), but not with each other, and it is their sustained separateness that matters. There is no terrifying merging of souls here, but rather a simple social contract that seems to point a way past the gothic scenarios that have filled its pages, and yet one must pause. Remembering Locke's statement that marriage is a contract in which a husband still has "conjugal power" over his wife (1988: 174 [I, §48]), and remembering Pateman's argument that a man's sexual right over his wife is at the basis of any patriarchal structure, one sees that the change registered in the novel's final pages is limited. Catherine and Hareton may no longer be locked into the gothic nightmare that characterized their parents' experience, but their lives are still shaped by social conventions that reinforce a muted – and more "civilized" – version of the same dynamic.[9]

Jane Eyre

Jane Eyre appeared in the same year as *Wuthering Heights*, and is implicitly in conversation with it.[10] Charlotte Brontë's tale of Jane and Rochester is at least as legendary as Emily Brontë's story of Cathy and Heathcliff. At its heart is another orphan whose story provides an opportunity to explore questions about the relationship between home and the *unheimlich*, and about the relationship between individual identity, the identity of a beloved, and the gothic entrapment that can result if the two coincide. Where Emily Brontë explores from the perspective of the Earnshaws and the Lintons how Heathcliff exposes and exacerbates the gothic aspects of their lives, however, Charlotte Brontë does the reverse and examines from Jane Eyre's perspective the events that threaten to turn her into a gothic victim. Heathcliff and Jane are oddly alike when we first meet them: both are described as "interlopers" in their first homes (*Wuthering Heights*, p. 29; *Jane Eyre*, p. 48), both are seen as disrupting the families they enter, and efforts are made to contain them both. Where Heathcliff perpetuates the gothicism of his own life by imposing similar experiences on everyone around him, however (a point discussed in Meyer 1996: 118), Jane finds a way out of the episodic gothic of her life.[11]

As was true of *Wuthering Heights*, critics began very early to comment on *Jane Eyre's* obvious debts to gothic fiction: the nightmare of life in the Reed household; the oppression at Lowood school; the fact that Bertha Mason is hidden away in Rochester's attic, whence she descends like a malignant spirit to threaten both Jane and Rochester. While the novel's gothic aspects have often drawn negative responses, they have also drawn considerable critical appreciation. When Sandra Gilbert and Susan Gubar titled their massively influential study of women writers and women's literary tradition *The Madwoman in the Attic* (1979), they testified to the importance they place on Brontë's engagement with the gothic. Their still compelling analysis argues for the novel's movement beyond the genre of "moral gothic," or "myth domesticated," to which it has often been assigned (1979: 337), yet at the same time sees that Jane's escapes from the gothic scenarios of her life constitute the bulk of its action. At the center of that action, they place Jane's encounter with the character they see as her "truest and darkest double": Bertha Mason (1979: 360). They implicitly locate the novel's gothicism in its dealing with the uncanny, then, and it is on this that I want to build. If the presence of the uncanny in Jane's life defines her experience as gothic, then it is her growing ability to re-imagine the uncanny as a familiar and even intimate part of her life that allows her to transform the gothic into something else.

Gilbert and Gubar argue that Jane's movement from Gateshead to Lowood, Lowood to Thornfield, Thornfield to Moor House, and finally Moor House to Ferndean marks her story as a "female *Bildungsroman*" in which she moves from "the imprisonment of her childhood to the almost unthinkable goal of mature freedom" (1979: 339). That movement might also be described in terms of Jane's transformation from an outsider to an insider: she is an unwanted but nonetheless acknowledged member of the family at Gateshead, an initially tortured and eventually treasured resident at Lowood, a servant who becomes central to life at Thornfield, and a refugee who ends up providing for the cousins she discovers at Moor House. In that reframing one sees more clearly how the uncanny initially manifests itself in Jane's life. Her suspension between the roles of "outsider" and "insider" literally unsettles her, creating in her a divided or doubled identity. That division is for much of the novel imagined as a suspension between the realms of spirit and of body, the incorporeal and the corporeal, and it is Jane's failure to understand the connection between these realms that gives so much of her experience its frightening edge.[12] Only when she apprehends that connection – in moments of sensibility that partake as much of one realm as the other – does the uncanny metamorphose into the familiar, and the gothic story of her life give way to a happier domesticity.[13]

The nightmarish quality of Jane's childhood is associated with her doubled identity from the novel's opening pages, when she describes her life with the Reed family. As an adult looking back to her childhood, she can "see . . . clearly" why her years in their household were so difficult:

> I was a discord in Gateshead Hall; I was like nobody there; I had nothing in harmony with Mrs Reed or her children, or her chosen vassalage. If they did not love me, in fact, as little did I love them. They were not bound to regard with affection a thing that could not sympathize with one amongst them; a heterogeneous thing, opposed to them in temperament, in capacity, in propensities; a useless thing, incapable of serving their interest, or adding to their pleasure; a noxious thing, cherishing the germs of indignation at their treatment, of contempt of their judgement. (p. 47)

Her careful account of what it was to be an outsider to the family in which she lived differs dramatically from her terrified experience of the same thing when she was a child, however. Then she knew only that she had been taken in and protected by her uncle Reed when he was alive, but that after his death she was forever victimized by her cousins and her aunt. Indeed, her worst experience in this household comes when a quarrel with her cousin John ends with her being punished by confinement to the "red room" in which her uncle had died. Her exile to this room emphasizes her marginal position in the family, even as it also recalls her tie to her uncle and her legitimate claim to be in the household, and proves particularly terrifying in the way it brings these two perspectives together.

Locked in this dark and shadowy chamber, Jane for a time seems to avoid its more fantastically gothic qualities by keeping her attention on the all too real difficulties of her day-to-day existence at Gateshead. She first imagines that she might escape the "insupportable oppression" of life at Gateshead by "running away, or if that could not be effected, never eating or drinking more, and letting [her]self die" (p. 47). While one would like to read this last statement as a sign of childhood bravado, it is important to remember that Catherine Linton follows through on just such a promise and actually dies. Escaping the body is one way out of the kinds of physical suffering that the young Jane endures, and while for the moment she refuses it, the fact that she does not have other good options available means that it quickly resurfaces in variant form.

While Jane may not want to escape imprisonment by letting herself die, getting help from the dead is another story. Realizing that her deceased uncle would never have sanctioned this harsh treatment of her, she begins to wonder whether "Mr Reed's spirit, harassed by the wrongs of his sister's child, might quit its abode – whether in the church vault or in the unknown world of the departed – and rise before me in this chamber" (p. 48). That she can imagine receiving comfort from a ghost breaks from most of gothic tradition, in which ghosts are generally threatening. While this is an idea that she finds "consolatory in theory," however, she feels it "would be terrible if realized," and one has to wonder why. Her expectation of a "preternatural voice" or "some haloed face, bending over [her] with strange pity" is perhaps sufficient explanation, for who could be other than frightened by such an occurrence? What she is imagining is an uncanny experience that frightens in part by its strangeness and in part by its insubstantiality. Jane will always resist any force that threatens to pull her away from the material world, and when later in her life she actually hears a preternatural voice as eerie as any she fears at this time – Rochester's, reaching out to her over the distance from Ferndean to Moor House – she will find a way to respond that does not threaten her in the same way. That eventual comfort with the uncanny is one sign – indeed, the major sign – of how effectively she will disarm the gothic over the course of the novel. How she gains that comfort is the question that needs answering.

Jane's time at Lowood Institution is more explicitly oppressive than eerily gothic, yet insofar as it leads her to reaffirm her commitment to embodied experience over insubstantial visions, it contributes to what I have just called her disarming of the gothic. On her arrival at Lowood, Jane finds herself once again viewed as an outsider whose conduct deserves punishment. After three short weeks during which she suffers like everyone else under the school's abusive treatment of its students, the frightening Mr. Brocklehurst arrives. This unwelcome "apparition" (p. 94) has learned from Mrs. Reed the story of Jane's life and presents her to the other students as someone who does not belong. When she breaks her slate, her punishment is to stand on a stool in front of the other students while he describes her as "a little castaway – not a member of the true flock, but evidently an interloper and an alien," an ungrateful liar sent to Lowood "to be healed, even as the Jews of old sent their diseased to the troubled pool of Bethesda" (pp. 98–9).[14] Echoing Jane's description of her place in the Reed household, Brocklehurst's rhetoric identifies Jane as a diseased and foreign body in the Lowood community, but also sets the stage for her to be drawn firmly inside it.

Where Jane's time in the red room led to terrifying reflections on the ramifications of her ties to the Reed family and a strong if temporary desire to escape her bodily existence, her punishment on the stool does the reverse. Just when she was about to panic, Jane recalls, "a girl came up and passed me: in passing, she lifted her eyes. What a strange light inspired them! What an extraordinary sensation that ray sent through me! How the new feeling bore me up! It was as if a martyr, a hero, had passed a slave or victim, and inspired strength in the transit" (p. 99). In this moment of sensibility, Jane begins to find a way past her humiliation, making an almost palpable connection with the girl who walks by her, and gaining a "strength" that seems as much physical as anything else. That movement is reinforced when Helen Burns contrives to walk by her with a smile that Jane reads as "the effluence of fine intellect, of true courage" (p. 99), and again, it is the fact that Helen's "intellect" and "courage" are embodied in her smile that facilitates the connection described here. Thus begins a healing process quite different from the penance Brocklehurst imposed, as Jane begins to feel herself not a "noxious thing," but part of the community at Lowood.

At Lowood, Jane learns to find comfort in the community with which she makes an ever more strongly felt connection. In this she differs significantly from her dear friend Helen Burns, who says that dying from consumption makes her "happy" insofar as she will "escape great sufferings," and who takes consolation in the Christian thought of life after death with a God who is her "father" and "friend" (p. 113). Where Helen implicitly argues that transcending the body is a viable way to escape the oppression of earthly existence, Jane clings to that existence – literally clings to Helen on her deathbed – and to her discovery that the life of the body can also be a life of the spirit. This insight is reinforced through Jane's relationship with Miss Temple, who is identified by Gilbert and Gubar as the Victorian "angel in the house" – but "even more house than angel" – and it is she who nurtures Jane during her time at Lowood (Gilbert and Gubar 1979: 345). She is the "place" in which Jane had taken refuge from Brocklehurst and other evils, a grounded mother figure to counter Helen's divine father, and when she leaves, she takes with her "the serene atmosphere [Jane] had been breathing in her vicinity" (1979: 116). With this metaphor Jane suggests a sustaining connection between the worlds of spirit and body that revises the terror of the red room, and takes her forward.

As others have discussed, Jane longs for activity and expanded horizons, and she eventually moves from Lowood to Thornfield, not simply because Miss Temple has gone, but because she "remembered that the real world was wide, and that a varied field of hopes and fears, of sensations and excitements, awaited those who had courage to go forth into its expanse, to seek real knowledge of life amidst its perils" (p. 116). Thornfield will offer the greatest challenge yet to Jane's efforts to hold on to that "real world," however. Her residence there marks her as a hard-working governess on the one hand and as the fairy creature with whom Rochester falls in love on the other. Rochester sees Jane as an almost disembodied creature, and while Jane consistently reasserts her flesh-and-blood reality in the face of his playful but persistent assertions to the contrary, his vision gradually takes over even her sense of things.

Critics have commented in various ways on the fairy-tale-like frame around Jane's relationship with Rochester. When she meets him in the woods, she imagines his dog as the gytrash of folklore – "a lion-like creature with long hair and a huge head" (p. 144) – and he later says that, on first encountering her, he "thought unaccountably of fairy tales, and had half a mind to demand whether [she] had bewitched [his] horse" (p. 153), which has thrown him. Through the rest of the novel, Rochester will persist in seeing Jane as "an 'elf'" (p. 272), a "fairy" (p. 273), an "angel" (p. 288), and when she returns to Thornfield after a month at Gateshead, her quiet re-entry on foot prompts him to tease her because she did not "send for a carriage, and come clattering over street and road like a common mortal," but instead chose to "steal into the vicinage of [her] home along with twilight, just as if [she] were a dream or a shade" (p. 272).

Jane longs to be "at home" at Thornfield, but the closer she comes to realizing this desire, the more everything about her seems just the opposite. After Rochester has finally asked her to marry him, the world around her becomes increasingly hard to hold on to. The night before their wedding is to take place, she tells him, "Everything in life seems unreal," while he himself is "the most phantom-like of all" (pp. 306–7). This feeling that reality is fading stems most immediately from her experiences two nights before she is to be married to Rochester. First she dreams that Rochester leaves her, walking away down a road while she is left behind with a baby; then she dreams again that he leaves her, this time riding away while she stands on the crumbling walls of Thornfield, again with a baby; finally, she awakens to the surreal vision of her wedding veil being torn in half by a woman who reminds her of "the foul German spectre – the vampire" (p. 311). The "vampire" is none other than Rochester's first wife, Bertha Mason, and Rochester's acknowledgment of her existence is also an acknowledgment that Jane was right to see her life as "unreal." It was. Bertha represents the return of the real with a vengeance.

In coming face to face with Bertha, Jane confronts a woman whose physical presence points to the complicated reality of the world in which they both live. We read that Bertha is the West Indian woman whom Rochester married to please his family, though also thinking that he loved her; that she is tall, dark, and was once thought beautiful; that madness runs in her family, and that she herself was incarcerated as a madwoman four years after Rochester married her, first in Jamaica and then for ten years at Thornfield. Described as a "beast" (p. 321), a "wild animal" (p. 321), a "demon" (p. 322) and a "monster" (p. 336), both her appearance and behavior suggest that we are to see her through British imperial eyes as a colonial savage, and yet such a reading would be much too simple.

Born in Jamaica to a now decaying aristocratic family, Bertha is a Creole – a term that "was used in the nineteenth century to refer to both blacks and whites born in the West Indies" (Meyer 1996: 68) – and a member of the increasingly decadent and dysfunctional Jamaican plantocracy (Sharpe 1993: 45). The novel describes her in language that "insistently and conventionally mark[s] Bertha as black" (Meyer 1996: 69), even as it acknowledges that Bertha "is a woman whom the younger son of an aristocratic British family would consider marrying, and so she is clearly imagined as white – or as passing for white – in the novel's retrospective narrative" (1996: 67). She is the product of British imperialism, embodying its tensions and contradicitions, a nation's uncanny double come back to haunt those who made her.

These readings of Bertha's political identity complicate earlier feminist readings of her as Jane's double.[15] In a contrast that echoes that between Victoria and Lilla in Dacre's *Zofloya*, Bertha is literally the tall, dark counterpart to the small, fair Jane, arguably a "monitory image . . . for Jane," but still more often read – in a description cited above – as Jane's "truest and darkest double: she is the angry aspect of the orphan child, the ferocious secret self Jane has been trying to repress ever since her days at Gateshead" (Gilbert and Gubar 1979: 360). Gilbert and Gubar develop this reading by demonstrating the likeness of the two women in their rage at their own oppression, in their own and others' tendency to imagine them as mad and/or monstrous in some way, and in their insistence on rebellion.[16] Bertha is kept under lock and key, yet, with all the force of Dacre's Victoria, manages to set Rochester's bed on fire, to stab and claw her brother when he visits, to visit Jane in her bedroom and destroy her bridal veil, and finally, to burn down Thornfield in its entirety, killing herself as well. The orphaned Jane is equally restrained by the Reeds, Mr. Brocklehurst, and even Mr. Rochester, yet she finds her way to independence in spite of them. In Rochester's lexicon, Bertha is a "demon" to Jane's "fairy," and that language – casting both as other-worldly creatures, as Gilbert and Gubar also note (1979: 361) – brings them together as a single uncanny "other" guaranteed to haunt his all too human existence.

To describe Bertha as Jane's uncanny double is to say that she reflects back to Jane a distorted image of herself, and Jane herself comes to understand that there is a connection between them. When Jane accuses Rochester of cruelty in hating Bertha, who "cannot help being mad," he says she does not understand the situation. "If you were mad," he asks, "do you think I should hate you?" "I do indeed, sir," she replies, and with that response, she makes clear that she does not see herself as so different from Bertha after all. That said, however, it is worth adding to this insight – true as it may be – that to see these two women *only* as doubles for each other limits our understanding of both. Shifting the lens just slightly, Bertha emerges as not uncanny but sublime, a heroine out of Edmund Burke's *Enquiry* – large, dark, terrifying – with the potential to overwhelm both Jane and Rochester. Rochester she does injure and almost annihilate. Jane she arguably helps return to herself, forcing her to see the realities of her life in Rochester's house, and it is precisely that clear vision that lets Jane then act autonomously and walk away.

Jane's final struggle with her roles as insider and outsider, her last negotiation between the familiar material world she inhabits and a world that points beyond the material, comes at Moor House. There she is taken in by Mary and Diana Rivers after three days of homeless wandering, and the revelation that the Rivers are related to Jane – along with her inheritance of twenty thousand pounds from their uncle – would seem at last to ground her in an almost perfect domestic life. A threat to that life comes from the aptly named St. John, however, who is going to India as a missionary and wants Jane with him as his "helpmeet," "fellow-labourer," and "wife" (pp. 427–8). While after initial resistance she agrees to support him in his religious work, she cannot imagine doing so as his wife, and says his efforts to persuade her otherwise are "killing" her (p. 438). In the end, however, he exerts a force so overwhelming that she almost yields. "All men of talent . . . provided they be sincere, have their sublime moments, when they subdue and rule" (p. 443), Jane states, and in one such moment, everything changes: "Religion called – Angels beckoned – God commanded – life rolled together like a scroll – death's gates opening showed eternity beyond: it seemed, that for safety and bliss there, all here might be sacrificed in a second" (p. 444).

St. John's appeal to Jane constitutes what Gilbert and Gubar have described as the strongest and perhaps "most irresistible" threat yet to her autonomy (1979: 366). Sharpe reads it as an effort to transform Jane into the sort of self-sacrific-ing English woman that the novel consistently associates with India, where Hindu widows practicing sati "were burned alive on their husbands' pyres" (1993: 49, 53), in contrast to the self-indulgently destructive women that it just as con-sistently associates with the Caribbean (1993: 45). Jane herself recognizes that to go with him would be "to rush down the torrent of his will into the gulf of his existence, and there lose [her] own" (p. 443), and only the infamous telepathic communication from Rochester stops her from saying "Yes" to him anyway.

The mysterious call that takes Jane back to Rochester has drawn responses both positive and negative (Yeazell 1979). While it can seem more supernatural than natural, more of the spirit than the body, I read it as bringing those two realms together in the most fully imagined form of sensibility that we have seen. Jane experiences Rochester's call as a physical sensation that is inextricably tied to emotional and psychological sensations. Having lamented her "inward dimness of vision," Jane longs for divine guidance and in response feels her heart

Confronting the Uncanny

"still to an inexpressible feeling that thrilled it through, and passed at once to [her] head and extremities . . . not like an electric shock, but . . . quite as sharp, as strange, as startling" (p. 444). Then comes the voice of Rochester speaking to her "in pain and woe, wildly, eerily, urgently" (p. 444), and while she allows the possibility that all of this is "the effect of excitement," she nonetheless acts on it. Where as a young girl Jane had backed away from the mere idea of her uncle's ghostly voice, she now moves toward Rochester's in a moment of remarkable self-empowerment: "It was *my* time to assume ascendancy. *My* powers were in play and in force" (p. 445). She is like Catherine affirming that she *is* Heathcliff, and yet there is a difference. Cathy and Heathcliff lose themselves in a sublimity whose desirability I have all along been questioning. Jane and Rochester do not.

Writing ten years after her marriage to Rochester, the physicality of their connection is still apparent, as is the fact that they are separate people within that connection. "I know no weariness of my Edward's society," Jane writes, "he knows none of mine, any more than we do of the pulsation of the heart that beats in our separate bosoms" (p. 476). The image of two people with one heart suggests an almost unimaginable closeness, as does Jane's statement that she is "ever more absolutely bone of his bone and flesh of his flesh" (p. 476). This passage echoes Genesis 2: 22 to suggest that Jane and Rochester are a latter-day Adam and Eve, yet they clearly revise that archetypal relationship. Rochester's flesh is weak, and his physical strength derives as much from Jane as vice versa. When Jane finds him at Ferndean, he has been maimed and blinded from the fire in which Bertha jumped to her death, and she becomes "his vision" as well as "his right hand," so that "he saw . . . through [her]" even as she is "never . . . weary of gazing for his behalf" (p. 476).

Jane and Rochester develop a relationship that grounds intangible connections of spirit firmly in the physical world. They live in "perfect concord" and are "happy" (pp. 476–7), not looking for the sublime rewards that will be experienced by the saintly St. John and lucky to have avoided the sublime injustice that was visited on Bertha Mason. In the figures of St. John and Bertha, however, one realizes that the gothic has not been vanquished, but simply pushed out to the margins of the story. It takes place in the far reaches of empire, and that is where we must go next.

7

The "Unhomely" Nation of Gothic Narratives
Charlotte Smith, Charles Brockden Brown, and Matthew Lewis

relatively recent and extremely productive approach to gothic fiction focuses on its rhetorical contribution to the work of defining a national identity. One might wonder why this line of analysis has emerged so late, given that the very term "gothic" bore directly on eighteenth-century discussions of what it meant to be English. As I noted in my introduction, the term "gothic" condensed into a single concept a complicated perspective on historical events. Ian Duncan summarizes:

> An unofficial, oppositional movement, populist and proto-nationalist in its appeal and with its ideological roots in the radical Whiggery [i.e. progressive politics] of the last century, was reclaiming "Gothic" culture as the ancient constitutional source of British liberties usurped by the Norman Conquest and subsequent aristocratic rule. . . . At the same time, the establishment conception of "Gothic" was that of barbarian forces that had overthrown a civilization, and the long cultural darkness haunted by despotism and anarchy, superstition and enthusiasm, out of which the present British dispensation, modelling itself on classical principles, had only lately emerged. (1992: 21–2)

The Goths are thus associated both with an ancient sense of "Englishness" and with the loss of that identity to invading forces. The term "gothic" is thus divided at its heart, and, as Duncan summarizes, "the Gothic novel describes the malign equation between an origin we have lost and an alien force that invades our borders, haunts our mansions, possesses our souls" (1992: 23).

If the term "gothic" suggests that we should see the very idea of nationhood not in terms of absolutes, but in terms of division and difference, we can see why English gothic novelists so often set their stories elsewhere. We can see as well why they so often embed in stories of one culture characters drawn from another. To talk about somewhere else is to talk about home at the same time, and this point emerges all the more clearly when the "somewhere else" is in fact a British colony.[1] The relation between mother country and colony is not just one of difference, but also one of likeness, an uncanny doubling that is by definition gothic, and that makes clear the uncertain ground on which terms like "nation," "mother country," and "colony" really stand.

A powerful model for thinking about the uncertain identities produced by colonial experience comes from Homi Bhabha's *The Location of Culture*. Writing primarily about colonial and post-colonial fictions, he builds an argument for what he calls the "unhomely" lives of those who inhabit them. "Unhomely lives" have been shaped by what Bhabha calls "extra-territorial and cross-cultural initiations," forms of cross-cultural contact that bring the outside world in, that blur the boundaries between what is public and what is private, and leave people with "a vision that is as divided as it is disorienting" (1994: 9). The "unhomely" experience is at once cultural and psychological, producing a double vision that Bhabha for good measure identifies as uncanny. That the "unhomely" is a version of the uncanny would have been clear in any case, however, for both words are translations of the single Freudian concept of the *unheimlich*, and as such contribute to experiences that Bhabha all but directs us to see as gothic. "The unhomely moment creeps up on you as steadily as your own shadow," he writes, "and suddenly you find yourself . . . taking the measure of your dwelling in a state of 'incredulous terror'" (1994: 9).

Bhabha sees that the unhomely life develops from the same pattern of doubling that is at the heart of uncanny experience, and from the same root interest in "home" as a place that can be both familiar and utterly strange. He presses Freud's thinking one important step further, however, when he argues for the importance of women in this experience. Where Freud repeatedly saw the woman at the center of the uncanny experience only to set her aside as less than important, Bhabha sees the female figures at the center of his analysis. He is attuned to the ways in which patriarchal societies have tended to efface women, and consciously builds on feminist criticism when he urges us to remember that this effacement effectively constitutes – and also hides – an "unhomeliness" at the heart of (our own) civil society (1994: 10).

Bhabha's analysis gives us a way of conceptualizing the gothic nature of lives shaped not just by colonial experience but more generally by situations that ask people to "negotiate the powers of cultural difference" (1994: 9). Those who build their lives around those negotiations will in all likelihood find themselves "unhomed," their identities fractured – but also constituted – by the double vision characteristic of their situation. Turning back to the world of eighteenth- and nineteenth-century gothic fiction, where the contours of those experiences are just emerging through their narratives of nation-making, empire-building, and colonial rebellion, we find the powerful and the subordinated alike struggling against the uncertainties of the unhomely.

National Anxieties: Charlotte Smith and Charles Brockden Brown

Katie Trumpener has grouped Charlotte Smith's novel *The Old Manor House* (1793) with others of this period that are "shaped by the conjunction of Gothic and Jacobin influences," observing that this novel – like those others – "structures a plot of cultural comparison around the traverse between Britain and its colonial possessions" (1997: 168). That said, Smith is also rather unusual in focusing specifically on Britain's relationship with America at the time of the revolutionary war. Smith disapproved of the British policy that led the Americans to rebel, though she could not quite see the war as anything other than a European conflict played out on American soil. In Smith's novel, the British loyalists fight the British rebels in a war whose most significant violence is displaced on to the Native Americans used by both sides, and yet even that displacement is not enough to maintain British identity intact. Her hero is unmade and remade as a result of his experiences abroad.

The Old Manor House tells the story of Orlando Somerive and his beloved Monimia. He is the younger son of a family struggling to get back into the good graces of his elderly aunt, Mrs. Rayland, who has disinherited them because of their grandfather's marriage to a woman of a lower class; she is the impoverished niece of the old woman's companion, Mrs. Lennard. The lovers' story does not emerge in one continuous narrative, however, but is interrupted for several chapters in volumes III and IV by the tale of Orlando's experiences fighting against the American rebels in the 1776 revolution. Trumpener rightly suggests that this movement in the novel's plot "relativizes the worldview of the English aristocracy, even as it demonstrates their inability to grasp their place in and impact on the rest of the world," and places on Orlando the burden of "bring[ing] the war home, to explain the wide-ranging consequences of domestic politics" (1997: 168–9). The novel does not go so far as to put American views at its center but, rather, imagines America as a mirror held up to the mother country to show those in Britain what they really look like. In other words, America is imagined as Britain's uncanny double come back to haunt her.

Britain is depicted as a place where romance narratives battle with the seamy realism of "things as they are" to shape everyday life. As that description implies, the narrative of Orlando and Monimia reads like a hybrid of Ann Radcliffe and William Godwin. Like Radcliffe, Smith spins a tale with all the trappings of high gothic fiction but the supernatural, and, like Godwin, she locates the real evils of this world in an oppressive class structure. The orphaned Monimia has been raised by an aunt who treats her like a servant by day, locks her into a bedroom tucked away in a turret of Rayland Hall at night, and does everything she can to prevent her from developing a relationship with Orlando. Orlando is at once her lover and protector, and is himself held in thrall by his own elderly aunt from whom he hopes to inherit a fortune. The two manage to meet secretly, thanks to the staircase hidden in the wall behind her bed by which she escapes her nightly confinement, and, while the household gradually grows suspicious about their relationship, they are safe to the point at which Orlando leaves for the war.

Orlando's relationship with Monimia has been read as one that conservatively places him in the role of active hero and her in the role of passive heroine. More recently, criticism has suggested that their relationship complicates this structuring of gender roles, for while it does move to a happy ending in which they are entirely reinforced, it does so by a rather subversive route. Joseph Bartolomeo (1993) argues that the novel gives us a hero who is gently satirized by his tendency to model himself on heroes of romance even as he fails in key ways to fulfill the chivalric role he has assigned himself, while at the same time creating a heroine who proves well able to move beyond the passive role assigned to her as she fends off would-be ravishers and finds work to support herself as well as her family. The novel's desire to hold on to and at the same time question the gender conventions of gothic romance takes on a still more complicated aspect when one realizes that it is tied in to a discussion of national politics as well. For England is the site of gothic romance, and America the site of a far grittier history.

The novel's engagement with gothic romance is self-consciously built around a central irony. Orlando insists that Monimia free her mind of any propensity to the superstition associated with such stories, without realizing that he himself is driven by something very similar. When Orlando first escorts Monimia down the secret staircase from her bedroom, across the courtyard, and through the chapel to his own room, Monimia nearly faints when she reaches the chapel. She is frightened by the place, and explains why:

> It is haunted, you know, every night by the spirit of one of the Lady Raylands, who
> I know not how long ago died for love, and whose ghost now sits every night in
> the chancel, and sometimes walks round the house, and particularly along the
> galleries, at midnight, groaning and lamenting her fate. (p. 40)[2]

Orlando laughs away her concerns, which he sees as having "violated [her]
natural good sense" (p. 40), and indeed, when the pair is later terrified by intrud-
ers who are eventually identified as smugglers, the novel does not for a moment
suggest that the unexplained visitors and the various noises they make stem from
supernatural causes.

As Bartolomeo also notes (1993: 650), while Orlando is criticizing Monimia's
romantic propensities, he is at the same time indulging his own, and we see evidence for this in the way that Orlando's father responds to his son's confession
of his attachment to the "angel" Monimia. "An angel! Every idle boy that reads
ballads or writes them, every scribbler that sends his rhymes to a magazine, calls
the nymph who inspires him an angel; and such an angel is this Monimia of
yours! and from such sort of reading you have learned to fancy yourself in love
with her" (pp. 264–5). Orlando may not believe in ghosts and goblins, but he is
as much a product of sentimental reading as Wollstonecraft's Maria will be after
him. The difference is that his reading serves him well. By the novel's end, his
faith in what his father would describe as pure romantic fiction has been justified: he has married Monimia, been named the heir of the Rayland estate, and
successfully litigated for its recovery when it was stolen out from under him on
the basis of an outdated will. Indeed, as he enters Rayland Hall with a warrant
to search for the will that establishes him as its rightful possessor, we read that
he

> could not . . . help fancying, that the scene resembled one of those so often met
> with in old romances and fairy tales, where the hero is by some supernatural means
> directed to a golden key, which opens an invisible drawer, where a hand or an head
> is found swimming in blood, which it is his business to restore to the inchanted
> owner. (p. 527)

Orlando knows he is a hero following a script. The saving grace is that this script,
flawed as it may be, seems to be better than the others available to him.[3]

The other narrative model that the novel holds up as possible model for
Orlando's life comes from British history. His time in the army represents not
simply a discrete series of adventures, but a way of modeling action and identity
that originates in historical narrative. Orlando joins the army for reasons of both
principle (he needs a profession) and self-interest (this one will appeal to Mrs.
Rayland), though he is entirely ignorant of what he will be required to do once
he has his commission. He gradually begins to question the logic of his actions,

and on arriving at the Portsmouth docks, where ships are loading for the trip to America, he "for the first time enquire[s] of himself what all this was for?" (p. 345) He asks that same question again when they are at sea:

> when he considered a number of men thus packed together in a little vessel, per-
> ishing by disease; such of them as survived going to another hemisphere to avenge
> on a branch of their own nation a quarrel, of the justice of which they knew little,
> and were never suffered to enquire; he felt disposed to wonder at the folly of
> mankind, and to enquire again *what all this was for?* (pp. 347–8)

His answers are many, but they are all unsatisfactory in the end.

Trying to convince himself that he is fighting for "the glory of his country," he reasons that no price is too high, then wonders "if it was not from a mistaken point of honour, from the wickedness of governments, or the sanguinary ambi-tion or revenge of monarchs, that so much misery was owing as wars of every description must necessarily attain." He turns for comfort to "history – Our Henries and our Edwards, heroes whose names children are taught to lisp with delight . . . and he trie[s] to believe that what these English Kings had so glori-ously done, was in their descendants equally glorious, because it went to support the honour of the British name" (p. 348). He is not sure they did right, however, and he has even less faith in the "modern directors of war . . . who [incur] no personal danger, nor [give] themselves any other trouble than to raise money from one part of their subjects in order to enable them to destroy another, or the subjects of some neighbouring potentate," or the "subordinate departments, to whom the care of providing for troops . . . [is] entrusted," and whose provi-sion of inadequate rations has killed off the troops even as it enriched themselves (pp. 348–9). Both official histories and official governments are presented as corrupt and providing no justification for war of any sort, and other arguments fall apart equally quickly. Orlando's "fellow soldiers" try to make him see "the English Americans as men of an inferior species, whose resistance to the mea-sures . . . of the mother country, [deserve] every punishment that the most fero-cious mode of warfare could inflict," and his friend Fleming insists that "a soldier never thought of examining into such matters": "the sword is my argument," he states, "and I have sold that to my King, and therefore must use it in his service, whatever and wherever it may be pointed out to me" (p. 358). None of these arguments convinces Orlando, who has only to see the results of battle to decide that war is "not to be justified by *any* cause" (p. 358).

Smith's progressive politics are often discussed, and here she clearly speaks through Orlando against war in any form, even as she speaks just as clearly against the war of 1776, which she saw as a war waged by Britain against its own people and its own principles. Having "always been told, that the will of the people was the great resort in the British Government," Orlando is appalled to think that this war is being waged "at ruinous expence" and "in absolute contradiction to the wishes of the people who were taxed to support it" (p. 358). To see this war as a civil war is to limit one's perspective on it, however, and this is perhaps why Smith stops short of articulating the American view of the conflict. She writes a scene in which British officers guard an American prisoner of war, during which Orlando has "an opportunity . . . of hearing the American party tell their own story" (p. 359). While she describes the "pity, not unmixed with respect" that Orlando feels in response to the story, along with his "astonishment" at "the infatuation of the British Cabinet, or rather the easy acquiescence of the British people," she never tells us what the story was (p. 358). That gap in the narrative speaks volumes.

As much as anything else, the gap announces that Smith's interest in America turns on what it can tell us about the British more than on what it can tell us about the colonies. She offers a predictable depiction of the landscape drawn from books (as were Radcliffe's views of Italy and France), gesturing toward a characteristic sublimity that distinguishes it from the landscape of England, as "[e]very object seemed formed upon a larger scale" (p. 357). More interesting to her than nature, however, are the people of the place – not the rebel colonists, or even the loyalists, but Native Americans. Her portrait of their "savage appearance, and the more savage thirst of blood which they avowed" makes them just as stereotypical as the villainous Italians and Spaniards who populate other gothic novels (p. 360). Less typical is her willingness to consider that these villains have something in common with her hero.

While the revolutionary war pitted the British against the American colonists, Smith portrays this conflict almost in passing. We read of families driven from their homes by the defending troops of the mother country, but do not see the battles that displaced them. Instead we see Native Americans, who are first allies and then enemies of the British.

As allies of the British, Native Americans were cast in opposition to the colonists, and the British public, including Smith, debated the merits of this decision. In a long footnote that rehearses debates about the "humanity" as well as "policy" of relying on Native Americans for defence, Smith notes the "humanitarian" concern that, in their battles with the colonists, "Indians" would be "capricious, inconstant, and intractable; their rapacity insatiate, and their actions cruel and barbarous" (p. 360). While arguments against unnecessary cruelty in war (paradoxical as they may be) are always articulated, one might see here a displacement onto Native Americans of not just blame for the cruelty that the British themselves were inflicting on the rebels, but the very role of "enemy." Smith reinforces this sense in her novel, when she more than once shows us native warriors with scalps in their hands, including those of women, children, and the elderly (pp. 360–1), while no Englishman is ever shown injuring a colonist.

British debates about the "policy" of relying on Native Americans to fight for them expressed concern that their "services" were "uncertain" and that "no dependence could be placed on their engagements" in battle (p. 360). While Smith's novel again suggests the validity of this reservation, the reasons she gives for the Native Americans' outright betrayal of British troops shift the perspective on their relationship considerably from that represented in her footnote. When Orlando and his party are attacked by Native Americans, Smith makes clear that it is because "the English had not dealt fairly with them . . . they got nothing . . . but had lost some of their best men in defending the lines," and so "were going home to their own lands" (p. 378).

Smith both demonizes and sympathizes with the Native Americans of her imagination, then, and their double-edged role in the novel is further complicated by Orlando's friendship with a young Iroquois named Wolf-hunter. They share a "secret sympathy" that "between generous minds seems to exist throughout the whole human kind" (p. 361). Orlando learns from Wolf-hunter some of the language and "a good deal of the customs of the Indians of North America" (p. 362), and when the Native Americans rebel against their British allies, it is Wolf-hunter who first saves Orlando from death and then "equip[s] him like an Indian warrior. His fine hair was cut off, all but a long lock on the crown of his head – and he was distinguished from an Iroquois by nothing but his English complexion" (p. 380). Orlando has unwillingly "gone native," though he resists this perception, seeing himself as "condemned" to live with "barbarians, deprived of all human intercourse, and in a kind of living death" (p. 381). He spends four months in the company of the Iroquois before he is able to make his way to Quebec, then to New York and onto an English ship. That he is captured by the French on his way home, and forced to detour through France to England, reminds one of the French–English tensions lurking behind the battles for the colonies.

Orlando's lurching return to England occurs in tandem with an equally lurching return to his English identity. In Quebec he is "once more restored to the appearance of an Englishman," though he is still "much changed by the hardships he had undergone, and by the loss of his hair, which had been remarkably fine" (p. 388), and the commander of the French ship on which he is taken prisoner ensures that he has a "proper passport" for his travel home (p. 389). Nearly all that he has acquired is taken from him by the smugglers who take him from France to England, however, and when he seeks shelter in a British alehouse, his appearance is a motley mix that marks all of the stages of his journey. His hair is still "in the mode of the Iroquois, and now presented what is called a shock head," while his clothing includes a waistcoat from Quebec, a French coat, and a hat given to him by the smugglers (p. 395). He is a pastiche of cultural identities, and people do not know how to place him: "Some took him for a Frenchman, and some for an Exciseman . . . All agreed that he was a spy, and heartily wished him away" (p. 392). That said, the problems posed by his appearance are trivial compared to those posed by the fact that most people think him dead, though regaining the appearance of an Englishman eases the way to regaining his place in society as well.

While Orlando's time away from England initially seems to have stripped him of his identity entirely, it would be more accurate to say that the role he is to fill – and his ability to fill it – have both expanded. The most tragic events in the story of Orlando, Monimia, and the Somerive family occur during, and to a degree result from, Orlando's absence from his family while he fights in the American war. While he is away, Mrs. Rayland dies, his family's claim to her estate is usurped, his father dies, his sister Isabella elopes and disappears, his elder brother becomes even more debauched, and Monimia is increasingly persecuted. In his absence, he is cast as the patriarchal figure who can resolve all problems, and he just about does. While he cannot undo the fact of his father's death, or keep his brother from the early death that results from hard living, he does manage to find and marry Monimia, draw Isabella back into the family, and successfully expose the corruption that has robbed him of his inheritance.

In this last venture he is helped significantly by an elderly, impoverished military officer, who at first sight recalls to him "[a]ll the horrors of which he had been a witness in America" (p. 461). The man has lost his leg, and before even meeting him, Orlando sees him as someone who,

> trembling on the verge of life, seems to have none of its common necessaries; yet perhaps has been disabled from acquiring them by having lost his limb in the service of what is called his country, that is, in fighting the battles of its politicians; and having been deprived of his leg to preserve the balance of Europe, has not found in the usual asylum a place of rest, to make him such amends as can be made for such a misfortune! (p. 461)

By the end of the novel, this "military mendicant" has been made a "tenant for life" on Orlando's estate, and it is to him – as well as his relationship with Orlando – that the novel's final paragraph is devoted (p. 533). Thus the novel remembers its excursion to America and the costs of that war at home, if not abroad. The maimed soldier mirrors the romance hero, and, in recognizing that, Smith takes a small step to ensure that her country will remember and not be haunted by the ghosts of its past.

Five years after Smith wrote *The Old Manor House*, American-born Charles Brockden Brown self-consciously adapted gothic tradition to American experience. His address "To the Public" at the beginning of his 1799 novel *Edgar Huntly* makes this point explicit: "That new springs of action, and new motives to curiosity should operate; that the field of investigation, opened to us by our own country, should differ essentially from those which exist in Europe, may be readily conceived. The sources of amusement to the fancy and instruction to the heart, that are peculiar to ourselves, are equally numerous and inexhaustible" (p. 3).[4] As a writer he claims for himself the "merit . . . of calling forth the passions and engaging the sympathy of the reader, by means hitherto unemployed by preceding authors" (p. 3). Where "[p]uerile superstition and exploded manners; Gothic castles and chimeras, are the materials usually employed for this end," he asserts that "[t]he incidents of Indian hostility, and the perils of the western wilderness are far more suitable; and, for a native of America to overlook these, would admit of no apology" (p. 3). His sense of responsibility to his newly formed nation is clear here, as is his sense of its distinctiveness, and that same consciousness informs the three other gothic novels that he published in the years 1798–9. While his claims are forceful however, his novels demonstrate what critics have shown to be the difficulty of forging a national identity in the new republic. *Wieland or The Transformation: An American Tale* announces its national identity in its subtitle, and yet the novel's plot focuses above all on threats to that identity. Those threats take different forms, but are finally all rooted in what Mark Seltzer (1978) helps us see as the power of language to make and unmake the world.

Wieland was published in 1798, but Brown specifies in his "Advertisement" to the novel that it is set "between the conclusion of the French and the beginning of the revolutionary war," that is, between 1763 and 1776 (p. 4).[5] While much criticism of the novel has elucidated its commentary on the politics of the newly independent nation in which Brown wrote, it is worth remembering that the novel itself portrays a colony that had not yet gained its independence. The only explicit reference to politics comes near its beginning, when Clara Wieland – the novel's narrator – contextualizes her tale relative to the recently concluded French–Indian war:

> Six years of uninterrupted happiness had rolled away, since my brother's marriage. The sound of war had been heard, but it was at such a distance as to enhance our enjoyment by affording objects of comparison. The Indians were repulsed on the one side, and Canada was conquered on the other. Revolutions and battles, however calamitous to those who occupied the scene, contributed in some sort to our happiness, by agitating our minds with curiosity, and furnishing causes of patriotic exultation. (p. 29)

These sentences point to a moment in the consolidation of what would soon become an independent American identity, though that struggle fades in the face of the drama of the Wieland family, or perhaps is displaced onto it (Weldon 1984;

Samuels 1996). Whether the life of the nation can be represented by the life of a single family is a question that the novel asks us to consider. If it can – as many critics have argued – then the story of the Wieland family is a cautionary tale indeed. For it is very nearly destroyed by the end of the novel.

The Wieland family consists of Clara Wieland, her brother Theodore, Theodore's wife Catharine, and their two children. Their circle also includes Catharine's brother Pleyel, whom Clara will eventually marry, and a motherless child named Louisa Conway. When we meet them they seem blissfully happy, and the suffering they are about to undergo seems almost unimaginable. So what goes wrong? There are many possible answers to that question, but I will focus my attention on two: one the seemingly supernatural cause of the family's disasters and the other the altogether human cause of them.

As was true in the English gothic novels discussed earlier, the seemingly supernatural story turns on religion. As a young man living in England, Clara's father discovered the writings of a French Protestant sect called the Camissards, and became an evangelical Christian as a result. With the advent of his faith, "[t]he craving which had haunted him was . . . supplied with an object," and he left England for an America that would be more tolerant of his extreme religious views (p. 9). There he married, had a family, and lived a solitary life built around a religious practice that "had been expressly prescribed to him" (p. 13). His death by fire in the austere temple he built for worship suggests the severe price of this faith. It is intimated that he was a victim of spontaneous combustion, though the novel is purposefully vague on the causes of the fire, and while his children deliberately turn away from his religious extremism, they cannot in the end avoid it.

Even as his inwardly turned religion satisfied a "craving" in Clara's father, so does the equally inward-looking social circle of Clara, her brother, and her brother's friend/wife Catherine seem to fill the gap left by the death of the Wieland parents. The education of Clara and her brother "had been modelled by no religious standards," and while Clara takes pains to tell us that they were not unreligious, she emphasizes that their "devotion was a mixed and casual sentiment, seldom verbally expressed or solicitously sought, or carefully retained" (pp. 24–5). When they inherit their father's property, they convert the temple he built to a place of secular recreation where they "sung, and talked, and read, and occasionally banqueted" (p. 26). It becomes a temple of arts and learning, its connection to the classical world of humanism emphasized by its neoclassical design, as well as by its furnishings of a bust of Cicero (which may or may not be a copy of an Italian original) and a harpsichord. With the return of Catherine's brother Henry, their idyllic circle is complete.

The laws of literature, if not of life, demand that this perfection be punctured (the story of perfection is mere stasis and repetition, no narrative at all), and the

fall begins when the members of the Wieland household begin hearing mysterious voices warning them to behave in one way or another. The sense of strangeness builds, until one terrible night Theodore Wieland kills his wife, his children,
and Louisa Conway. When he finally gives an account of the crime, he speaks of
a "vision" that "dazzled" his senses, and "nameless fear" that "chilled [his] veins."
"It is forbidden to describe what I saw," he goes on. "Words, indeed, would be
wanting to the task. The lineaments of that being, whose veil was now lifted,
and whose visage beamed upon my sight, no hues of pencil or of language can
pourtray" (p. 190). Wieland's sublimely indescribable vision of divinity is not the
end of the encounter, however. The divinity speaks to him, and its words are
appallingly clear: "Thy prayers are heard. In proof of thy faith, render me thy
wife. This is the victim I chuse. Call her hither, and here let her fall" (p. 190).
That sacrifice accomplished, Wieland receives a second command: "Thou hast
done well; but all is not done – the sacrifice is incomplete – thy children must be
offered – they must perish with their mother!" (p. 197) Its clarity notwithstand-
ing, there is a sublime force in this voice too, for it possesses Wieland entirely,
and he does its bidding unhesitatingly.

Did Wieland really hear God talking to him? Was he enacting a latter-day
Abraham and Isaac story? Perhaps, for even when we learn that at least some of
the voices might have been ventriloquized by an intruder named Carwin, we still
do not have a fully rational explanation of what Wieland heard. But, as Elizabeth
Barnes points out, we do know what Wieland did. In a crime that betrays the
very patriarchal order in which he participates, Wieland kills "those who are
legally, financially, and most important, emotionally tied to [him] and in whom
[he has] an emotional investment" (Barnes 2002: 47). Why? We might begin by
noting that he seems in some obscure way to be carrying out a "duty" that we
know his father passed on to a future generation. We might then follow Barnes
in noting further that "the father–son relation symbolized political conflict for
Americans in the revolutionary era," and that America had figured itself as the
"abused son of a tyrannical parent" when it rebelled against England (Barnes
2002: 53).[6] As Barnes understands this dynamic, however, the son has now
stepped into the role of father and is abusive in turn. In the world of the novel,
"good and evil, love and aggression, are inextricably intertwined," and "[p]aternal
love is no defense against the world's evil. In fact, quite the contrary: it magni-
fies the violence" (2002: 54).

If fathers inevitably betray their sons, it is worth remembering that this father
acts in the name of religion. The Protestant religious fervor that allows Wieland's
direct and dangerous relationship to God counters the Catholic religious fervor
that creates the equally dangerous figures of Lewis's Ambrosio or Radcliffe's
Schedoni. The Protestant version of religious corruption privileges individual-
ism to a dangerous degree,[7] while the Catholic version creates a church that inter-

feres far too much in the lives of its adherents, but they are in the end equally dangerous. Patriarchal religion will maim America even as it has maimed Europe, it seems, and yet religion is not the only or even the principal villain in the piece.

As in the novels of Walpole, Lewis, and Maturin, the seemingly supernatural narrative of Wieland's self-destruction is countered by a story that is firmly based in the world of human experience. This is the story in which the wonderfully independent Clara, who has inherited half of her father's property and lives alone in a house near her brother's, finds herself manipulated in ways that echo with a difference what happened to her brother. She too is "haunted" by mysterious voices that undermine her sense of reality and severely threaten her place in the world. Her fall turns not on religion, however, but on reputation, and is undoubtedly the result of Carwin's ventriloquizing.

Clara narrates the novel, and feels an attraction to Carwin from the start, though what draws her she cannot quite say. Even before she knows who he is, he catches her attention with his "rustic and aukward" way of walking, his "ungainly and disproportioned" person, his clothing "not ill adapted to such a figure" (p. 57). She is drawn even more strongly to the unknown person whom she hears talking with her servant. "The voice was not only mellifluent and clear, but the emphasis was so just, and the modulation so impassioned, that it seemed as if an heart of stone could not fail of being moved by it" (p. 59). When the two turn out to be one and the same person she is initially shocked and then still more attracted to him. In his face, she sees the same disjunction repeated, for while "[e]very feature was wide of beauty," his forehead, the lustre of his eyes, and "something in the rest of his features, which it would be in vain to describe," all convince her that he has a "mind of the highest order" (p. 61).

Carwin completely captures Clara's imagination, and as their relationship unfolds, the connection between them becomes ever more complicated. Following her first meeting with Carwin, Clara is so preoccupied with him that she stays home to sketch his picture, rather than spend the evening with her brother, and the next day she spends "alternately looking out upon the storm" that has arisen and "gazing at the picture . . . upon a table before [her]" (p. 62). And almost as if she had conjured it, that night in bed she is terrified by "a whisper, which, at first, appear[s] to proceed from lips that [are] laid close to [her] ear" (p. 64). She eventually identifies the voice as coming from the closet by her bed, and when she then hears what she takes to be two men plotting her murder, she flees her home. The whisperer is Carwin, of course, and he continues to manipulate her as the novel proceeds. The next incident occurs when she is in a small retreat by the river. She has just had a dream in which her brother has been identified as dangerous to her, and she awakens to a voice telling her to leave that place and not return. The climactic episode, though, is again in her bedroom.

The second time that Carwin hides in Clara's bedroom closet is at the end of a day that has been consumed by worry for Pleyel, whom Clara has finally revealed she loves. Her thoughts of Pleyel have shifted to thoughts of her father, and sitting in her room at night, she decides to read the memoirs he left. She rises to get them from the closet and suddenly realizes that she is "alone, and defenceless" (p. 96). She remembers the supposed murderers who had hidden there earlier: "The words of that mysterious dialogue, their fearful import, and the wild excess to which I was transported by my terrors, filled my imagination anew" (p. 96). Memory alone has taken her to the verge of a sublimely terrifying experience, and while she regains her composure momentarily, she almost immediately gives way to further fears, convinced that "some being was concealed within [the closet] whose purposes were evil" (p. 96). Almost at that moment, there is indeed a shriek from the closet. She is at first terrified: "My frame shook, and the vital current was congealed," she writes (p. 98). And then she starts to think. Logic tells her there is "a ruffian . . . hidden in the closet," but the memory of her dream leaves her convinced that her brother is the source of danger here, and in a surprisingly bold move, she opens the closet door. The person who comes out is neither a ruffian nor her brother, however, but Carwin.

The scene is remarkably dense. The slippage of her thoughts from Pleyel to her father to her brother to Carwin suggests an identification of all four men with each other, and eroticizes all of the connections. The fact that the intruder is Carwin and not her brother reinforces an established pattern in which Carwin repeatedly intrudes on the brother–sister bond (often read as nearly incestuous) and nearly breaks it. That said, critics have also noted that, while Carwin steps into a sexually charged role, his failure to attack Clara sexually at this moment marks him as the would-be gothic villain who does not play the role assigned him. Such a reading misses an important point, however, for Carwin's weapons are always words rather than anything physical, and so they are again in this situation. While he does not harm Clara physically, after he leaves her house he deliberately feigns a conversation between Clara and a seeming lover that is overheard by Pleyel, and that destroys – with Pleyel, at least – her reputation as an honorable woman. The scene recalls the moment in Samuel Richardson's *Pamela*, when Mr. B – cross-dressed as a maid – springs on Pamela as she is undressing. He does not rape her either, but instead tries to negotiate the terms on which they will conduct their relationship. Nancy Armstrong has read the scene in *Pamela* as evidence that what is really at stake in the struggle between Pamela and her master is control over the language that shapes the reality of their relationship (1987: 116), and the same thing is true in the relationship between Clara and Carwin. Where Pamela gets what she wants from Mr. B, however, Clara does not. She lets Carwin walk out of her room, not even realizing the harm he has done and will do.[8]

So who is Carwin, and how can he wreak so much havoc? Brown asks us to think of him as a "biloquist," and understanding the full weight of that label takes us far in coming to terms with him. The etymology of Brown's word "biloquist" tells us that Carwin is someone who can literally speak (Latin *loqui*) double (*bi*). Carwin is a "double-voiced" devil whose language threatens the very stability of the world that the novel portrays. Mark Seltzer (1978) has demonstrated how the breakdown of cause-and-effect sequences in the novel makes way for forms of "magical causality." Thus, as reason appears ever less adequate to explain the events of the novel, other causes of the action appear, and one of those is language. Seltzer draws attention to the novel's privileging of books as sources of authority: Wieland's father learned his religion from books; Wieland and Pleyel argue over the classics; Wieland's confession is in the form of a written document; the novel itself is a letter written by Clara. Spoken words have great authority as well, as we see in the power of Carwin's disembodied threats and warnings. Language shapes life in this novel, and Seltzer's point hits home when he turns to Tzvetan Todorov's discussion of the fantastic in literature. As Seltzer summarizes, Todorov's understands the fantastic as a "genre characterized by hesitation between explanations (natural and supernatural)" (1978: 87). The fantastic presents us with a view of reality as doubled or uncanny (a word Todorov himself uses, though he intends it to conjure only that sense of "hesitation" and not the psychoanalytic frame that goes with Freud's uncanny). "If the fantastic constantly makes use of rhetorical figures," Todorov writes, "it is because it originates in them. The supernatural is born of language, it is both consequence and its proof" (cited in Seltzer 1978: 87).

Carwin's accomplishment is to suspend everyone in the novel in the realm of the fantastic. The "uncertainty" created by his biloquism is at the centre of the novel. The idea that he might have manipulated Theodore Wieland undercuts the reading of Wieland as a man directed by clearly supernatural forces, even as the fact that he does manipulate Clara Wieland undercuts the idea that empirical knowledge of the world is reliable. He destroys the security of the Wieland family and – insofar as they figure the nation – of America as well. Nicholas Rombes has described Carwin as "curiously foreign" (1994: 44), and his phrase is well chosen.[9] Near the conclusion of the novel, Carwin tells Clara that he was born in America (p. 227), yet Pleyel remembers meeting him in Spain, where he had seemed to be English, though he appeared "wholly Spanish" and was "indistinguishable from a native, when he chose to assume that character" (p. 77). He is both American and European, and his lineage reaches back through England to Spain, as if to the heart of the gothic novel. He emblematizes the trouble that the new nation faces from without and from within. As Shirley Samuels has argued, he is an "outsider" who proves to be an "insider" as well. "By his intrusion into . . . normal domestic scenes," he manages to "expose the shaky underpinnings" of the family and – she might have added – the nation (1996: 56). His doubled or even tripled national identity sits alongside the seeming disjunction between his looks and his voice that I noted above, and alongside his biloquism, giving a distinctly political edge to both. Akin to the radically "unhomed" figure that Bhabha describes, he embodies the plasticity and uncertainty of national identity at the very moment of its seeming consolidation.

Representing Jamaica: Revisiting Matthew Lewis

Smith's America stands as an ironic double of England, demonstrating in extreme terms what happens when a government turns against its own people. She does not consider that America might be seen in other terms as well – as uneasy in its role of double, as truly wanting the independence that it finally achieved – and so manages to evade the much more difficult problems that emerge with such consideration. For that we need the American citizen Charles Brockden Brown, who knew first-hand both the complicated nature of America's ties to England and why they needed to be broken. In this section I will look at a single work that in itself offers competing representations of Jamaica. Matthew Lewis's *Journal of a West India Proprietor* (1815–16) records his first trip to Jamaica, where he had inherited two plantations and several hundred slaves. As he grapples with the contradictions between his desire to be perceived as a humane landlord and his participation in a slave economy whose disruption he fears, he makes clear the gothic nature of Britain's relationship with its colonies, and of life within those colonies. His Jamaican "home" is without doubt "unhomely."[10]

One might approach the gothicism of Lewis's *Journal* from a number of angles, but that which interests me most derives from its incorporation into a fact-based narrative a long poem that is essentially a fictional counterpart to the journal's account of everyday life. Entitled "The Isle of Devils," the poem interrupts the prose narrative near its conclusion, and while the two parts of the text were perceived as sufficiently distinct that the poem was eventually published independently of the prose narrative, they have a great deal to say to each other. The prose narrative documents Lewis's efforts to establish himself as a patriarch whose benevolence ensures that colonialism will thrive. In contrast, the poem's story of a European woman twice raped and twice impregnated by a "demon king" makes clear that colonialism is a violent enterprise whose survival hinges on women's ability to mother children who will perpetuate the system. Prose narrative and poem thus double but also oppose each other, working together to articulate a complicated story of how race and gender relations define what it means to be "at home" in this colony.[11]

Lewis's Prose Narrative: Patriarchy and
the Making of a Colonial Home

Jamaica provides Lewis with a home whose deep uncanniness emerges only when its gothic trappings are pushed aside to reveal its much more disturbingly gothic structure. H. R. Malchow's observation that Lewis "indulges with some relish in a gothic representation of stories of Obeah poisonings and brutal acts of revenge perpetrated by escaped slaves" (1996: 16) encourages one to see Lewis's "gothicization" of Jamaican culture as a deliberate way of coping with its obvious foreignness, while a closer reading of the text makes clear that Lewis finds Jamaican culture unsettling not just in its foreignness but – as Bhabha's work leads one to expect – in its uncanny familiarity. Those aspects of colonial culture that look like British culture are what prove most difficult for Lewis to handle, for he finds himself unable to determine the sincerity with which they have been produced, and suddenly aware that cultural identity may be no more than the result of good acting.[12] Unsettled but not undone by the recognition that clever performances may lie at the heart of colonial culture, Lewis fights back by himself playing a part whose genuineness is surely just as difficult to judge: that of the benevolent patriarch.

Lewis's initial hours in Jamaica emblematize the complex way in which political identity is enacted in colonial culture. He arrives on January 1, walking into a festival whose main participants are the slaves on the island, and whose cultural range spans from the West African-derived John Canoe to the portrayal of British culture in a procession of the Blues and the Reds. The John Canoe (a dance or procession led by a masquerader) is – as Lewis notes – an "indispensable" part of the celebrations (p. 36).[13] But – as Orlando Patterson rightly notes in response – the contest between the Blues and the Reds is the real center of attention (1969: 239). Lewis contextualizes it thus:

> It seems that, many years ago, an Admiral of the Red was superseded on the Jamaica station by an Admiral of the Blue; and both of them gave balls at Kingston to the *"Brown Girls"*; for the fair sex elsewhere are called the "Brown Girls" in Jamaica. In consequence of these balls, all Kingston was divided into parties: from thence the division spread into other districts: and ever since, the whole island, at Christmas, is separated into the rival factions of the Blues and the Reds (the Red representing also the English, the Blue the Scotch), who contend for setting forth their processions with the greatest taste and magnificence. (p. 37)

In this procession that re-creates the rivalry between successive generations of the British military in Jamaica, black people offer competing representations of the whites who enslaved them. Patterson notes that each set of slaves thus manages to "safely displace tensions against the white group in the direction of the rival set of slaves" (1969: 248), and states further that festivities like these also allowed for the expression of aggression against whites in such socially accepted forms as mimicry, caricature, and satire. That there might be a critical edge to the performance is a possibility that Lewis does not explicitly register, though he clearly sees and even enjoys its playfulness. The Blues go so far as to commemorate the British victory at Waterloo in a presentation led by

> a strange uncouth kind of a glittering tawdry figure, all feathers, and pitchfork, and painted pasteboard, who moved most reluctantly, and turned out to be no less a personage than Britannia herself, with a pasteboard shield covered with the arms of Great Britain, a trident in her hand, and a helmet made of pale blue silk and silver. (pp. 37–8)

While this unwilling Britannia – a slave owned by "the mistress of the hotel from whose window [Lewis] saw the show" (p. 37) – gives Lewis pause, he chooses not to interpret her hesitation to embrace British culture as anything other than a reflection of her own shyness. Reading the account now, however, it seems impossible to miss the fact that her resistance emblematizes the resistance of all those around her to the culture that held them captive, impossible to miss the fact that her tawdry costume comments on the tawdriness of the nation it represents, impossible to miss the fact that Britannia is figured but also disfigured by the procession as a whole.[14]

Elsewhere in the *Journal*, Lewis is more obviously alive to the double-edged relationship of colonizer and colonized. He comments constantly on the possibility that things said to him may be false, then deliberately sets aside this possibility. When former slaves promise to bid him goodbye before he leaves the island, he writes: "All this may be palaver; but certainly they at least play their parts with such an air of truth, and warmth, and enthusiasm, that, after the cold hearts and repulsive manners of England, the contrast is infinitely agreeable" (p. 59). So agreeable, in fact, that Lewis goes on to say: "I find it quite impossible to resist the fascination of the conscious pleasure of pleasing; and my own heart, which I have so long been obliged to keep closed, seems to expand itself again in the sunshine of the kind looks and words which meet me at every turn, and seem to wait for mine as anxiously as if they were so many diamonds" (p. 59). In the face of what may be pure acting, Lewis acts in return. His heart "seems" to expand, and for a moment is at home in the place that has seemed "unhomely."

Lewis controls his sense of Jamaica's strangeness by consciously choosing to interpret ambiguous behaviors in ways that suit his purposes, and by trying to manipulate public perception of his own behavior in return. The very doubleness that can be so threatening to him is thus also desirable, and there are occasions when Lewis in fact makes an ambiguity that he does not find. Witness, for example, his response to a celebration honoring his arrival. "Nothing could be more odd or more novel than the whole scene," he writes,

> and yet there was something in it by which I could not help being affected; perhaps it was the consciousness that all these human beings were my *slaves*; – to be sure, I never saw people look more happy in my life; and I believe their condition to be much more comfortable than that of the labourers of Great Britain; and, after all, slavery, in *their* case, is but another name for servitude, now that no more negroes can be forcibly carried away from Africa, and subjected to the horrors of the voyage, and of the seasoning after their arrival . . . (p. 42)

Lewis apparently eases his own conscience by deciding that Jamaican slavery is better described as servitude, though in fact more than just conscience is at stake here. Following the above passage comes a description of a young man who introduces himself to Lewis with the words, "Massa not know me; *me your slave!*" (p. 42). Lewis balks at this description, for "[t]he word 'slave' seemed to imply, that, although he did feel pleasure then in serving me, if he had detested me he must have served me still. I really felt quite humiliated at that moment, and was tempted to tell him, – 'Do not say that again; say that you are my negro, but do not call yourself my slave'" (p. 42). Lewis's humiliation makes clear that he feels not just conscience-stricken, but subordinated by the situation, and he asks his slave to make him feel less vulnerable. This flicker of insight into what Patterson has called the parasitic nature of the master–slave relationship – this revelation that "the dominator, in the process of dominating and making another individual dependent, also makes himself (the dominator) dependent" (1982: 336) – makes clear how contingent Lewis's power really was, and makes clear too that the relationship could last only as long as both parties played their roles.

In trying to rescript the master–slave relationship, Lewis was undoubtedly trying not only to ease his own conscience, but to help himself in more material ways as well. He arrived in Jamaica at a crucial moment in Britain's colonial history – 1815 – only eight years after England had abolished its international trade in slaves. While abolition had not eliminated the institution of slavery outright, James Walvin notes that "[i]n general it was hoped that it would lead to amelioration in slave conditions. The argument ran that planters, unable to buy new slaves, would be obliged to treat their existing slaves better and hence make good the demographic shortfall" (1982: 10). This did not happen – a fact that was instrumental in the British government finally legislating for an end to slavery in 1834[15] – yet it is nonetheless easy to see that Lewis might have had more than a simply moral interest in improving his relationship with the slaves that he owned.[16]

The complicated relationship between Lewis's interest and that of his slaves emerges particularly in the way he manages his plantation, for he develops ways of controlling them that are less physically violent than those of his peers, though no less coercive. Resolutely opposing such practices as whipping slaves for disobedience, he routinely defends slaves he does not own if they come to him for help, and takes pride in the fact that his "over-indulgence to [his] negroes" (p. 135) is said to be the cause of an order to the Jamaican grand jury to be "particularly vigilant and attentive" in their enforcing of the laws pertaining to slaves (p. 135). Yet Ronald Kent Richardson says rightly that Lewis knows how to exert authority over his slaves by "substitut[ing] a psychological motivation for a physical one, an internal imperative for an external one" (1987: 62). James Carson further shows how Lewis develops mechanisms that encourage his slaves to internalize the idea of servitude and so subject themselves to him in ways that at least seem voluntary. Carson comments, for example, on Lewis's decision to establish a series of holidays meant to honor the duchess of York, himself, and "picaninny-mothers" (p. 118), thereby making sure that his slaves will be loyal to Britain, to him, and to the women whose children ostensibly guarantee the survival of the plantation (Carson 1986: 118–25) – a point to which I will return.

Lewis plays the part of benevolent patriarch in a way that blurs the boundary between acting and genuine affection, and hopes that his slaves will follow his cue in moving beyond pretended loyalty to forge an affective connection with him. And on leaving, Lewis is almost – but not entirely – convinced that he has succeeded: "and when I came down the steps to depart, they crowded around me, kissing my feet, and clasping my knees . . . And this was done with such marks of truth and feeling, that I cannot believe the whole to be mere acting and mummery" (p. 147). He may or may not be reading his slaves accurately, even as they may or may not be reading him accurately,[17] and, as if in response to the possibility that his whole stay has been a polite fiction, on the way back to England Lewis writes down a poem he composed on the way out, called "The Isle of Devils." The title alone suggests the poem's opposition to the officially benevolent view of Jamaica that Lewis adopts in the Journal proper, but I will summarize its story to provide some context for the next part of my argument.

"The Isle of Devils": Motherhood and the Undoing of the Colonial Home

The poem's plot recalls that of Shakespeare's play The Tempest and its various sources.[18] It tells the story of a young woman named Irza, who is separated from her beloved Rosalvo in a shipwreck, washed up on an island, and – having been threatened by "monstrous dwarfs" – is taken to safety by a creature "Gigantic as the palm, black as the storm, / All shagged with hair, wild, strange in shape and show" (p. 169). This black giant saves Irza only to imprison her in a grotto, kill her lover when he appears on the scene, and impregnate her twice. Aware of neither pregnancy until she gives birth, Irza produces one child who is monstrous and likened to his father, another who is beautiful and likened to his mother. Indeed, Irza's role as mother becomes increasingly important as the poem proceeds, and her eventual rescue from the island is complicated both because it separates her from these children and because it causes the black giant, or "demon king," to dash the beautiful, golden-haired child on the rocks as a prelude to drowning himself and the monster child. Irza lives out her life as a "poor lay-sister" (p. 182), a source of comfort to others, but herself comfortless as a result of her experiences on the island.

The poem is clearly the double of the prose narrative that makes up the rest of the *Journal*, rendering explicit the gothic motifs of the latter.[19] The poem's portrait of the demon king's home as a space that is at once a safe haven (the dwarves cannot reach her) and an uneasily controlled place of confinement (Irza cannot leave, and the demon king has constant access to her)[20] comments ironically on Lewis's efforts to make a home of his seemingly safe yet really unstable plantation. Home as the poem portrays it is always gothic, always threatening in its uneasily dual character, always just beyond the master's control. The poem goes so far as to suggest that women rather then men ultimately control not just home but the social order in which it participates, identifying mothers as those who have the capacity to stabilize but also to disrupt that social order. And this last fact – that improper mothering can produce monsters who by their very existence threaten to destroy the home altogether – is finally what frightens Lewis most.

The poem makes its comment on the *Journal* largely through the figures of the demon king and Irza, both of whom have affinities with colonizer as well as colonized. The demon king can be aligned with European colonizers through his role as master, and, pushed just a little, that reading suggests that even Europeans harbor within them a savage or "black" quality – an *Unheimlichkeit* – that is truly frightening. Of course, the demon king can also be more directly associated with black slaves through his dark, monstrous appearance, especially with the victors in the slave revolts that had occurred in the Caribbean since the 1790s, and that Lewis himself feared.[21]

Similarly, Irza is clearly aligned with Europeans by virtue of her stated race and nationality, but might also be linked with black slaves by virtue of her subordination to the demon king. Playing out the first of these readings, and thinking of Irza as a European woman who is apparently raped by a black man, one might be tempted to see her story as a precursor to those discussed by Jenny Sharpe. In her work on nineteenth-century India, Sharpe notes that "the

European fear of interracial rape" comes into being at those moments when "colonial structures of power" are threatened (1993: 3). However, whereas in the scenarios she discusses, rape fears and rape fantasies promote the colonial order by allowing the Europeans to oppress the supposed rapists in turn, here something rather different happens.[22] The Europeans who "rescue" Irza from the demon king do not seek to perpetuate the colonial project, but to undo it. Faced with a being they cannot subdue, they flee altogether rather than risking defeat, and make clear that, ideally, "island culture" and European culture would be completely separate from each other. And this, of course, does not – perhaps cannot – happen. Irza returns to Portugal, but even there she is not only stained by "her fancied crime" (p. 182) but to some degree identified with the race of people with whom that "crime" put her in contact. Indeed, she refers to herself as "a demon's wife" throughout the end of the poem (p. 182).

Playing out the second of these readings, and thinking of Irza as a woman who is enslaved, one might want to argue that her experiences link her with black women in the colonies, and perhaps demonstrate the oppression of women across cultures.[23] Such a reading is helpful to a point, and yet it is clear that European women generally are oppressed in different ways from the women who are Lewis's slaves. Indeed, one might even argue that European women are at least indirectly implicated in the oppression of Lewis's slaves, as he tries to impose the values associated with the former onto the latter. Lewis's *Journal* makes clear the way in which he does so, documenting both the psychological and the underlying economic imperatives for controlling first European women and – through them, or his idea of them – Caribbean women as well.

What initially seems to drive Lewis's treatment of women is his desire to identify them with home. Soon after arriving in Jamaica, he writes a poem called "Landing" that opens with the question,

> When first I gain'd the Atlantic shore,
> And bade farewell to ocean's roar,
> What gracious power my bosom eased,
> My senses soothed, my fancy pleased,
> And bade me feel, in whispers bland,
> No Stranger in a Stranger-land? (p. 47)

The answer comes quickly. "Approaching sounds of female tongue" made the narrator feel at home – not the sounds of "Venus," but the voice of someone likened to a "friend," a "mother," a "sister," and finally simply "woman" (p. 48).

In defining "woman" in the way he does – as nurturing, caring, comforting but definitely not erotic – Lewis calls on European notions of gender. Felicity Nussbaum (1995) has argued that British women in the eighteenth century were imagined as domesticated creatures who were happiest as mothers, while the women of the empire were imagined as sexual beings who came from and in themselves represented "torrid zones." Lewis's poem effectively seeks to transform the island on which the narrator lands into a British woman, then, and if one moves from the poem to the *Journal*, one sees that Lewis's treatment of his female slaves essentially seeks to make them into British women as well. His success in this project serves not only to make Jamaica feel like home, however, but to ensure the financial success of the plantation and the very existence of home, at least in a material sense.

Lewis tries to guarantee the economic viability of his plantation by urging his female slaves to become mothers.[24] His action is predictable given that, after the abolition of the slave trade in 1807, he "needed to take steps to reduce the death-rate and increase the birth-rate if the slave labor supply was to remain sufficient and plantations were to remain profitable" (Carson 1986: 121). As early as 1774, Edward Long's *History of Jamaica* had argued for the importance of encouraging women to have children, suggesting at one point that "[a] premium might be assigned for every new-born child" (1774: 2. 439), and Lewis seems to follow Long's advice in devising a series of material incentives for mothers. He offers them "a dollar each . . . for every infant which should be brought to the overseer alive and well on the fourteenth day [of its life]" (p. 125), as well as "a scarlet girdle with a silver medal in the centre," which they are to wear on various occasions as a means of gaining special favors (p. 79). Further, "[o]n every additional child an additional medal is to be affixed to the belt, and precedence is to follow the greater number of medals" (p. 80). Finally, as mentioned earlier, he institutes the holiday in honor of the "picaninny-mothers," while he himself volunteers to be godfather to every child born on the plantation (p. 54).

No matter how hard he tries to encourage women to have children, however, he cannot guarantee that they will live long enough to serve him, and this is a continual source of anxiety.[25] His stipulation that women should receive the dollar he had promised them only after their children reach two weeks of age is an effort to force the women to care for their children in ways he approves, for he believes the "best-intentioned mothers" to be "heedless and inattentive" (p. 63),[26] and it is with regret that he notes – on his return visit to Jamaica in 1817–18 – that "among upwards of three hundred and thirty negroes [on the Cornwall estate,] and with a greater number of females than men, in spite of all indulgences and inducements, not more than twelve or thirteen children have been added annually to the list of the births" (p. 202). Lewis here suggests that it is the female slaves' ability to "mother" children in all senses of the word that determines whether the colonial slave system will stand or fall, developing a line of thought consistent with existing discussions of the ways in which "[p]lantation culture depended on the female capacity to reproduce" (Sussman 1993: 214).

What he does not say, and may not consciously have known, is that even successful reproduction can be threatening, undermining the clear cultural oppositions that marked the early stages of the colonial encounter and making it difficult if not impossible for the colonial power structure to endure.[27]

The story of how the demon king and Irza deal with their children initially seems to place blame for the tragedy squarely on the parents. Irza's first child is described as a "monster" whose "shaggy limbs, and eyes of sable fire, / Betray'd the crime, and claim'd its hellish sire!" (p. 172). Her feelings for this child conflict with each other so much that, "Loathing its sight, she melts to hear its cries, / And, while she yields the breast, averts her eyes" (p. 173). She mothers this child biologically, but cannot bring herself to look at it, or to form any kind of social connection with it. When she shudders during the act of feeding, the demon king grabs the child from her, and clutches it to his own breast, in a striking act of maternal surrogacy. Irza's second child seems to redeem the whole situation, however, for this infant is "[i]n small the model of her beauteous self" (p. 177) and holds both her complete attention and Lewis's. Where only four lines describe the appearance of the monster child, at least sixteen (maybe more, depending on how one counts) are devoted to describing this baby's smooth pink skin, his blue eyes, his golden locks, his ivory brow and his coral lips. One's attention is meant to be drawn by this mother–child bond, which is so powerful that even the demon king no longer feels a need to lock Irza in a cave every day, feeling sure that "her child to home would chain her feet" (p. 178).

In assuming that an internalized sense of the duties of motherhood will keep Irza on the island, the demon king behaves much like Lewis when he works to establish such a sense in the women on his plantation. And just as Lewis could not in the end force the women on the plantation to deal with their children in all the ways that he wished, so is the demon king frustrated in his belief that he has learned how to control Irza. When the abbot who was with her when she was shipwrecked finally shows up to rescue her, she is reluctant to leave the island, fearing that "her flight might quite destroy her child" (p. 180). Leave she does, however (the abbot really gives her little choice), and while she mourns the loss of her child, she also weeps for joy at her release, much to the anger of the demon king, who appears on the beach carrying the "beauteous babe" and pleading for her return (p. 180). When she does not come back, we are told that he "[w]hirl'd the boy wildly round and round his head / Dash'd it against the rocks, and howling fled" (p. 181). Notably, one seems to see this event and what follows through the eyes of the demon king, who apparently kills the child in order to wound the mother, even as he then kills himself and his first child because Irza has wounded them. His suicide is prefaced by a wild scene on a cliff that is meant to highlight this fact, as he gesticulates in at way that

> . . . seem'd to say, with action wild,
> "Look, mother, look! this babe is still your child!
> With him as me all social bonds you break,
> Scorn'd and detested for his father's sake:
> My love, my service only wrought disdain,
> And nature fed his heart from yours in vain!
> Then go, Ingrate, far o'er the ocean go,
> Consign your friend, your child to endless woe!
> Renounce us! hate us! pleased, your course pursue,
> And break their hearts who lived alone for you!" (p. 181)

These lines are problematic, for while they explicitly describe the tragedy of the end of the poem in terms of Irza's desire – or lack of desire – to mother her children socially, it is the demon king himself who actually destroys his children. Where to place the blame for what happens is not the only or even the central issue here, however. Rather, one is being encouraged to read in purely personal terms a drama that really has much larger political implications.

Miscegenation and/as the *Unheimlich*

If one looks again at the family made up of the demon king, Irza, and their two children, thinking about not the parents, but the children, the issues shift. At the heart of the situation are two children who are the products of a mixed-race relationship, but show no signs of miscegenation. Why not? Eighteenth-century colonizers were obsessed with defining the racial status of children whose parents were of different races.[28] Indeed, Lewis includes in his *Journal* a variant of Edward Long's five-generational path to "whiteness" (Long 1774: 2. 260), which specifies that

> The offspring of a white man and a black woman is a *mulatto*; the mulatto and black produce a *sambo*; from the mulatto and white comes the *quadroon*; from the quadroon and white the *mustee*; the child of a mustee by a white man is called a *musteefino*; while the children of a musteefino are free by law, and rank as white persons to all intents and purposes. (p. 68)

In light of this kind of obsessive categorizing, the question of how to talk about the race of Irza's children becomes ever more interesting and urgent.

If Lewis's interest in Irza's children is tied to his interest in the children of his slaves, one can come to an understanding of the former through the latter. Many children on plantations were born of mixed-race relationships, and there has been considerable discussion about whether – as B.W. Higman suggests – "the chances of manumission increased as the slaves approached whiteness" (1976: 143).[29] By this line of reasoning, a child who was whiter than its mother might not have been considered suitable to be a slave, and so the social order on the plantation would have been destabilized. Lewis at least seems aware of this as a possible problem when he talks about the case of Nicholas, "the son of a white man, who on his death-bed charged his nephew and heir to purchase the freedom of this natural child. The nephew had promised to do so," but six months later "broke his neck, and the property went to a distant relation" (p. 51). Lewis continues the story by saying that

> Application in behalf of poor Nicholas has been made to the heir, and I heartily hope that he will enable me to release him. I felt strongly tempted to set him at liberty at once; but if I were to begin in that way, there would be no stopping; and it would be doing a kindness to an individual at the expense of all my other negroes – others would expect the same; and then I must either contrive to cultivate my estate with fewer hands – or must cease to cultivate it altogether – and, from inability to maintain them, send my negroes to seek bread for themselves – which, as two thirds of them have been born upon the estate, and many of them are lame, dropsical, and of a great age, would, of all misfortunes that could happen to them, be the most cruel. (p. 51)

Lewis's reasoning gets somewhat sophistical here, but at the heart of his ruminations is his concern that to free Nicholas would set a precedent that would damage the economy of his plantation, and the only reason Nicholas had a chance at freedom in the first place was because he had a white father.[30] It is his mixed racial heritage that sets events in motion, then, and that – as others have also noted – points to miscegenation as the root cause of the problem here.[31]

If miscegenation threatens to destabilize the existing social order and perhaps even to undermine it altogether, one might speculate that Irza's seemingly monstrous child and her seemingly beautiful child are the product of wishful European thinking about how cultural interactions might work. If the meeting of European and Caribbean cultures could simply produce people who clearly belonged to one culture or another, as opposed to a visibly mixed race of people like Nicholas, then the world could go on as it always has.[32] This cannot happen, however, and even in Lewis's poem the notion that it has happened is only an illusion. Both of Irza's children are actually products of miscegenation, and while each appears to represent only one culture, each in fact has ties to two. They thus upset the social order much more covertly than do people like Nicholas, and so are perhaps more dangerous still.

Irza's children finally emerge as metonymic representations of the *unheimlich* or unhomely culture of the colonized Caribbean. They are dangerous not just because of their doubled cultural ties, but because that doubleness is hidden – because they are not what they seem – and they indicate a long-standing interest in British culture about how to identify people of mixed race. Citing *The London Chronicle* for September 9, 1766, Folarin Shyllon draws attention to two marriages between black men and white women, one of which produced a child "intirely Black, and in every particular of colour and features resembling the father," and one of which produced a daughter who was "as fair a child to look at as any born of white parents, and her features exactly like the mother's." So far, this scenario is much like that of Lewis's poem, but now things change. One learns no more of the first child, but the picture of the second is complicated by the statement that the father got proof of his parentage when a nurse "undressed the infant, and showed that the baby's 'right buttock and thigh' were as black as the father" (Shyllon 1977: 103–4). The report directs one to paternity as the key issue in the identification of that second child, but paternity is above all a way of determining the child's race. This child will never be able to pass as fully European, and that – surely – is the point.[33]

Certainly the possibility of passing is clearly what concerns Lewis as well. Irza's "monstrous" child has unperceived ties to European culture, even as her beautiful child harbors a "monstrosity" that Europeans have learned to fear. While the former may be undesirable, the latter is a real threat to the "purity" of European culture, and so Lewis – through the abbot – chides Irza for her unwillingness to leave her beautiful child behind:

> The fiends most dangerous are those spirits bright,
> Who toil for hell, and show like sons of light;
> And still when Satan spreads his subtlest snares,
> The baits are azure eyes, the lines are golden hairs. (p. 180)

When Lewis kills off the children who embody the *unheimlich*, kills off as well the creature who fathered them, and confines to a convent the woman who mothered them, he rids the world of one sort of gothic horror. Children of mixed race will no longer threaten European culture, will no longer be produced by European women who will never be acceptable mothers simply because they are connected with "monstrous" men. He eliminates this horror with a violence that is itself horrifying, however, and so it goes.

Lewis's Jamaica is gothic from the start, a home that is not home, a place that is at once desired and feared, a culture that is defined by contradictions that finally threaten not only its stability but its very existence.

8

Feminist, Postmodern, Postcolonial
Margaret Atwood and Ann-Marie Macdonald Respond to the Gothic

Gothic has not only remained a popular form, but is probably more popular now than it ever has been. It is constantly being reinvented in ways that address the realities of our current historical moment, and this ongoing reinvention tells us many things, not least of which is that forms of oppression – the essential element for any gothic tale – persist as well. Even as gothic novels change they stay the same, then, always turning on dichotomies that must be at least momentarily disrupted for the story to move to its resolution. The theoretical frameworks provided by the aesthetic of the sublime, the uncanny, and the unhomely indicate how gothic writers blur the seemingly rigid divisions that structure the worlds they portray, and while one is grateful for these moments of confusion – in which villains and victims are no longer so clearly defined – one also wishes for more lasting solutions to the problems these novels show us.

There are late twentieth- and early twenty-first-century writers who have developed other and better ways through the impasse of the gothic, realizing that the best way past this black and white structure is through complication, through the embrace of the plural and often fractured visions that we associate with postmodern fiction and a multicultural world. In this final portion of my argument, I look at late twentieth- and early twenty-first-century writers who work within but also against the tradition of British gothic discussed here. Of the many writers who might fit this bill, those that interest me most are working not in Britain but in Britain's former colonies, writing back – as it were – to the mother country. As I suggested in the last chapter, colonial relationships would seem to be by definition gothic, colonizer and colonized standing as doubles of each other in a relationship that is not so much hierarchical as haunting. Britain is shadowed by its colonies and vice versa. What can one do to change this relationship and allow each place its independence?

Answers to this question vary with the writer's time and place. If one takes Canadian literature as a case study, Margaret Atwood stands out as writer who has arguably been rewriting gothic tradition from the beginning of her career.[1] Her acute consciousness of the structures that trap women – their bodies, their homes, social convention, the stories that model their lives – informs virtually every novel she has written. She announced a specific engagement with the genre when she published *Lady Oracle* (1976), a novel that moves from Canada back to Britain and even back to Italy, the site of so much classic gothic fiction,[2] and over the course of her career has returned to the issues she raised in that early novel, most recently in her Booker Prize-winning novel *The Blind Assassin* (2000).[3] Both novels develop an aesthetic that finds a way past gothic experience through the maintenance – rather than blurring – of differences. From a sustained discussion of Atwood's career as a gothic writer, I then turn my attention to the work of Ann-Marie Macdonald, who was known primarily as a playwright and actress when her first novel was published in the late 1990s. *Fall on Your Knees* conjures a multicultural present moment that puts Canadian culture in play with Lebanese, African Canadian, and American cultures, eventually shattering the dualisms of gothic with its multifaceted vision.

Gothic, Satire, Science Fiction: Margaret Atwood Anatomizes the Gothic

As Coral Ann Howells notes, Atwood herself has said that *Lady Oracle* is "a realistic comic novel colliding with gothic conventions," her version of Jane Austen's *Northanger Abbey* (1996: 65).[4] Austen's Catherine Morland is so influenced by her reading of the novels of Ann Radcliffe that she expects gothic terror around every corner, and, while she is roundly chastised by the ever sensible Henry Tilney for thinking such horrific things of people (including Henry's father, whom Catherine believes must have either locked up or murdered his wife), she is not altogether wrong to see that enlightened British society exercises enormous and not always benevolent power over women. Similarly, Atwood's Joan Foster faces over and over again the task of differentiating – but also seeing the connection – between the life she lives and the gothic novels she not only reads but also writes. That Joan writes costume gothics for a living makes her at least potentially a very different heroine from Catherine, however, for Joan has control over the gothic script in a way Catherine does not. She can change the all too familiar story.

How Atwood manipulates gothic convention is one of the most engaging aspects of the novel. She starts with Joan Foster's life, which is something of a gothic story in itself. If Austen's somewhat plain, wilful, tomboyish Catherine Morland "did not seem 'born to be an heroine'" (Austen 1995: 13), the over-weight and ungainly Joan Foster would seem to be even less so. On second thought, however, one realizes that Joan is actually quite a bit "like a heroine," though perhaps a heroine turned inside out. Traditional gothic heroines are imperiled by all sorts of dangerous forces, as we've seen – absent or over-whelming mothers, predatory fathers, societies that will not let them act for themselves. Most of all, though, they are trapped by societies that will not rec-ognize the heroine's plight as caused by factors external to her, but instead blame that plight on the simple fact that she is female. Mary Wollstonecraft saw this clearly, showing in the story of Maria and her daughter the ways in which women can seem to be betrayed by their own bodies. Atwood sees it too, creating in Joan Foster a heroine who for the first two decades of her life is literally trapped by her body.[5] Initially this entrapment would seem to be the result of her obesity, and yet when Joan loses weight, she is still trapped. There would seem to be no way to win. To inhabit a woman's body is to be a gothic heroine. End of story. Unless – and here we circle back to a point already made – we change the story.

What are the narrative options? What choices can Joan make? What would it mean to escape one's body, and is such a thing possible, or even desirable? These are questions that gothic novels are well equipped to answer, replete as they are with supernatural beings whose disembodied state is arguably a large part of their power, and what they tell us is that if one can imagine life beyond the body, the reality comes at too high a price. One can temporarily move beyond one's body through some sort of transcendent experience, perhaps (recall Radcliffe's heroines), but the only real way out is death (recall Dacre's). Joan sees this, staging for herself a series of symbolic deaths throughout the novel, as she sheds one persona, adopts another, and finally fakes her own death. Joan's efforts to escape the limitations of her own life fascinate in part simply because they involve such constant reinvention of herself, but more because they demonstrate once again that gothic heroines elude the men who would confine them only after they have worked out their relationships with the women who do the same. Caught between her mother and her Aunt Lou, Joan tries to reject the former and embrace the latter, only to find out that she needs them both.[6]

Joan's mother models a costly kind of female propriety: she is married to an anesthetist, overly concerned with physical appearances, unhappy, and, finally, alcoholic. Her relationship with her daughter turns almost entirely around the issue of the latter's physical size. Overweight from childhood, by the age of 13, Joan

> was eating steadily, doggedly, stubbornly, anything I could get. The war between myself and my mother was on in earnest; the disputed territory was my body. I didn't quite know this though I sensed it in a hazy way; but I reacted to the diet booklets she left on my pillow, to the bribes of dresses she would give me if I would reduce to fit them . . . to her cutting remarks about my size, to her pleas about my health . . . to the specialists she sent me to and the pills they prescribed, to all of these things, with another Mars Bar or a double helping of french fries. I swelled visibly, relentlessly, before her very eyes, I rose like dough, my body advanced inch by inch towards her across the dining-room table, in this at least I was undefeated. I was five feet four and still growing, and I weighed a hundred and eighty-two pounds. (p. 73)[7]

Joan's body is both weapon and prize, and in the way she wields the former against her mother, Joan might be judged a winner of sorts. The victory is not satisfying, however, and Joan seeks other ways to find her freedom.

The alternative to Joan's mother is her Aunt Lou. Abandoned by the hand-some gambler she married as a young woman, Louisa K. Delacourt has a career in the marketing department of a feminine hygiene company, lives alone, has a boyfriend, and is happy. Aunt Lou's escape from life as a wife to life as a working woman marks her as yet another woman who understands that women's way out of a gothic existence is through economic self-sufficiency. The fact that Aunt Lou's money comes from marketing pamphlets about an aspect of female sexu-ality underlines the connection between economic and sexual freedom. Given Aunt Lou's departure from most of the traditional narratives for women's lives, how should one explain the fact that she is also a born romantic who takes Joan to movies, judging their quality by how much they "made you cry" (p. 86), or that she takes Joan to a church run by "Spiritualists" (p. 115), where the Reverend Leda Sprott passes on messages from the dead (and one from Joan's not yet dead mother)? Aunt Lou spends her free time seeking out exactly the kinds of sensa-tional experiences that she has been fortunate enough to escape in her day-to-day life. She does not so much turn her back on gothic (the excess of sentiment, the belief in the supernatural) as put it in its place.

In allying herself with her aunt rather than her mother, Joan embraces a model of femininity that allows her to shape her own life, rather than be shaped according to others' expectations and desires. What, then, is she to think when her aunt dies and leaves her a $2,000 inheritance conditional on her losing one hundred pounds? Is her aunt just another version of her mother? Yes and no. Like Joan's mother, she believes that one's body size will affect how one is able to make one's way through life. Unlike Joan's mother, however, she presents the issue as one of personal freedom rather than the reverse. As Aunt Lou tells the story, control over one's body brings with it economic freedom and physical autonomy.

Joan's decision to do as her aunt has asked comes during her recovery from an all too significant accident. Recovering from a wound inflicted at a sportsmen's show, where she has been shot in the leg by an arrow – made into unwitting prey – Joan once again thinks about the troubling landscape of her body:

> One day, while I was sitting up in bed . . . I happened to glance down at my body. . . . There, staring me in the face, was my thigh. It was enormous, it was gross, it was like a diseased limb, the kind you see in pictures of jungle natives; it spread on forever, like a prairie photographed from a plane, the flesh not green but bluish-white, with veins meandering across it like rivers. It was the size of three ordinary thighs . . . I thought, This can't possibly go on. (p. 133)

Joan sees herself first as "native," then as expansive open land – both of them objects of conquest in any number of histories – and then rejects that map of identity. She moves out of her mother's house soon after, and becomes "a different person" (p. 157).

Joan's escape from the confines of both her parents' home and her own body is only partially successful, however. She takes many of her troubles with her, as she continues to be haunted, both figuratively, by visions of her earlier self, and literally, by visions of the fat lady at the circus, as well as by her mother, whose death precipitates her ghostly reappearance in Joan's life. Long fascinated by the fat lady (whom she has never seen), Joan fantasizes about her in awkward situations, and near the end of the novel – having faked her own death, and buried the clothes she was wearing at the time – she imagines "the clothes [she'd] buried there growing themselves a body. It was almost completed; it was digging itself out . . . a creature composed of all the flesh that used to be [hers] and which must have gone somewhere" (p. 353). She imagines this creature as featureless, "smooth as a potato, pale as starch . . . a big thigh . . . a face like a breast minus the nipple," and then sees:

> It was the Fat Lady. She rose into the air and descended on me as I lay stretched out in the chair. For a moment she hovered around me like ectoplasm, like a gelatin shell, my ghost, my angel; then she settled and I was absorbed into her. Within my former body, I gasped for air. Disguised, concealed, white fur choking my nose and mouth. Obliterated. (p. 353)

Joan's vision of being smothered by her own living flesh – her own body – reads the female body as an annihilating rather than predictably nurturing force. This is the Fat Lady's final appearance in the novel, and not long after comes the counterpart to this scene: the final appearance of the ghost of Joan's mother.

Joan's mother begins her ghostly appearances even before she dies, though the Reverend Leda Sprott is the only one to see her. Not her material but her astral body arrives with a message to Joan, who protests: "I . . . didn't like the thought of my mother, in the form of some kind of spiritual jello, drifting around after me from place to place, wearing (apparently) her navy-blue suit from 1949" (p. 121). She next appears just after her death, wearing the same suit, crying, her make-up running, and Joan sees her this time, in the living-room of her London apartment. Why her mother has visited her Joan doesn't know. "What did she want from me? Why couldn't she leave me alone?" (p. 194) The last visit comes at the end of the novel, when Joan – in Italy after her own mock-death – awakens in the night to exactly the same vision of her mother. This time Joan asks her mother what she wants, getting in response a smile that draws the two of them together. All that stops Joan from merging with her is a locked door, and, having escaped that fate, Joan realizes what the problem has been: "She'd never really let go of me because I had never let her go" (p. 363).

The moment when Joan is able to cut her tie with her mother is the moment when she sees clearly both her mother and herself, and this insight comes with – or through – insight into her work as a writer. Joan writes books under two names, neither entirely her own. Using the name of her aunt, Louisa K. Delacourt, she writes costume gothic novels, and using her married name she writes an experimental poem called "Lady Oracle." That these two strands of Joan's work are not all that different she herself understands, noting that "Lady Oracle" was "a lot like one of my standard Costume Gothics, but a Gothic gone wrong. It was upside-down somehow. There were the sufferings, the hero in the mask of a villain, the villain in the mask of a hero, the flights, the looming death, the sense of being imprisoned, but there was no happy ending, no true love" (p. 259).

Joan's costume gothics announce their literary genealogy in their titles. *The Lord of Chesney Chase* is her first; she is writing *Escape from Love* when she meets her future husband Arthur, and *Stalked by Love* when she feigns her own death and flees to Italy. Their focus on strong, virile men, their concern with themes of pursuit and entrapment, are easily recognized. They are the most formulaic fiction imaginable, a reinforcement rather than a rewriting of the narrative tradition in which she is working, and yet at the same time they intersect with and finally provide Joan a way out of the confines of her own life. These novels intersect with her life in obvious ways, echoing as they do her long-standing feelings of entrapment by her life, and in more subtle ways as well, as – for example – she works through writer's block by acing out problematic scenes in real life, to see what should come next. She meets Arthur in the midst of one such re-enactment, when she is imagining herself as *Escape from Love*'s Samantha Deane, running from the unwanted advances of Sir Edmund DeVere, and screams aloud as Sir Edmund / Arthur lays his hand on her arm. Life and art come together, and it is in working through the narrative problems of *Stalked by Love* (how can Charlotte the maid escape the very different attentions of her master Redmond and his mistress Felicia?) that she will come to understand some of the key problems of her own life (how can she herself resolve her relationships with the various men in her life on the one hand and the various women on the other?). Her costume gothics provide both the imaginative impetus and the financial resources for her to extricate herself from the web of relationships that has constrained her.

The resolution that her work as a gothic novelist will eventually provide cannot take place until "Lady Oracle" has done its work, however. "Lady Oracle" is more than once described as "a mixture of Khalil Gibran and Rod McKuen" (p. 251), though it actually begins as a side-note to one of Joan's costume gothics. It grows out of one of her attempts to resolve a plot difficulty in a novel she is writing – *Love, My Ransom* – by enacting the scene in question. Concerned that the occult is becoming a necessary ingredient in such fictions, she has her heroine of the moment drink from an "exotic flask" and stare into a mirror. What happens next is a mystery to her, and so Joan herself does the same thing, only to find herself drawn into the mirror as if into a physical space. Her repeated journeys into the mirror for a time take precedence over the fiction-writing, and each time she emerges from the mirror she discovers she has written something – words and phrases that she eventually combines in an experimental poem about a "powerful" woman who is "almost like a goddess" though with "an unhappy power" (p. 248), and has a relationship with a man who seems alternately evil and good. The woman is "The dark lady the redgold lady / the black lady oracle / of blood, she who must be / obeyed forever / Her glass wings are gone / She floats down the river / Singing her last song" (p. 252). The poetry may be bad, but the figure it imagines deserves comment. She is a sort of literary pastiche, combining characters as disparate as Rumpole's wife (consistently referred to as "she who must be obeyed" in the popular British fiction series about Rumpole of the Bailey) through Tennyson's Lady of Shalott (admired by Joan, who wants "to have someone, anyone, say that [she] had a lovely face, even if [she] had to turn into a corpse in a barge-bottom first" (p. 159)), to Joan herself (with her "redgold" hair). Joan does not fully make sense of the lady, though, until that moment when her mother's ghost appears and then disappears on her balcony in Italy. Then she realizes:

It had been she standing behind me in the mirror, she was the one who was waiting around each turn, her voice whispered the words. She had been the lady in the boat, the death barge, the tragic lady with flowing hair and stricken eyes, the lady in the tower. She couldn't stand the view from the window, life was her curse. How could I renounce her? She needed her freedom also; she had been my reflection too long. What was the charm, what would set her free? (p. 363)

This woman represents not only Joan and her mother, but all the women who have ever felt themselves trapped in a gothic nightmare, and Joan explicitly seeks a way out of the scenario that forces all of these women into a single mold, though the recognition of their sameness is perhaps her most profound insight. This desire for separation seems tied to the related recognition – when in the next chapter she turns back to *Stalked by Love* – that all of the significant men in her life have been versions of the same person. When Charlotte walks into the maze that lurks at the heart of that story, she encounters a man whose physical appearance metamorphoses as she watches him. One after another, he takes on the appearance of all the men with whom Charlotte – and also Joan – have been involved: the novel's hero, Redmond, but also Joan's father, the Polish count, the Royal Porcupine, the evil/good man of "Lady Oracle," Arthur himself, and a skull or death's head. In this story of the heroine trapped by a man – good or evil – one sees that the only way out is not to be a "heroine." Having finally cut the invisible tie that bound her to her mother, Joan is able to see clearly the other ties she must cut as well, and on deciding to re-enter the world of the living, she resolves: "I won't write any more Costume Gothics . . . I think they were bad for me" (p. 379). Seeing that the narratives of life and art clearly have some bearing on each other, she quite literally decides to change the genre in which she writes: future-oriented science fiction is next. (Whether that's really any different is another story, as we will see in discussion of *The Blind Assassin*.)

Where *Lady Oracle* comments wryly on the ways in which – even now – women's lives still seem inescapably shaped by those patriarchal forces we know so well from gothic tradition, those same wry/comic tones effectively undercut the whole scenario. For Joan, as for the Radcliffean heroines that preceded her, financial independence is absolutely key to a life that is anything other than gothic in its lineaments. Also like Radcliffe's heroines, she needs to see and be able to set aside the ties that bind her, but in this she distinguishes herself from her literary predecessors. Radcliffe rejected sublimity as the vehicle by which truth was made known, though she exploited the affective possibilities of the sublime in her repeated use of the seeming supernatural. Austen took Radcliffe one step farther, imagining seemingly supernatural effects that inevitably turned out to be the result of natural causes, and finding the humor in the gap between appearance and reality. Atwood builds on and surpasses both, resurrecting what she dares us to read as the supernatural (Joan's mother appearing in her navy blue suit from 1949 on one end of the spectrum and Joan's trips into the mirror on the other),[8] imagining this supernatural world as a barely displaced version of the natural, and at the same time satirizing this tendency to collapse one into the other. Indeed, satire replaces sublimity as the keynote of this modern gothic, and, as it happens, the formal mechanisms of satire reverse those of the sublime, asserting a distance between subject and object.

Satire is a genre that makes its points by positing a distance between ourselves and that which we are satirizing, and in Atwood's novel that opportunity for difference becomes a privileged possibility for survival. Satire not only lets Joan Foster maintain her difference from a world that would swallow her up, but lets her multiply different "selves" as well, in a pattern that does not so much dangerously fragment her identity as ensure her survival.[9] Atwood's satiric mode, then, is a powerful weapon against the gothic formula with which she engages.

The Blind Assassin

One might say that *The Blind Assassin* begins where *Lady Oracle* left off nearly twenty-five years earlier. Atwood is again pondering the relationship between gothic romance and science fiction, but this time seems more interested in exploring their points of connection. While gothic fiction has traditionally looked to the past and science fiction to the future, both present uncanny images of the "real world" in which they are written, and they present uncanny images of each other as well. Gothic and science fiction are flip sides of the same coin, in other words, and *The Blind Assassin* sees this. The novel imagines a world in which the shaping power of these fictions is so strong that one can no longer easily distinguish between what is meant to be "real" and what is meant to be fiction. The real and the fictional emerge as versions of each other. Where in early gothic fiction this uncertain grounding would have signaled disaster, however, here it is liberating. The more realities one can construct, the better chance one has of finding one in which oppression is not the order of the day.

The novel's complicated structure shows us a primary story that doubles and then doubles again, with narrative lines that seem endlessly to refract and comment on each other. *The Blind Assassin*'s story, told by 83-year-old Iris Chase, runs parallel to a second story, whose chapters are interspersed with those detailing Iris's life. Also called "The Blind Assassin," the embedded narrative has been published posthumously under the name of Iris's sister Laura, though we eventually find out that its author was Iris herself. And the embedded narrative of the "The Blind Assassin" divides yet again. Its primary plot tells the story of an unnamed narrator's relationship with a man who was her lover; its secondary plot consists of a fantastic story that the lovers invent to amuse themselves – part historical romance, part science fiction – about a blind assassin and a mute virgin in a place called Sakiel-Norn. In the mythology of Sakiel-Norn, blind assassins begin their lives as children who weave exquisite carpets but lose their sight in the process, then become prostitutes famed for their touch, and then become professional killers. The mute virgins are bred to be sacrifices to gods in whom people no longer believe, and their tongues are cut out to prevent them protesting their fate. Their lives are sacrificed to a state ruled by a tyranny more brutal than that in any gothic novel we have discussed so far, yet Atwood imagines one assassin saving one mute woman and the two of them escaping their oppressive existence. Why? Are we really to believe that women's killers will turn into saviors? Is this the liberation that we are to expect from fiction? *Lady Oracle* suggests that such liberation will never be good enough, and that the only way women can escape entrapment in gothic scenarios is by refusing to participate in them. *The Blind Assassin* complicates that vision by suggesting that resistance can take place within the gothic structure. The point is not to transform the woman's killer into a savior, but rather, to watch the woman leave her killer behind and save herself.

How a woman can accomplish that is told through the twinned stories of Iris and her sister Laura, who from girlhood find their lives shadowed as much by strong women as by men. They are the granddaughters of one Adelia Montfort, who was "from an established family, or what passed for it in Canada – second-generation Montreal English crossed with Huguenot French" (59).[10] The socially pretentious Adelia has worked hard to identify herself as English rather than Canadian, going so far as to name her home Avilion. She "took the name from Tennyson," intending it to conjure a magical place "Where falls not hail, or rain, or any snow, / Nor ever wind blows loudly; but it lies / Deep-meadow'd, happy, fair with orchard lawns / And bowery hollows crown'd with summer sea . . ." (pp. 60–1). As Iris points out, however, "Avilion was where King Arthur went to die," and it just as likely signals how far she is from the glamorous social life of her imagination, "how hopelessly in exile she considered herself to be" (p. 61). Adelia herself starts to look something like a gothic heroine, trapped in a place that is at best an imitation of the place she really wants to be, and the architectural details of the house confirm this identification. Her home is "a merchant's palace, with a curved driveway leading to it, a stumpy Gothic turret, and a wide semi-circular spooled verandah overlooking the two rivers" by which it is situated (p. 58). The house is so fully identified with Adelia that it remains unchanged after her death, her influence sufficiently palpable that Iris can say without irony, "Laura and I were brought up by her. We grew up inside her house; that is to say, inside her conception of herself" (p. 62). The grandmother's house holds them the way any gothic castle holds any gothic heroine, and Iris knows that they need to leave (recall Kahane's argument that gothic fiction is about the daughter's separation from her mother). They endure life on what Iris later describes as a "thorn-encircled island, waiting for rescue" (p. 43).

The sisters' life at Avilion is unusual. Their family is at its most functional when it is run by women, though these women are hardly in positions of unambiguous power. Even as their socially ambitious grandmother gave distinctive character to a house in which she was to some degree trapped, so their mother gamely keeps the family business running when her husband is fighting in the First World War, but is in the process transformed into a woman old before her time, who dies after a third child miscarries. The sisters both inherit something from these strong but oddly disempowered women.

Iris takes over some of the responsibilities for mothering her sister, though she becomes increasingly resentful of the way she is "needed at home" (p. 173), and as she grows older she seems to be adopting some of her father's responsibilities as well. She eventually even goes to work for her father at the Chase and Sons factory, filling the role of "son" in the family business. Her acceptance of this position is no feminist victory, however, but an unwilling act of duty performed in spite of the fact that she sees herself as having "no business abilities" (p. 197). Iris's strength and her weakness lie in her ability to make compromises, to do what she must to maintain the status quo, and as her life progresses, it is increasingly defined by the gap between appearance and reality.

Laura takes after her mother in her devotion to social causes, working in a soup kitchen as a girl living at Avilion, and later in a hospital, when she lives in Toronto. Unlike her mother or her sister, however, she has little interest in maintaining appearances for their own sake, and she is seen as "different" primarily because of her unwillingness – maybe even inability – to engage in the double-talk of daily life. Iris learns very young not to tell her sister to go jump in the lake, because she just might. And yet Iris can see that

> perhaps Laura wasn't very different from other people after all. Perhaps she was the same – the same as some odd, skewed element in them that most people keep hidden but that Laura did not, and this was why she frightened them. Because she did frighten them – or if not frighten, alarm them in some way; though more, of course, as she got older. (p. 89)

Laura functions as an uncanny other to her sister and to others as well, letting that which has been repressed rise to the surface, or, more accurately, never repressing anything at all. It is her refusal to open up that gap between appearance and reality that makes her dangerous, her interest in "essences" above all (p. 45).

Iris and Laura are their mother's daughters, but they are their father's as well, and his story is one of progressive failure. Descended from Americans who came from Pennsylvania in the 1820s (well before Canada became a nation in 1867), he inherited from his father a fortune earned by the family button factory. Forced to run the factory when he does not want to, he watches his business decline so badly that he seeks to save it by marrying Iris to a competitor named Richard Griffin. This is the "rescue" that the sisters have been waiting for, and predictably, it leads to an even grimmer form of entrapment than what they knew before. The marriage destroys Chase industries entirely, and nearly destroys not just one but both sisters as well.

Married to Richard Griffin at the age of 18, Iris finds herself in an upper-class Toronto life that completely masks her unhappiness. Living in a house every bit as pretentious as the one she grew up in, wife of a man whose very touch bruises her, Iris is still more confined than she was as a child, and when Laura comes to live with them as well, her experience largely parallels that of her sister, right down to the sexual abuse. Laura keeps Richard's treatment of her secret, even when her eventual pregnancy results in her being committed to an asylum, where her child is aborted and her stories discounted. While she eventually tells Iris something of what had happened, she does not name the man who assaulted her, and Iris does not realize that it was her husband. On the contrary, she assumes it was a man named Alex Thomas – a man who has long interested both sisters – and in this spectacular act of blindness becomes an unwitting assassin herself. Her failure to see what has happened is followed by Laura getting into her sister's car and driving it off a bridge. Only after Laura's death does Iris find out the extent of her husband's guilt, at which point she leaves him, and soon after publishes under Laura's name the story of a woman – perhaps Iris, perhaps Laura, perhaps a fictional combination of both – who has an affair with a man very much like Alex Thomas.

Both as girls living at Avilion and as young women living in Toronto, the sisters' lives have been shaped by the well-known mechanisms of gothic narrative. Theirs is yet another story born of abusive patriarchal power that takes the form of violence, incest, and the incarceration of women who cannot be otherwise contained, and – like all gothic heroines before them – they have sought ways out of their situation. At different times and in different ways, both sisters turn to Alex Thomas in the seeming hope that he can release them from their limited existences, and while he cannot, there are reasons why they turn to him first. They meet Alex when they are young girls at their father's company picnic, and he is in every way ambiguous: "a young man – a man, not a boy – a darkish man, with a light-coloured hat. His style was indeterminate – not a factory worker, but not anything else either, or nothing definite" (p. 176). He claims to be an orphan "found sitting on a mound of charred rubble, in a burned-out house" somewhere in eastern Europe, says that he then found himself among Presbyterian missionaries (p. 189), and enters the story as a suspected union agitator and political radical. Alex is in crucial ways like Brontë's Heathcliff. The housekeeper at Avilion judges that "[h]e's most likely some half-breed Indian, or else a gypsy" (p. 182), and his lack of national or family ties certainly marks him as an outsider to the community into which the sisters try to draw him.

Laura attaches herself to Alex first, meeting him at different places, and eventually hiding him at Avilion when he is suspected of being behind a fire that burns down the button factory. It is Iris who meets him years later in Toronto and has an affair with him, however, and it is Iris who really learns the lesson of the story that Alex told her in his saga of Sakiel-Norn. I mentioned earlier the story's suggestion that a woman's killer can become her savior, and it is important to say now that the salvation offered to the woman is short-lived. Both the blind assassin and the mute virgin he saves die soon after they escape the land in which they had been so oppressed, even as Alex himself provides the sisters with only temporary respite from the difficulties of their lives. A more permanent solution to their problems can come from them alone, and while Laura's suicide is one way out, Iris's decision to become a writer is another. Atwood sticks by what she knew as early as *Lady Oracle* when she suggests that writing is a way to reshape the gothic narrative of one's life. As in *Lady Oracle*, however, she again confronts us with a woman who writes not in her own name but in another's, and again we must ask what this means.

Before considering Iris's decision to publish her own story under Laura's name, pause for a moment to consider why she does not publish under her own. Reflecting on what she did so many years ago, the elderly Iris explains:

> I wrote it . . . when I was waiting for Alex to come back, and then afterwards, once I knew he wouldn't. I didn't think of what I was doing as writing – just writing down. What I remembered and also what I imagined, which is also the truth. I thought of myself as recording. A bodiless hand, scrawling across a wall. (p. 512)

The book is written to fill the void left by the loss of Alex, even as its publication fills the void left by Laura's death, and it is perhaps ironic, perhaps inevitable, that as it replaces these missing people it correspondingly reduces Iris herself to the role of shadow. She is no longer a whole person, but a disembodied hand writing a story of loss.

That image of the hand recalls the image of Laura's suicidal drive off the bridge, wearing white gloves. It also recalls a photograph taken of Iris and Laura, with Alex Thomas between them. The photograph was taken at the company picnic on the day they met, and marks the beginning of their strangely triangulated relationship. I mentioned earlier that Laura hides Alex at Avilion for a time, and when she eventually lets Iris in on the secret, they come "closer together than [they] had been for a while" (p. 216). The sisters fantasize about Alex in different ways, and when he finally leaves, Laura hands Iris a print of the photograph. She herself has made the print, and has "cut herself out of it – only her hand remained. She couldn't have got rid of this hand without making a wobbly margin," and has "tinted" it "a very pale yellow" (p. 220). Iris is distressed by the picture, and recalls: "The sight of Laura's light-yellow hand, creeping towards Alex across the grass like an incandescent crab, gave me a chill down the back of my spine" (p. 220). Laura explains the photograph by saying to Iris, "that's what you want to remember," and acknowledges having made another print for herself, this one with all of Iris cut out except for the hand. These images of happy couples with a hand sneaking up on them make clear the dynamic of the sisters' relationship, which persists in spite of – or maybe because of – being always mediated by a male figure. They at once shadow and sustain each other, and it is when the man is replaced by the book about the man that their closeness becomes most evident.

Knowing all this, it comes as no surprise that Iris explains her decision to publish "The Blind Assassin" under her sister's name as an acknowledgment of the truth. "Laura didn't write a word of it," she says, and then she qualifies that statement. "Technically that's accurate, but in another sense – what Laura would have called the spiritual sense – you could say she was my collaborator. The real author was neither one of us: a fist is more than the sum of its fingers" (p. 512). Appealing as that image of the sisters joined in solidarity may be, however, their relationship never becomes quite that simple. They always shadow each other, each functioning as the other's "left hand," Iris tells us (p. 513). The reference here is to images of a Christian God with his son at his right hand, and no one at his left. Puzzling about what this might mean, Laura decides that this vision is simply a matter of perspective. We never hear about anyone sitting at God's left hand, she reasons, because he sits at a circular table, and "everyone sits at everyone else's right hand, all the way round." Turn your head, look the other way, and everyone is on the left. The sisters do that, changing the way we look at things with their "left-handed book" in which "one of [them] is always out of sight, whichever way you look at it" (p. 513).

The Blind Assassin thus finds a way out of the gothic not by turning its back on it, or by insisting on its difference from the world of lived experience, but by acknowledging its terrible reality even as it acknowledges its transformative power. In this novel, the division at the heart of the gothic is what makes escape possible. Iris survives her sister's death by displacing part of her own identity on to her, even as she survives her marriage by displacing something of her own life into that of Alex Thomas (whose fantastic stories she also helps to write). This view is less rosy than that of *Lady Oracle*, for it acknowledges the maintaining of difference – of divisions within oneself as well as between oneself and other people – not as victory but as a simple survival strategy.

Fall on Your Knees

I opened this book by quoting a passage from Ann-Marie Macdonald's *Fall on Your Knees*, and it is with delight that I circle back to this novel, which appeared in Canada in 1996, and in the United States two years later.[11] The novel marks itself as gothic with its epigram, taken from *Wuthering Heights*: " 'Why canst thou not always be a good lass, Cathy?' 'Why cannot you always be a good man, father?' " Father–daughter relationships will be at the core of this novel, which will again take the patriarchal family and gender relations as its central subjects. The marriage of Scots Irish James Piper to a 13-year-old Lebanese girl named Materia Mahmoud inaugurates a gothic nightmare that persists through several generations of the family story. James and Materia have three daughters – Kathleen (who is later raped and impregnated by her father), Mercedes, and Frances – and most of the novel focuses on the efforts of the Piper women to escape their nightmarish household. Seeing past the paternal to the maternal initially seems to be the way out – as in the novels of Ann Radcliffe – and certainly this recentering of value and authority loosens the ties that bind. In this novel, however, gender and family politics are complicated by the connection with racial politics, and both are complicated by the colonial context in which much of the novel takes place. Any real escape from the traps of this particular gothic plot is going to mean thinking through a whole series of oppositions – male / female, white / black, colony / mother country, Western / non-Western, national / international – and, amazingly enough, Macdonald manages to do this. Her novel remembers and re-creates the gothic in its literally catholic – or universal – embrace of difference.

Macdonald knows exactly how a gothic plot is supposed to go, and has great fun letting us see this. Early in the novel, Materia goes to work at the pointedly named Empire Theater, where she provides the piano accompaniment for one silent film after another. It is here that we find the passage I discussed in my first chapter, with the audience watching, "breathless, eager for the next terror," as a typically gothic tale appears on screen. You remember:

> A man in evening clothes has cornered a young woman in a slinky nightgown halfway up a clock tower. No narrative preamble required, *all ist klar*, the shadows lurk, the tower lists, the music creeps the winding stair, the villain spies a grace note of silken hem and he's on the chase in six-eight time up to where our heroine clings to a snatch of girlish melody, teetering on the precipice of high E,

overlooking the street eight octaves below. Villain struggles with virgin in a macabre waltz, Strauss turned Faust, until, just when it seems she'll plummet, dash her brains on the bass clef and die entangled in the web of the lower stave, a vision in tenor crescendos on to save the day in resolving chords. (p. 50)

The bravura performance of this gothic plot in miniature deserves our applause. The young woman trapped in the tower, threatened by one man and rescued by another, could be any heroine from Walpole or Lewis or Radcliffe; her persecutor could be Manfred or Ambrosio or Schedoni, her rescuer Theodore, or Lorenzo, or Vivaldi. One might read the scene as a struggle between two sublime forces – one evil, one good, but both destined to kill (either literally or figuratively) the heroine caught between them. One might read it as the uncanny opposition of virtue and vice, which turn out to be versions of the same thing and still threaten to quash the heroine caught between them. One might extrapolate from that and follow the lead of René Girard and Eve Sedgwick, seeing in it a story of mimetic desire in which the important contest is between the two men, who are interested more in each other than the young woman (think of Polidori's *The Vampyre*). In all these readings of the story, though, one thing is constant. The woman in the scene is impossibly positioned, and would be much better off if she could fashion yet a third way out.

Finding that third way is Macdonald's task in the narrative she spins around this one. She begins her story in the same place, with the story of the piano-playing Materia, who leaves her father's house to elope with James when she is only 13. Materia's leave-taking is figured not just as a move from the house of the father to that of the husband, but also as a move from the "Old Country" (the Lebanese culture of her parents) to the brave new world of Canada and Cape Breton Island. Materia initially believes herself to be trading a patriarchal home in which she has been quite literally trapped (locked into her bedroom at night) for a desirable alternative; the reader, however, is never allowed to think this way. When we learn that Materia's father actually builds the house in which she and James take up residence, we understand that this new residence is not an alternative to that which she leaves behind, but another version of it. As the narrator reminds us, "just because [the house] was new, doesn't mean it wasn't haunted" (p. 25), and haunted it is – by the "Old Country" that Materia did not quite leave behind when she eloped with James, by the family that she also did not quite escape, and, most chillingly, by Materia herself. Described as dead to her parents the moment she elopes, identified by a curious neighbor as "a ghost" who haunts the nearby cliffs (p. 33), Materia gradually metamorphoses into a figure ever so quietly reminiscent of Charlotte Brontë's Bertha Mason. Living in her "big two-story white frame house, with attic" (p. 25; note that attic), she is caught in a world shaped largely by her father and her husband, two men who are alike in their control over her, but utterly unlike in their cultural heritage and moorings, and so in their specific demands on her. She is not the good Catholic Lebanese daughter her father wanted, but neither is she the good Protestant Scots Irish wife, and especially mother, into which James tries to make her. Gradually overwhelmed by a sense of her own "badness" (p. 58), Materia responds to the pressures on her first by letting her "mind ebb away" (p. 59), and finally by dying with her head in an oven, after the particularly acute crisis provoked by the circumstances of her daughter Kathleen's death.

Against Materia's story one can read those of her daughters, Kathleen, Mercedes, and Frances, each of whom repeats her mother's story to an extent, but each of whom also starts to find a way to transform the gothic narrative. Kathleen is the eldest of the three girls, and seems at a glance to be entirely unlike her mother. Defined above all by a phenomenal musical talent that she perhaps inherits from her mother the pianist, Kathleen is destined to be a diva. She sings before she can talk, carries a tune at eighteen months, and from that young age her exceptional talent – as well as her exceptional beauty – set her apart from virtually everyone around her. The course of her life seems antithetical to that of her victimized mother, and yet the two are not as different as one might think.

Kathleen's life is from the start carefully shaped by her father. James controls every aspect of it, cultivating her sense of her own uniqueness to such a degree that she voluntarily holds herself apart from the world around her. Having accomplished this, James doesn't need to actually lock his daughter up in the house to control her – she has effectively taken on the role of her own jailer. In a striking description that equates the castles in which gothic heroines are typically imprisoned with Kathleen herself, Macdonald writes: "Kathleen's fortress, her tower of creamy white, is steep and terrible. No one comes in or out. Except for her father, Sister Saint Cecilia [a teacher] and a select few minions necessary to support life" (p. 95). Kathleen is the gothic heroine *par excellence*, trapped in her own magnificence. All that changes, however, when – having moved to New York to study music – she takes as her lover the extraordinary Rose, a cross-dressing black woman who plays jazz piano. This is an action that violates in as many ways as possible her father's sense of what she should be doing: his own incestuous desire for her has all along precluded his allowing her any kind of even nascent sexual connection with another person, and a same-sex, interracial relationship is beyond his imaginative capacity. When he discovers Kathleen and Rose in bed together, he literally pulls them apart, first throwing Rose into the hall, then raping and repossessing Kathleen. And now Kathleen knows what she did not before – that she is and perhaps has been all along a character in a gothic plot of the worst kind.

Is she, though? Have there not been moments when she is not involved in such a story? We have seen that gothic plots focus not only on women's

struggles against fathers and father-figures, but also on their efforts to shape relationships with their mothers: at times daughters need to separate from their
mothers, at others to rediscover them and build or rebuild their relationships with
them. With this in mind, Materia's relationship with Kathleen bears consideration. Materia worries from the time Kathleen is born that she does not love her
daughter, and Kathleen – for her part – merely tolerates her mother, "try[ing]
not to breathe" when her mother holds her in her arms. The distance between
them persists, and it is only when they are truly separated – when Kathleen is in
New York – that it starts to close. Kathleen sees a woman on a streetcar with
"Mumma's hands" (p. 436), and she is shocked when she sees that "she was a
colored woman" (p. 436). This is perhaps the point at which Kathleen begins to
see her mother in an accurate light, and the very physical kind of knowing that
is suggested here culminates in the moment of Kathleen's death. Pregnant as a
result of the rape, she spends her pregnancy in the attic of the home in which
she grew up, and once she goes into labor it is clear that either she or her
children must die. Her mother has to choose, and – understanding that her
daughter does not want to live – makes sure that Kathleen gets what she wants.
Kathleen's death thus marks an uneasy movement toward a mother to whom
she was never close in life, even as it marks Materia's equally uneasy movement toward a daughter she has always found herself unable to love, and certainly it suggests a way out of Kathleen's gothic nightmare, though hardly one
we would want to endorse.

A more constructive version of what one might call the "maternal dynamic"
of the novel, however, comes as a result of Kathleen's singing. At her first
concert, she sings from *Rigoletto*. People do not understand the words, but tears
come to their eyes, "because a real and beautiful voice delicately rends the chest,
discovers the heart, and holds it beating against a stainless edge until you long to
be pierced utterly . . . the voice is everything you do not remember. Everything
you should not be able to live without and yet, tragically, do" (p. 75). Kathleen's
voice sends her audience back to what the psychoanalytic critic Julia Kristeva
(1980) would call the semiotic, that pre-Oedipal moment when one is still bonded
to the mother, has not yet separated and joined the symbolic world of the
father.[12] When she sings, in other words, Kathleen brings her audience back to
the maternal, and in so doing rescues them – and herself – from the gothic world
in which she and they all live. That rescue is but temporary, however. It is not
something they can hold on to, and brings with it the threat of sublime self-loss
that I discussed in relation to Radcliffe. (Indeed, as Kathleen is taking her bows
for this very concert, she is interrupted on stage by a man announcing that Great
Britain is at war with Germany, and that Canada, heeding the call of the mother
country, is at war too – a commentary on the destruction of self inherent in the
maternal bond if ever I heard one.) Macdonald faces the problem that Radcliffe

faced before her: if a return to the pre-Oedipal mother is not possible and not even desirable, if we live inevitably in the world of patriarchy, the world of the symbolic, the world of difference, what then can one do to escape the sorts of nightmares we have seen? The only possible answer is that we must somehow transform that world, and while such transformation may be easily invoked, it is not so easily accomplished. There are ways to bring it about, however.

If remembered maternal ties threaten a self-loss not much preferable to the violent repression that seems to go hand in hand with paternal authority, then one way out would seem to involve escaping the patriarchal family altogether. Macdonald suggests that such escapes come not from severing all family connections however, but from seeing in them an exuberant multiplicity that opens up the possibility of a different life. When Kathleen lands in New York to study music, she revels in the fact that "her mixed Celtic-Arab blood and her origins on a scraggly island off the east coast of a country popularly supposed to consist of a polar ice cap are enough, by American standards, both to cloak her in sufficient diva mystery and to temper the exotic with a dash of windswept North American charm" (p. 120). Identity here is constructed in terms of race and place above all, as Kathleen claims both her father's and her mother's ethnic origins, both Canada and the United States, as places to live. The cultural crossings that earlier in the novel have registered simply as problematic here become sources of power, and it is hard not to think that the novel's trope of "no man's land" – repeatedly represented as a dehumanizing space between clearly defined opposites – is here transformed into a space of human plenitude. Kathleen is not one thing but two (Celtic and Arab), not two but four (Celtic, Arab, Canadian, and American), and as she actively claims for herself these many identities she effectively rewrites the gothic plot that has cast her as trapped and/or haunted by these doubled and redoubled versions of herself.

Kathleen's expansive sense of her self for a time lifts her out of a home and a life whose gothic possibilities she has never fully appreciated, and yet it is not enough to protect her from the sheer physical force of the father who forces her back into the world she has tried to leave. Once she finds herself pregnant and trapped in the attic of her childhood home, her only options seem to be either to live out the gothic nightmare with which she is faced, or to escape it through death. The breech birth of her children, Ambrose and Lily, takes that choice out of her hands and puts it in her mother's, who cuts the twins out of her with scissors, and in so doing lets her daughter die. This is said to be the right choice for a devout Catholic like Materia, and yet she "die[s] a few days later of a guilty conscience," knowing that "what she did, although correct in the eyes of the Church, was murder in His all-seeing eyes." She goes on: "the real reason I let my daughter die is because I knew she was better off that way. I didn't know her well, but I knew she didn't want to live anymore. She preferred to die and I allowed her to do so" (p. 134). Kathleen ends up like Wollstonecraft's Maria, her body literally a "tomb" for the children to whom she gives birth (p. 139). She nearly managed, however, to escape the patriarchal nightmare into which she was born, and her sisters enact a still more ambivalent version of the same struggle.

Mercedes seeks whatever freedom can come from living by embracing patriarchal authority without question, while Frances devotes herself to defying it in every way possible. Their relationship with their father, and with the Catholicism that so strongly defined their mother, determines the course of their lives. Informed by James after the deaths of Materia and Kathleen that she will now need to be strong for the family, Mercedes self-consciously takes on the role of mother. She cooks, cleans, and shops; she is a stellar student; she is a relentlessly devoted Catholic. Even as she fulfills all of these roles, however, she longs for something different. She longs to build on her intellectual talents and "wants . . . badly to go to college" (p. 239). She hopes to transform her domestic life by marrying Ralph Luvovitz, a neighbor with whom she falls in love. She reads and rereads *Jane Eyre*, seeing in Jane perhaps the model of a woman who finds freedom in just these ways, and yet she herself goes nowhere. Family responsibilities keep her at home, and she ends up a high school teacher; Ralph goes off to college, and he meets and marries someone else. Only her Catholicism keeps her going, and it becomes an ever narrower form of religion that limits rather than expands her own life. Her finest moment – and it is not negligible – comes when she lies to her father in order to keep him from further hurting her sisters. Recognizing that this is "simply the cost of doing business with God," she emerges as "neither a saint nor a sinner," but "somewhere in between" (p. 361). Achieving this measure of humanity is the fullest escape she can manage.

Frances responds to the deaths of her mother and her sister very differently from Mercedes. From this moment on, she becomes an insistent and entertaining critic of the patriarchal stories with which she was raised. Faced with the task of repairing Mercedes' statue of "The Old-Fashioned Girl" – an ornament that plays "Let Me Call You Sweetheart" and "holds a yellow parasol" – she puts the head in place of the parasol and vice versa. Mercedes looks up to see "The Old-Fashioned Girl . . . daintily holding up her own head of ringlets to the sun while the insensate yellow parasol is implanted in the empty neck like a flag" (p. 243). Perhaps worse, Frances writes an epilogue into Mercedes' copy of *Jane Eyre*, "wherein Mr. Rochester's hand, severed and lost in the fire, comes back to life and strangles their infant child" (p. 212). Mercedes is hurt and angered by both of these acts, but Frances is simply saying what she knows. Old-fashioned girls lose their heads when they follow patriarchal plots, and even the good men in those plots are not all that good in the end (she did, after all, grow up with James as her father).

Frances's rejection of these stories brings with it a complex rejection of Catholicism as well. Judging by the roles she chooses to play in the sisters' riotous re-enactments of the stories in "The Children's Treasury of Martyrs," Catholicism too is a world best left to old-fashioned girls. Over and over again she plays the part of girls who lose their heads:

> Saint Barbara, whose father was a pagan and when she wanted to be a Christian he took her up a mountain and cut off her head while she was praying for him. Or else Saint Winnifred, who once knew a man who wanted to do wrong with her but she said not so he cut off her head but her kind uncle put it back on her leaving only a thin white scar. Or sometimes she was Saint Dymphna, who had a father who wanted to do wrong with her but she wouldn't so she escaped with the court jester, but her father found her in Belgium and cut her head off. (p. 190)

In her own life she seeks to turn those plots upside down, so that they look like the same old story but in fact place her in charge. That said, though, she also imagines herself in the role of Jesus in their Catholic version of "Little Women Doing the Stations of the Cross." She is the daughter who tries to baptize Kathleen's new babies in the night, and she is the daughter who arguably does give her own life to save that of her sister Lily.

Even more important than what Frances rejects is what she claims for herself, for she romanticizes and reclaims a Lebanese heritage she does not really know, even as she rewrites those narratives of Western patriarchy that make her life so untenable. She and Lily speak a secret language whose words are half-remembered Arabic from Frances's childhood, half-made up. She cooks Lebanese food. She steals back the life her mother was forced to give up when she married James, sneaking into the home where her mother grew up and inhabiting it like a ghost. She spies on her grandfather, takes things from the house (including a braid that has been cut from her mother's head), even clothes herself in Arabic dress and dances before her grandfather – in a hazy, dreamy moment – as her grandmother had before her. Less romantically, she becomes an exotic dancer and sex worker at her uncle's speakeasy, making of it an ironic "cultural Mecca" (p. xx). And, less romantically still, she at times even identifies with the abusive men she wishes to fight, playing the part of the woman caught in a classically patriarchal scenario only to turn the tables at the last moment.

While still in school, Frances seduces "Puss-Eye Murphy" – a boy known by some as "Pious-Eye" for his sense of "priestly vocation" – luring him into an outhouse on the pretense of needing advice about "a terrible sin someone had confessed to her" and then sexually abusing him (pp. 273–4). As a slightly older girl, she convinces a black man named Leo Taylor that she is an abused woman and that he must protect her. While she is indeed both physically and sexually abused by her father, she draws Leo in by actually injuring herself and letting him think her father responsible for her state. She talks Leo into taking her to an abandoned mine where she says she will be safe, then seduces – or, more realistically, rapes – him with the aim of becoming pregnant. That this event happens in a mine reminds us that the dying Kathleen was also described as an "abandoned mine" (p. 132), and suggests that her action must therefore be seen as not only horribly abusive but also oddly restorative, a recovery of territory – her own body and her sister's – that she thought she had lost.

Frances' efforts to reclaim the story of her mother even as she rewrites the story of her father culminate in her telling her sister Lily that she is pregnant not by Leo, but by Leo's sister Teresa. Teresa worked in the home of Frances's grandfather, and was eventually fired for the various thefts that Frances herself had committed. When she learns of Frances's sexual manipulation of her brother, she shoots her in the abdomen, and Teresa's bullet becomes for Frances the cause of her pregnancy. One might well read as delusional her insistence on reading an attack as an act of love, and yet she flourishes from that moment on. She actually does have a child – Anthony, whom Mercedes tells her has died when he has not – and following his birth she becomes a larger-than-life maternal figure. She cooks and bakes not just for her family, but for the community in which she lives. Through her, the dysfunctional Oedipal family gives way to something larger and more capacious.

If Kathleen, Mercedes, and Frances try with notably limited success to move beyond the gothic scenario of their mother's life, the next generation of the family – Lily and Anthony – does much better. Lily comes into the world primed for the role of gothic heroine, for her life is defined in crucial ways by her relationship to the dead. Ambrose, the twin with whom she was born, drowned when Frances tried to baptize him. She was also born the near-double of her deceased mother, whom she resembles in her red hair, her creamy skin, and her strong will, though her physical difference from her is also marked in a crippled leg. Lily is smart enough to know that her own identity depends on her understanding her connections to these people, whose stories in various ways are doubles for her own, even as she seems to know that losing herself in remembering them would be destructive.

Lily's knowledge of Ambrose develops only gradually. She hears stories of him but does not know if they are true or not, and in trying to come to terms with her family history, she steals Mercedes' careful drawing of the family tree and adds to it an image of a treasure chest that she says holds Ambrose within it. Frances tells her that "Ambrose is just a story," but immediately upsets her own fiction by suggesting that maybe he isn't, and the two of them bury the family tree in virtually the same place that Ambrose is buried.

Knowledge of a different kind comes when Ambrose appears to Lily as she is "in between" waking and sleeping, caught in that "no man's land" that the book thematizes as such a dangerously liminal place. We read that he is

> naked except for the decomposing bits of Frances's old white nightgown in which he was laid to rest. . . . Safe and soundless in his garden womb, he has not been dreaming because he has not been asleep. He has been growing. His body is streaked with earth and coal but otherwise he is pale as a root. Although he is exactly the same age as Lily, he is full-grown like a man whereas she is still a little girl. This is because their environments have been so different. (p. 213)

A little later still, Lily again sees him standing at the foot of her bed when she "is in that place between the lines," and when she asks who he is, "[h]e opens his mouth and the water pours out but Lily stays in the in-between place and does not make a sound until she and the bed and Frances sleeping next to her are soaked" (p. 258). In the midst of what her sisters perceive as a fever, Lily has just been doused with what the book asks us to see as the water that both baptized and drowned her little brother, and when she asks yet again who he is, Ambrose answers, "I am No Man" (p. 273), to which she responds, "Don't be afraid. We love you. . . . Hello" (p. 272). The Catholicism that killed him is revived in her, as she acknowledges this entirely liminal figure with a generosity that seems truly catholic – or all-embracing – in its reach. Much later, she digs up the body of her brother from nearly the same place in which she and Frances buried the family tree, and at that point she is ready to find her mother as well.

Lily learns that Kathleen is her mother from Frances, who to that point has herself filled that role in Lily's life. Frances is the pre-Oedipal mother whose "face first looked [Lily] into existence" (p. 416), and – newly delivered of her son, Anthony – she actually takes Lily to her breast and nurses her before sending her off to New York. Financed by money from Frances, carrying Kathleen's journal, and wearing Kathleen's green silk dress, as well as red boots made by her father James, Lily walks all the way from Cape Breton Island to Manhattan. Her journey is a pilgrimage: where Mercedes had wanted her to travel to Lourdes to have her crippled leg healed, and eventually be canonized as a saint, Lily instead goes on a "hejira" that ends not in Mecca but New York. The path she follows is her mother's, and when she arrives at Rose's apartment, three "older ladies" recognize her at once, one of them saying aloud what the others are surely thinking: "That red-haired devil who ruined our Miss Rose has come back to life as a shrunk-down raggedy cripple" (p. 486). While Rose does initially look at Lily as if she were a ghost, and address her as "Kathleen," this uncanny effect is but momentary. Indeed, it is Lily's presence that allows Rose to acknowledge what happened so long ago, and convinces her of Kathleen's death. Uncertainty is thus resolved for Rose, even as it was for Lily when she came to know the truth about Ambrose, and a story that has been suspended in time now moves forward again.

Even as Lily's life is a story of lost doubles that must be recovered, so is Anthony's. He is the child of the mixed-race coupling of Frances and Leo, and so embodies a double cultural heritage of which he knows nothing. Mercedes sends him off to an orphanage for black children the moment he is born, telling everyone he has died, and then at the end of her life – regretting that she excluded him from the family – leaves him instructions for finding Lily and Rose in New York. He does as she asks, and the final scene of the novel shows us Lily, Leo, and Rose sitting together, looking at a family tree and sorting out their connections to each other. They are the product of true gothic horrors – rape, incest, terrifying violence – and yet in discovering, acknowledging, and choosing to maintain those connections, they will find another way to go on. Significant here is the fact that Anthony is an ethnomusicologist. Where Kathleen and Rose both made music that seemed effortlessly to break down boundaries between people, taking them for a time out of the punishing realities of their lives, Anthony will understand that these transports were not effortless. He will understand the multiple contexts that produced such transports, and he will understand that such knowledge is a power of its own. Anthony – like Lily, and like Macdonald herself – will see that the embrace and encouragement of such plurality is itself the answer to the problem of the gothic.

Coda

Criticism of the Gothic

C riticism of the gothic has over the last several years become almost overwhelming. Books, articles, even a journal titled *Gothic Studies* attest to the
genre's seemingly irresistible appeal within the field of literary study, yet
the path to academic legitimacy was long in the making. While gothic writing
began to attract serious critical attention as early as the 1920s, it was not until
the 1970s – when the very meaning of literary study was changing dramatically,
and when feminist criticism in particular was reshaping the literary canon – that
gothic took center stage.

That criticism of the gothic came of age in the 1970s makes sense given what
was happening both outside and inside the academy. As the women's movement
and the civil rights movement were changing the very structure of American
society, college and university curricula, the nature of academic inquiry, and even
what counts as knowledge were changing as well. Jonathan Culler contextualizes these developments in American education, noting that they were facilitated
by both the vast growth in "the scale and structure" of American universities
from 1920 to 1970 and the upheaval that characterized so many campuses toward
the end of this period. "In retrospect," writes Culler, "it seems possible to argue
that student protest movements, which energized and disrupted universities in
the 1960s, had the effect of disturbing a stable order and weakening the pre-
sumption of departmental control, so that when new critical and methodologi-
cal possibilities emerged, as they very shortly did, they could be more easily
introduced into teaching" (1988: 25).

What kinds of changes took place? Culler notes the emergence of entire new programs and departments – women's studies, black studies, comparative literature – that challenged the discipline-based structure that had been the norm. Even within traditional disciplines, what was taught and how it was taught started to change considerably. In English departments, for example, authors and subjects that had formerly been excluded from study – women writers and writers of color among them – started to make their way into course reading lists. As what was read started to change, so too did ways of reading. Culler has traced the development of literary criticism over the course of the twentieth century, from its beginnings as an exercise in history-writing and philology above all, through the decades of the "new criticism" with its focus on the rhetorical nuances of texts rather than contexts, to the changes that began in the 1970s and have not stopped yet. At that point, he notes, literary criticism began to draw on "various theoretical perspectives and discourses: linguistics, psychoanalysis, feminism, Marxism, structuralism, deconstruction" (1988: 15), transforming itself into the field now generally called "theory." And what is "theory"? It is, says Culler, "the discourse that results when conceptions of the nature and meaning of texts and their relations to other discourses, social practices and human subjects become the object of general reflection" (1988: 22). In other words, it is any one of many modes of analysis that let us come to terms with how meaning is generated in literary and non-literary texts alike (1988: 15 – 25). All of this movement has been reflected in the single sub-field of gothic criticism, as critics have brought to bear on this literature, which itself consistently challenges established norms, everything that late twentieth-century literary theory had to offer. My purpose here is not to account for all of that criticism, but to outline the major forms that it has taken and provide a guide through some of the work that has been done.

Criticism of the gothic up to 1970 provides a further and important context for understanding what has been written since then. As early as the 1920s, Edith Birkhead's *The Tale of Terror: A Study of the Gothic Romance* (1921) traced the development of gothic from biblical stories through its development in England and America, while Eino Railo's *The Haunted Castle: A Study of the Elements of English Romanticism* (1927) detailed sources for and influences on specific gothic motifs. These histories are still instructive, even as they themselves invite rhetorical analysis. Both authors imagine the history of the gothic as gendered. Birkhead portrays Walpole as the father of the tradition, whose work "did not fall fruitless on the earth" (1921: 21), while "Mrs. Radcliffe . . . with her attractive store of mysteries" emerges as a seductive but also nurturing mother who "probably . . . saved the Gothic tale from an early death" (1921: 38). Similarly, Railo casts Walpole as father of the genre, albeit a father who "attempted to hide his paternity" until "assured of [his work's] success" (1927: 6), while he credits Clara Reeve with being the one who, "[i]nto the framework supplied by Walpole . . . pours the first leavening of female sensitivity" (1927: 8). Radcliffe is in his eyes the acme of the gothic tradition to this point – the only one of the authors mentioned so far to have any real understanding of the romanticism toward which gothic novels supposedly aim (1927: 15) – and presumably an amalgam of the male and female principles represented by Walpole and Reeve.

One wonders if these stories of male fertility and female nurture do not serve in part to contain the complicated accounts of gender formation that we see in the novels themselves, which seem to have at once fascinated and repelled both critics. Birkhead observes that "Mrs. Radcliffe's skeletons are decently concealed in the family cupboard," while "Lewis's stalk abroad in shameless publicity" (1921: 64), and Railo sharpens this critique into a diagnosis when he studies Lewis's "interest . . . in depicting an eroticism bordering on bestiality" and finds in his work "fruits of inflamed, neurasthenic, sexual visions, of a pathological psychology which betrays, unknown perhaps to the writer himself, an abnormal trait in his composition" (1927: 280). Certainly over the next three decades, the major critics of the gothic took it as their task to contain or render acceptable this literature that seemed in so many ways unacceptable. J. M. S. Tompkins' study of *The Popular Novel in England* (1932) argues in its preface for the importance of reading "tenth-rate fiction" in order to understand the sources of the "pleasure" it gave its first readers, and offers chapters on women writers, romance, and the gothic that even now are invaluable. Mario Praz's *The Romantic Agony* studies "the education of sensibility, and more especially of erotic sensibility" (1933: xi) in Romantic literature, including gothic, seeing in it not the pathology of the author but "a distorted image of characteristics common to all mankind" (1933: viii). Montague Summers's *The Gothic Quest* argues that the "gothic quest" has to do with "the spiritual as well as the literary and artistic seeking for beauty" (1938: 398), as does Devendra Varma's later study, *The Gothic Flame* (1957).

The emergence of feminist literary scholarship in the 1970s changed the criticism of gothic completely. The appearance of studies such as Patricia Meyer Spacks's *The Female Imagination* (1972), Ellen Moers's *Literary Women* (1976), Elaine Showalter's *A Literature of Their Own: British Women Novelists from Brontë to Lessing* (1977), and Sandra M. Gilbert and Susan Gubar's *The Madwoman in the Attic* (1979) did much both to legitimize the study of women's writing as a distinct subject, and to formulate ways of understanding it. As others have noted, among these seminal studies, Moers and Gilbert and Gubar have particular importance for the study of gothic.

Moers's work stands out for identifying the "female gothic" as a distinct subgenre that gives voice to women's fears of themselves. Moers builds her case partly around a discussion of *Frankenstein*, reading the novel as a "birth myth" that replaced cultural stereotypes of maternal bliss with a portrait of "revulsion against newborn life, and the drama of guilt, dread, and flight surrounding birth and its consequences" that for Moers is the "most interesting, most powerful, and most feminine" aspect of Shelley's novel (1976: 92–3). This analysis moves far beyond the conventional ideas of gender that informed those early studies by Birkhead and Railo, and yet – while Moers is too sophisticated to reduce women to their bodies alone – this reading does risk essentializing women. Gilbert and Gubar's *Madwoman in the Attic* allays this anxiety in its focus on women's cultural experiences. Taking their title from the figure of Bertha Mason in Charlotte Brontë's *Jane Eyre*, they give gothic fiction figurative pride of place in their study, and the novel becomes an emblem for their reading of the "female impulse to struggle free from social and literary confinement through strategic redefinitions of self, art, and society" (1979: xii). Juliann Fleenor's essay collection *Female Gothic* (1983) stretches definitions of female gothic still farther, including essays on women writers from the eighteenth through the twentieth centuries, and from Africa, Australia, Britain, Canada, and the United States. Nearly ten years later, Tamar Heller's *Dead Secrets: Wilkie Collins and the Female Gothic* (1992) demonstrates how this male writer uses female gothic "to write narratives about forms of power and authority – literary, familial, political – in Victorian culture" (1992: 9), while Diane Long Hoeveler's *Gothic Feminism: The Professionalization of Gender from Charlotte Smith to the Brontës* (1998) argues for gothic novels as texts that do not so much reflect the experience of women as teach them how to become properly feminized. When female gothic is understood as a cultural form that can be taught to both men and women, we have come as far from that early threat of essentialism as we can possibly get.

While "female gothic" quickly became an established critical category, criticism has not opened out into the hard and fast vision of "female" and "male" gothic traditions that one might have expected. Instead what we have seen are robust considerations of gothic that coalesce around specific issues and methodologies, making overarching arguments that often include consideration of the relationship between gender and genre (Miles (1993 and 1995), Ellis (2001), Williams (1995), and Kilgour (1995), for example, all discuss in some way the notions of "male" and "female" gothic). Among the most persistent approaches to the gothic are those that consider the genre's interest in the shaping of individual subjectivity, and while critics have addressed gothic from a number of perspectives, those of the past thirty years or so tend to have in common the recognition that identity is discursively constructed.

Among the earliest of these studies is Eve Kosofsky Sedgwick's *The Coherence of Gothic Conventions*, which explores the relationship between gothic's major conventions and identity formation (1980: 25). Robert Miles's *Gothic Writing 1750–1820: A Genealogy* reads the genre as "a discursive site, a carnivalesque mode for representations of the fragmented subject" (1993: 4). Maggie Kilgour's *The Rise of the Gothic Novel* discusses the genre as inextricably entangled in its multiple literary sources, "a Frankenstein's monster, assembled out of the bits and pieces of the past" (1995: 4) that nonetheless longs to recover a lost "wholeness, in which individuals were defined as members of the 'body' politic" (1995: 11). Even psychoanalysis – which, as Kilgour points out, is not so much a tool for reading gothic as it is "itself a gothic, necromantic form, that resurrects our psychic pasts" (1995: 220) – has come to be seen as a way of coming to terms with gothic's interest in the shaping of identity through various discourses. Thus Michèle Massé's *In the Name of Love: Women, Masochism, and the Gothic* reads "masochism and the Gothic as mutually illuminative explications of women's pain" (1992: 2). Terry Castle's *The Female Thermometer* (1995) traces the "invention" of uncanny experience in such eighteenth-century texts as Radcliffe's *Mysteries of Udolpho*. And Susan Greenfield's *Mothering Daughters: Novels and the Politics of Family Romance, Frances Burney to Jane Austen* draws on psychoanalysis to discuss "novels by women about missing mothers and their suffering daughters" (2002: 13), making clear that her purpose is "not to show that the novels affirm psychoanalysis but rather to suggest that they anticipate and help shape it" (2002: 19).

Related to this work on the discursive construction of identity is the range of research that has emerged in gender studies, gay and lesbian studies, the history of sexuality, and queer theory. Eve Kosofsky Sedgwick is again primary here. Her *Between Men: English Literature and Male Homosocial Desire* (1985) did crucial work in reading gothic fiction as a sign of a "homosexual panic" that targeted all men as potential victims of a homophobic society and thereby ensured that heterosexual relations would remain the norm. This work on the way that social organization shapes sexual identities and desires has a counterpart in the seemingly very different work on sensibility that began to emerge at about the same time as *Between Men*. From Coral Ann Howells's *Love, Mystery, and Misery: Feeling in Gothic Fiction* (1978), sensibility studies have steadily and inevitably opened out into studies of gender and sexuality. Recent work includes Claudia Johnson's *Equivocal Beings: Politics, Gender, and Sentimentality in the 1790s – Wollstonecraft, Radcliffe, Burney, Austen* (1995), which explores the male appropriation of sentimental discourse in the 1790s, as well as George Haggerty's *Unnatural Affections: Women and Fiction in the Later Eighteenth Century* (1998) and *Men in Love: Masculinity and Sexuality in the Eighteenth Century* (1999), which have focused sustained attention on same-sex relations in gothic fiction and other literature. Work on the body is also related to this early interest in sensibility: recent work includes Steven Bruhm's *Gothic Bodies: The Politics of Pain in Romantic Fiction* (1994) and Judith Halberstam's *Skin Shows: Gothic Horror and the Technology of Monsters* (1995).

As criticism has engaged with gothic's construction of subjectivity, gender, and sexuality, so too has it engaged with the related question of the genre's contribution to discussions of class, nation, and race. David Punter's major study, *The Literature of Terror* (1981), develops a reading of gothic tradition grounded in what Punter describes as "an underlying historical materialism" (1981: vol. 1, p. vii), and Kate Ellis's *The Contested Castle* (1989) examines the historical moment in which gothic emerged as a major genre, "investigat[ing] the relationship between . . . two epiphenomena of middle-class culture: the idealization of the home and the popularity of the Gothic" (Ellis 1989: ix–x, xvi). Issues of national identity come into focus in Ronald Paulson's *Representations of Revolution* (1983) and its discussion of English and Spanish responses to the French Revolution. In the 1990s, Ian Duncan's *Modern Romance and Transformations of the Novel: The Gothic, Scott, Dickens* (1992) charted the relationship between the genre of gothic romance and national identity, while Cannon Schmitt's *Alien Nation: Nineteenth-Century Gothic Fictions and English Nationality* argued that "Gothics pose as semi-ethnographic texts in their representation of Catholic, Continental Europe or the Far East as fundamentally un-English, the site of depravity," even as "a notion of Englishness is constructed in the novels" (1997: 2). Patrick Brantlinger's *Rule of Darkness: British Literature and Imperialism, 1830–1914* (1988) turned attention from questions of nation to questions of empire with a crucial chapter on "Imperial Gothic" that opened a path or inquiry for other writers. Gayatri Spivak's essay "Three Women's Texts and a Critique of Imperialism" (1985) offered crucial readings of *Jane Eyre* and *Frankenstein* that also paved the way for further work. Katie Trumpener's *Bardic Nationalism: The Romantic Novel and the British Empire* (1997) also provides both a broad and a deep context within which to read gothic fiction, which she discusses at various points. The recent essay collection *Empire and the Gothic: The Politics of the Genre*, edited by Andrew Smith and William Hughes (2003), draws on texts from the eighteenth, nineteenth, and twentieth centuries (it reaches as far forward as Salman Rushdie, Arundhati Roy, and J. M. Coetzee).

Finally, critical interest in the related questions of gothic aesthetics and the reception of the gothic has also gained momentum over the past twenty years. George Haggerty's *Gothic Fiction/Gothic Form* reads Gothic as an "affective form" designed to "elicit particular responses in the reader"(1989: 9). Rereadings of the genre's engagement with the sublime also interest themselves in affective responses to aesthetic experience, beginning with David Morris's essay "Gothic Sublimity" (1985), followed by sections of Anne K. Mellor's *Romanticism and Gender* (1988), Frances Ferguson's *Solitude and the Sublime* (1992), Vijay Mishra's *The Gothic Sublime* (1994), and Andrew Smith's *Gothic Radicalism: Literature, Philosophy and Psychoanalysis in the Nineteenth Century* (2000). E. J. Clery's *The Rise of Supernatural Fiction 1762–1800* (1995) has demonstrated how late eighteenth-century British culture created the vogue for a literature of terror. James Watt's

Contesting the Gothic: Fiction, Genre and Cultural Conflict 1764–1832 reads the gothic as a "category" whose retrospective coherence is belied by both "the diversity" of the works so classified and by "the antagonistic relations that existed between different works or writers" (1999: 1). Michael Gamer's *Romanticism and the Gothic: Genre, Reception and Canon Formation* argues that "the reception of gothic writing – its institutional and commercial recognition as a kind of literature – played a fundamental role in shaping many of the ideological assumptions about high culture that we have come to associate with 'romanticism'" (2000: 2). Finally, David Richter's *The Progress of Romance: Literary Historiography and the Gothic Novel* (1996) offers both a history of the gothic, and a discussion of gothic's relationship to history, as does Markman Ellis's more recent study *The Gothic Tradition* (2001).

So where are we now? Enough has been written on gothic fiction over the past thirty years to make one wonder if there is anything left to say. To that question the answer must be "Yes." Even as the university is both "the transmitter of a cultural heritage" and "a site for the production of knowledge" (Culler 1988: 33), so literary critics work to resurrect, preserve, and pass on literary traditions, and at the same to shape fresh readings of them. The "meaning" of a gothic novel (or of any other work of literature) will in important ways remain constant over time, and yet that "meaning" will change too. Stories will resonate differently in different historical moments, and for different readers. And so I end where I began, asking my readers to return to my opening questions, and to consider how their answers to those questions derive from the texts themselves, from the work of other scholars, and from their own learning and experience. It is the conversation among all three that will take us forward.

Notes

Introduction

1 Walpole's novel appeared on Christmas Eve 1764, though it bore the publication date 1765.

Chapter 1: Patriarchal Narratives

1 In a very different approach from mine, Anne Williams (1995: 21–2) argues that gothic takes the patriarchal family as its central myth.

2 For this section of my argument, I am greatly indebted to Laura Rosenthal, who initially directed me to Pateman's work. Rosenthal (1996) also discusses Filmer, Locke, and Pateman, and while I did not read her work until after I had written a version of the argument presented her, her readings of these texts complement and have helped to shape mine.

3 While the *Patriarcha* was published in 1680, this was 27 years after Filmer's death and perhaps 50 or more years after it was written. Composition of the text has been dated back to the 1640s, the 1630s, and (in the case of the first two chapters) the 1620s. See Sommerville's discussion of "The Authorship and Dating of Some Works Attributed to Filmer" in Filmer 1991: xxxii–xxxiv.

4 Pateman here builds on the work of Gordon Schochet's *Patriarchalism in Political Thought*.

5 For another perspective on the continuities and changes in early modern patriarchal society, see McKeon (1995).

6 Page references below are to *The Castle of Otranto*, ed. W. S. Lewis (Oxford, 1982); *The Old English Baron*, ed. James Rainer (Oxford, 1967).

7 For a reading of the sexual politics of this scene, and a reading that focuses generally on the sexual violence in the novel, see Haggerty 1999: 160–5.

8 Duncan (1992: 32) discusses his literalization of Alfonso's ghost as a "reduction of meaning and a failure of sublimity" that reveals the "insatiable yet hollow automatism of the patriarchal will, futilely craving a lost, original and absolute state, and complemented by passive or fugitive, feminine (though not always female) victims". Morris (1985: 311) makes an opposing argument.

9 In a reading that complements mine, E. J. Clery (2000: 31) characterizes Reeve's vocabulary as a mix of the "marvellous" (which stimulates the "strongest" and most "inward-directed" passions), the "probable" (which "makes the marvellous modern and palpable"), and the "sentimental" (which "facilitates the moral redemption of the passions, reorientating the narrative towards social integration").

10 This account of the origin of *The Castle of Otranto* comes from a letter Walpole wrote to the Revd William Cole on Mar. 9, 1765, and is cited by W. S. Lewis in his introduction to the edition of the novel quoted throughout this book.

11 For an extended treatment of the role of dreams in gothic novels, see Doody 1977. For the possibility that Reeve's use of dreams creates not realistic but uncanny effects see Haggerty 1998: 57.

12 Sedgwick's work is more complex than I can do justice to here. The ideas I discuss here Sedgwick relates particularly to Heidi Hartmann's discussion of patriarchy as "relations between men, which have a material base, and which, though hierarchical, establish or create interdependence and solidarity among men that enable them to dominate women" (cited in Sedgwick 1985: 3) and René Girard's discussion of erotic triangles as structures in which "the bond that links the two rivals is as intense and potent as the bond that links either of the rivals to the beloved" (1985: 21). See her introduction and ch. 1 for more on these ideas, and chs. 5 and 6 for readings of the gothic.

13 Haggerty (1998: 57–8) offers an interesting reading of Edmund's relationship with Harclay that stresses its eroticism.

14 Haggerty (1998: 58) reads her emphasis on "this *male* quality of the Gothic world" as evidence that she "may be mocking male relations at the same time that she seems to celebrate them."

15 Page references are to *The Recess*, ed. April Alliston (Lexington, 2000).

16 Cf. Clery (2000: 44), who argues that Lee's "innovation" was to use "the memoir form . . . primarily as a showcase and medium for the passions."

17 Lee was criticized for writing a history of Elizabeth and Mary that was in many ways not true to fact. Alliston (2000: xvii–xviii) notes that eighteenth-century writers distinguished between "two different kinds of historical truth: that of 'incident' (or plot) and that of character." She goes on to say that character was regarded as primary and determinative of incident, and thus – while Lee's novel did indeed diverge from standard eighteenth-century histories of Elizabeth and Mary in various ways – she nonetheless conformed to the practice of historical writers in emphasizing character above all in her writing.

18 For more on the relevance of the Gordon Riots to Lee's novel, see Clery 2000: 40–1.

19 For a sophisticated reading of Mary Stuart's legacy to her daughters, see Alliston 1990. Her argument that Mary – like all mothers in gothic novels – leaves her daughters "an education in virtue and the story of the mother's death" (1990: 112) emphasizes that this is all women can leave to their daughters. Ironically, this inheritance guarantees their continued compliance with – and so exclusion from – patriarchal societies that pass inheritances from father to son.

20 For more on communities of women in the novel see Isaac 1996, who argues that the enmity of Mary and Elizabeth is countered by the loving relationship of Matilda and Ellinor, both of whom she reads as consistently supported by the relationships with women. See also Haggerty (1998: 69), who sees this novel as one that "celebrates women-centered affection and eroticizes maternal relations with unswerving flair."

21 Doody has described this space as "a combined palace and prison, womb and grave" (1977: 555), while Haggerty reads it as not only "womblike" (1998: 66), but "equivalent . . . to female desire itself" (1998: 70).

22 As Alliston notes, the historical Lady Jane and her husband had at one point reigned for nine days (Lee 2000: 345 n. 17).

23 English–French rivalry was all the more fierce because the half-French Mary Queen of Scots had been seen as a means by which the French could gain power in England. English–Spanish rivalry had turned partly on Spanish efforts to conquer England, most notably in the Armada of 1588.

24 Thanks to my students at Barnard College, without whose help I might not have arrived at this reading.

25 Cf. Isaac, who comments on Lee's "paternalistic" portrait of Anana, but notes that "Lee is certainly progressive in her conviction that female friendships can bridge the gaps of race, class, and culture" (1996: 214).

26 Alliston (1990: 119) notes that she is the "primary (and so perforce more unambiguously) virtuous heroine."

27 Cf. Doody, who comments that the sisters "lead in a sense the life of phantoms – they cannot be real, they must not be known. They are the mystery of this gothic novel . . ." (1977: 555).

Chapter 2: The Aesthetic of the Sublime

1 For more on eighteenth-century interest in the sublime, see Ashfield and de Bolla 1996. For arguments that gothic literature is characterized by a distinctively "gothic sublime" that revises other forms of the sublime in a variety of ways, see Morris (1985), Mishra (1994), and A. Smith (2000).

2 Cf. Mellor (1993: 87), who comments that Burke's sublime focuses on psychological experience, while Kant's is an epistemology.

3 Indeed, Ferguson argues that Burke theorizes the sublime as an experience so well controlled that it is self-negating. While noting that "[w]ithout the distancing of death, there wouldn't, of course, be much to talk about," she sees the possibility that

"repeated exposure to the sublime may annihilate it altogether." As she elaborates, "[t]he sublime . . . dwindles as soon as familiarity converts the necessary distance of danger and death into an absolute banishment of those dreads" (Ferguson 1992: 46).

4 My current thinking about sublimity and difference draws on some of own previous work (Heiland 1992, 1997), and originated in conversations with Heather Weidemann. For related work on this subject, also see Mellor (1993: 88), who notes that "[i]n Kant's formulation of the sublime, corporeal distinctions – of sex, race, age, physical abilities – vanish. In his quest for pure reason, Kant erases the body, and hence the female, altogether." Finally, Bronfen (1992) also offers a sophisticated study of the connections between "death, femininity and the aesthetic" (to quote the subtitle of her book) that begins from the premise that "[f]emininity and death cause a disorder to stability, mark moments of ambivalence, disruption or duplicity" – a premise that complements my argument about gender and the sublime – and then goes on to show how "their eradication produces a recuperation of order, a return to stability" (p. xii).

5 Page references below are to *The Monk*, ed. Howard Anderson (Oxford, 1980); *Zofloya*, ed. Adriana Craciun (Peterborough, Ont., 1997); *Melmoth the Wanderer*, ed. Douglas Grant (Oxford, 1989).

6 For more on Lewis's revelatory strategies, especially in relation to Radcliffe, see Kilgour (1995: pt. III).

7 Hoeveler also cites this passage in her reading of Victoria as a "defective aristocrat" (1998: 146).

8 My understanding of Victoria's relationship with her mother, and with Dacre's creation of Victoria more generally, owes a great deal to the work of my student Kristen Roupenian.

9 Craciun implicitly makes this same observation when she notices that Victoria grows "larger and more masculine," as well as "darker," over the course of the novel (1997: 18).

10 Roupenian developed this idea in an unpublished paper and other work that she did for my Spring 2003 class on "Eighteenth-Century Gothic" at Barnard College. Hoeveler reads this scene in different but complementary terms, reading Victoria and Lilla as "inveterate enemies." Noticing that they struggle not for possession of a "castle" (as Radcliffe's heroines did – see ch. 3 below), and that Victoria even rids herself of a husband with considerable property "in order to sexually pursue the younger son, who has no wealth or estates in his own right," she too sees the scene as focused on a "sexual passion" that is "threatening to a culture that is predicated on their sexual discipline and control" (Hoeveler 1998: 154).

11 Developing a reading of the novel's specifically Irish politics, Backus notes that Biddy Branigan is a native Irishwoman who is to an extent opposed to the Anglo-Irish Melmoth family, though "[h]er immersion in the Irish oral tradition renders her largely impervious to hegemonic revisions of history." In other words, her sense of history has not been affected by the English presence in Ireland, and so she "is the only one who can tell Melmoth the story of his family's history" (Backus 1999: 113).

12 On the connection between the "unspeakable" and homosexuality in gothic fiction, see Sedgwick (1985), on which Backus draws in her reading of this scene.

13 Lydon (1988: 278–81) discusses the rebellion, noting that its leader Robert Emmet "has passed into Irish romantic folklore," while "his rebellion, while admired for its daring and bravery, has commonly been dismissed as foolhardy and little more than a farce in its execution" (1988: 279).

Chapter 3: Rethinking the Sublime

1 Letter to the George Keatses, Feb. 14, 1819 (Rollins 1958: 2. 62).

2 DeLamotte cites the *Critical Review* from Maurice Lévy, *Le Roman "gothique" anglais, 1764–1824*, series A 9 (Toulouse: Association des Publications de la Faculté des Lettres et Sciences Humaines de Toulouse, 1968), p. 51.

3 This statement grows out of Claire Kahane's more general contention that all gothic novels are really about this separation of the daughter from the mother (Kahane 1985).

4 Cf. Mellor, who reads Radcliffe as "displacing the horror of the Burkean sublime from nature into the home," and then "construct[ing] an alternative, more positive representation of the sublime" that is based in "a recognition of the *distance* of the perceiving self from the other" (1993: 94–5). Also of interest here is the work of De LaMotte (1990), whose reading of gothic fiction is structured around the genre's "anxiety" (p. viii) about the boundaries of the self, especially as those boundaries pertain to women. Kilgour (1995) also offers an interesting and very different perspective on the question of gender and difference. Her discussion of *The Mysteries of Udolpho* argues in part that Radcliffe sees individuals as threats to community, and that this anti-individualist stance helps explain why "the narrative seems to work towards a total identification of all women" with each other. That said, Kilgour demonstrates that "total identification" is something Radcliffe finally avoids, "distinguishing" her female characters from each other to a degree, though only to show the ways in which women are "opposed, gothic doubles of each other, bound in a sadomasochistic chain" (1995: 127–8).

5 Page references below are to *A Sicilian Romance*, ed. Alison Milbank (Oxford, 1993); *The Italian*, ed. Frederick Garber (Oxford, 1981).

6 Miles makes a related point when he discusses the importance of "thresholds" in Radcliffe, noting that if the "threshold is Radcliffe's recurring image, her recurring theme is women's subjection to 'impossible' choices" (1995: 96).

7 On the pre-Oedipal sublime, see Weiskel (1986), Hertz (1985), and Yaeger (1989). On the pre-Oedipal dynamic as central to definitions of the mother–daughter relationships in Radcliffe and other eighteenth-century novelists, see Greenfield (2002). Kahane (1985) also writes about the mother–daughter relationship at the heart of the gothic, insisting on the need for the daughter to separate from the mother.

8   This discussion of the female sublime began as part of a paper entitled "Forms of the Sublime in Jeanette Winterson's *Sexing the Cherry,*" delivered at the Apr. 1996 meeting of the American Society for Eighteenth-Century Studies.

9   Page references below are to *Romance of the Forest,* ed. Chloe Chard (Oxford, 1986); *The Mysteries of Udolpho,* ed. Bonamy Dobrée (Oxford, 1980).

10 Johnson (1995: 118) discusses the violence encoded in the sublime landscapes of *The Italian.*

11 Chloe Chard notes the connection to Rousseau in her notes to the Oxford edition of the novel, citing specifically the fact that the figure of La Luc is modelled on that of the Savoyard Vicar in Rousseau's *émile* (Radcliffe 1986: 385).

12 Here I am indebted to my former student Alexa Blasdel, who discussed with me her understanding of how Adeline and Theodore essentially switch roles half-way through the novel.

13 The links between the sublime landscapes and Montoni himself have been noticed by other critics. DeLamotte comments that Montoni's name "suggests that his personality extends beyond his castle to encompass the mountains landscape itself" (DeLamotte 1990: 119). Kilgour (1995) notes that Montoni's name "makes his generic plot function clear: he is to play the role of the forbidding father who keeps the lovers apart, just as the Alps do in Emily's imagination," though she complicates this easy equation of the landscape with the man when she notes that mountains also "offer protection and shelter" at various points in the text (Kilgour 1995: 119).

14 For an extended discussion of Radcliffe's use of the "explained supernatural" in this novel and more generally, see Miles (1995: 129–48) and Castle (1995).

15 Poovey (1979: 324) discusses Valancourt's susceptibility to "the charms of the salons and the temptations of the gaming table."

16 Kilgour (1995: 137) argues from a complementary perspective that the novel's "surface focus on revealing the identity of her mother conceals another concern with the role of the father."

17 Working with slightly different material, Kilgour (1995: 136) also notes that Emily's story concludes with her "recover[ing] some, though not all, of what she has lost," and comments particularly on the fact that she is reassured to learn that her father and mother – though deceased – "are still her parents after all."

Chapter 4: From the Sublime to the Uncanny

1   In addition to Bloom (1982), see Morris (1985), Mishra (1994) and A. Smith (2000), who offer extended discussions of the relationship between the sublime and the uncanny.

2   My former student Evangelia (Angela) Mazaris wrote a paper on Freud, Hoffman, and Olympia that helped my own thinking on this subject.

3   Page references below are *Enquiry Concerning Political Justice,* ed. Isaac Kramnick (Harmondsworth, 1976); *Caleb Williams,* ed. Maurice Hindle (London, 1988); *A Vindication of the Rights of Woman,* ed. Miriam Brody Kramnick (Harmondsworth, 1975).

4   For more on this, see Graham 1984: 47–59, esp. pp. 50–1.

5   On Godwin's use of the sublime, see Ferguson (1992), Fludernik (2001), Kaufman (1997), and Mishra (1994).

6   Kilgour expands on this idea, noting that "Caleb and Falkland are . . . a complex conflation of the relations of master/slave, father/son, hero/worshipper, and copy/imitator. They are even husband and wife . . ." (1995: 63). She comments further: "In its confusion of opposites, the relation between Caleb and Falkland has often been read as a prototype for the gothic double" (1995: 63).

7   Many critics have commented on the erotic aspects of Caleb's relationship with Falkland, but the best essay on this subject is still Alex Gold's "It's Only Love: The Politics of Passion in Godwin's *Caleb Williams*" (1977). Gold frames his reading in terms of Godwin's understanding of love as "the product of repressive social institutions and the enemy of equality, independence, and harmony" (1997: 137).

8   On Caleb's paranoia, see von Mücke (1996).

9   This reading is indebted to that of Peter Logan (1997), who reads Caleb's "nervous narrative" as a chronicle of the oppressive social conditions that produce this very nervousness. The paradox here is that nervous narrators cannot also be credible narrators – the disease they seek to document undermines their authority, or, in the terms I've been using, sensibility signifies gothic entrapment but does not offer a way out of it. Logan argues that escape demands leaving sensibility behind, as Caleb does when – in the novel's original ending – he repents his past conduct and speaks in Falkland's favor. Logan further complicates his argument when he notes that, for Godwin, sensibility is gendered feminine, while reason is gendered masculine. To leave sensibility behind is also to leave women behind – an all too familiar way of resolving the problem of gothic, if that is how Godwin resolves it.

10   Page references are to *Northanger Abbey*, ed. Marilyn Butler (London, 1995).

11   For two quite different readings of how Godwin's editing shapes Wollstonecraft's prose, see O'Quinn (1997) and Rajan (2000). Page references are to *Maria*, ed. Gary Kelly (Oxford, 1976).

12   On the politics of Maria's imprisonment, see Heller (1992); on Maria's captivity by the ideology of sensibility, see Poovey (1984); on the limits of imaginative escape, see Kilgour (1995).

13   I discuss in the next paragraph the same passages that O'Quinn does, building a reading that would not have been evident to me had I not read his argument.

14   Kilgour also describes this "vicious circle of domination, which, from a female perspective, reworks most closely the major concerns with class oppression and the lot of the servant from *Caleb Williams*" (1995: 83).

Chapter 5: Uncanny Monsters

1   Page references are to *Frankenstein*, ed. Marilyn Butler (Oxford, 1994).

2   Cf. Marie-Hélène Huet, who reads the novel as "a tale of disrupted filiation, a story grounded in the belief that it is sacrilegious to give birth when death surrounds us,"

and argues further that the novel's concentrically structured narratives constitute "a literal reproduction of the theory of *emboîtement* or *encasement*, the theory that posited that all future generations were contained in the seed of our first parents and that there would come a time when the last man or woman would be born" (1993: 142–3).

3   Mellor does not read the scene as incestuous, but does argue forcefully that "at every level Victor Frankenstein is engaged upon a rape of nature, a violent penetration and usurpation of the female's 'hiding places,' of the womb" (1988: 226).

4   For a reading that questions the monster's identification as an uncanny figure, see Gigante 2000: 567. Where Gigante reads the uncanny as the product of "childhood fixation" that seems to affect one person only, I rely on Freud's statement that the uncanny can also stem from a larger cultural repression that one must assume potentially affects the culture as a whole.

5   For complementary and more complex readings of the monster in relation to eighteenth-century thinking about sensibility, and especially in relation to Rousseau, see Marshall (1988), ch. 6.

6   My work on vampires began with a paper called "Anne Rice and the Enlightenment Vampire," presented at the 1993 Annual Meeting of the American Society for Eighteenth-Century Studies, a small part of which I repeat here.

7   Page references are to *The Vampyre*, ed. Robert Morrison and Chris Baldick (Oxford, 1997).

8   This work was attributed to Thomas Preskett Prest until the 1970s, but at this point Rymer's authorship is agreed on (Auerbach 1995: 27).

Chapter 6:   Confronting the Uncanny

1   Significantly, the three sisters published under male pseudonyms: Anne was Acton Bell, Emily was Ellis Bell, and Charlotte was Currer Bell. For more on their decision to publish under these names, see the "Biographical Notice of Ellis and Acton Bell" that Charlotte Brontë – still signing herself "Currer Bell" – wrote for the second edition of *Wuthering Heights*. That "Notice" appears in the edition cited throughout this book – *Wuthering Heights*, ed. Pauline Nestor (London, 1995) – and is discussed in Nestor's editorial notes (see p. 339). In the same discussion, Nestor also directs attention to Charlotte Brontë's preface to the third edition of *Jane Eyre*; this "Note" is also included in the edition cited throughout this book: *Jane Eyre*, ed. Q. D. Leavis (London, 1966).

2   Other critics have also discussed "home" as a central issue in the gothic. Ellis (1989) argues that "home" is at once safe space for women and a place of imprisonment; Kahane (1985) reads the homes in gothic novels as maternal spaces that threaten to engulf the heroine if she does not leave them; Fay (1988) grounds her discussion of the gothic in what she calls "home politics," by which she means the dynamic by which the domestic and political spheres interact (1988: 110).

3   For different perspectives on the nature of the Brontës' engagement with gothic tradition, see Heilman (1971) and Homans (1986), the latter of which focuses particu-

larly on questions of gender. In a study of ways in which nineteenth-century fiction explores women's relation to language, Homans argues that the Brontës' interest in gothic stems from the genre's engagement with the "literal" (and feminine) rather than "figurative" (and masculine). Working from the premise that gothic in general "literalizes the romantic imagination" (which is "predominantly masculine"), and noting further that "literalization is precisely what female figures embody in romantic myth," she reads the sisters' version of gothic as one that "both acknowledges and protests" this association of women with the literal (1986: 86).

4 For a different perspective on this "Preface," see Drew (1964).

5 Stevenson also discusses Heathcliff as a figure "alienated" from the environment of Wuthering Heights (1988: 67). Commenting on this passage specifically, he notes that Heathcliff "does not fit his 'abode,' but neither do his 'dress and manners' fit his looks," and goes on to argue that Heathcliff's "indeterminate origins" do not mean "that he is free to define himself, but that every character he comes in contact with (and every reader) is forced to mark him with a meaning they give" (1988: 69–70).

6 Kate Ellis comments interestingly on how the Earnshaw children defend themselves against Heathcliff (1989: 210–13).

7 Stevenson works from these passages as well, arguing not that Cathy is in danger of losing herself in Heathcliff, but that he is in danger of being overwhelmed by her. Their "likeness" comes from what Cathy projects on to him. His argument about likeness and difference opens out into a discussion framed by insights from anthropology about the need to find a mate who is "different from the family, but like the group" (1988: 73). He reads Heathcliff as both "brother and other" (1988: 75) and a figure that upsets the expected relationship with Edgar.

8 See also Stevenson (1988) and Ellis (1989) on this passage.

9 Building on her reading of the novel's relation to British imperialism, Meyer (1996: 122–3) offers a still more tempered reading of the novel's conclusion than mine, reading the "domestic bliss of the Cathy/Hareton ending" as ironic.

10 Homans notes that "*Jane Eyre* was begun just a few months after the completion of *Wuthering Heights*," and that "the sisters read their ongoing work aloud to each other" (1986: 299).

11 This reading complements existing criticism. Key reference points include Ruth Bernard Yeazell (1979), who argues that Jane's desire for love works in conjunction with her desire for independence to make possible her final return to Rochester. More recently, Massé (1992) has argued for Jane's escape from the gothic patterning of her life on the basis of Jane's refusal to equate love with the suffering inflicted by authority.

12 Bronfen (1992: 219–23) develops a reading of the novel that sits interestingly alongside mine. She sees Jane poised between the "liminal" figures of the spiritual Helen and the corporeal Bertha, and argues that they represent externalized forms of death over which Jane triumphs as she takes her place in masculine society. Homans's (1986: 84–99) reading of Jane's relationship to the "literal" and "figural" also speaks to the reading I develop here.

13 Here I disagree to some extent with Avery (1998), who argues that the gothic episodes in *Jane Eyre* are confined to the scenes at Gateshead and at Thornfield. While I would agree that these are the places where the traditional gothic trappings of ghosts and so forth are invoked, I wish to argue that the deeper dynamic of gothic fiction – focused as it is on the constitution of individual and especially female subjectivity in the face of pressures experienced as sublime, uncanny, or some variation thereof – structures the whole of the novel.

14 The reference here is to a pool whose waters would heal the first person to enter them after they had been troubled by an angel. See John 5: 2–9.

15 In addition to Gilbert and Gubar, see Yeazell, who reads "Bertha's insanity" as "a fit emblem of that chaotic disintegration of the self which Jane so deeply fears" (1979: 135).

16 Their whole chapter on *Jane Eyre* merits attention both for its excellence and for its status as a key feminist reading of the novel. On Bertha's relationship to Jane, see Gilbert and Gubar 1979: 359–62.

Chapter 7: The "Unhomely" Nation

1 On questions of national identity, see Schmitt (1997) and Trumpener (1997). On gothic and imperialism, see Brantlinger (1988), who was one of the first to open up this line of inquiry, as well as Trumpener, Meyer (1996), and Sharpe (1993).

2 Page references are to *The Old Manor House* (Oxford, 1969).

3 Bartolomeo (1993: 655–6) reads it as further evidence of Orlando's romanticism, but also as a sign of Smith's "canny self-consciousness that problematizes a romantic resolution which confers power of every kind upon the male hero."

4 Page references are to *Edgar Huntly*, ed. Norman S. Grabo (Harmondsworth, 1988).

5 Page references are to *Wieland*, ed. Jay Fliegelman (New York, 1991).

6 Barnes (2002) here builds explicitly on the work of Jay Fliegelman.

7 Barnes (2002) cites a related argument by Jane Tompkins, who sees Brown as "less concerned with loss than chaos. In her [Tompkins'] view, the absence of Wieland's father . . . contributes to Wieland's future collapse. In political terms, too much 'independence' is revealed by Brown to have 'horrifying consequences'" (2002: 53). Barnes draws from Tompkins' *Sensational Designs: The Cultural Work of American Fiction, 1790–1860* (New York: Oxford University Press, 1985), p. 44.

8 Samuels (1996: 56) also notes that Carwin effectively "invades" Clara's body, "albeit through the surrogate servant Judith, and through the ventriloquized sexual conversation that Pleyel 'overhears'."

9 Rombes then develops his observation along different lines than those I develop here, reading Carwin as a figure who mediates between the extremes of American politics in the 1790s, when the Federalist government's desire for "order" seemed threatened by the "rapacious abandon" of the Republicans.

10 This discussion builds on analyses of Lewis's *Journal* in Malchow (1996), Sandiford (1996), and Carson (1986), as well as on Kari Winter's (1992) discussion of

the connections between the situation of women in gothic novels and of female slaves.

11 Bohls' (2002) essay complements mine, arguing that Lewis's use of the picturesque is a not entirely successful effort to stabilize the variously doubled or divided relationship between Lewis and his slaves.

12 Bohls (2002) discusses the "staginess" of Lewis's interactions with his slaves; see especially pp. 63–4 and 72–4. For a discussion of mimicry in colonial culture, see Bhabha 1994: 85–92 ("Of Mimicry and Man: The Ambivalence of Colonial Discourse").

13 On the origin and significance of the John Canoe (alternatively identified as the "John Connu" or "Jonkonnu"), see Patterson 1969: 243–4.

14 Bohls (2002: 73–4) discusses this scene in terms similar to mine, commenting further on the Jonkonnu's performance in a picturesque setting that "could potentially cut two ways," either undercutting or reinforcing Lewis's status as "Massa."

15 Walvin (1992: 307) notes that "in return for compensation to the planters of £20 million, slaves were to be free on 1 August 1834. In fact it was only partial freedom. All children under six were freed. Others, however, became 'Apprentices' and had to work for their former owners for upwards of forty hours a week, for nothing, for a period of six years. Some islands (Antigua and Bermuda) decided to free their slaves immediately."

16 Sandiford (1996: 89–90) comments on the qualified nature of Lewis's efforts at amelioration. While his analyses and mine are differently framed, our observations and conclusions about this material – specifically about Lewis's ambivalence – basically agree.

17 Patterson (1982: 65) reads Lewis as "temporarily overwhelmed but . . . hardly deceived" by this display of seeming affection, reading it "as a thinly disguised form of sarcasm [that] signal[s] the failure of authority in this most brutal of slave systems." Bohls' (2002) discussion of theatricality is relevant here as well.

18 Lewis himself describes it as a "strange story" that he found in "an old Italian book, called 'Il Palagio degli Incanti,' in which it was related as a fact, and stated to be taken from the 'Annals of Portugal,' an historical work" (p. xxx).

19 See also Macdonald (1998: 193), who comments that "this fantastic and horrible poem . . . provides an allegorical frame for all the impressions of the island that Lewis recorded in his *Journal*," and develops a reading adjacent to mine in places, though different in its overall emphasis. On the more general question of gothic motifs in the journal and poem, Malchow's (1996) argument for the intertwining of gothic and thinking about race is borne out by this narrative in which gothic images of light and dark are clearly correlated with the fair European woman and the black male "demon" (see his chapter "The Half-Breed as Gothic Unnatural," pp. 166–237). Sandiford's (1996) demonstration of Lewis's use of the sublime as a way to express specific but also shifting political concerns could easily be extended to a reading of the poem's violence as sublime. Carson's (1986) argument for the importance of surveillance in both texts is clearly supported by this poem's crucial focus on efforts to control Irza, while Winter's (1992) discussion of the relationship between gothic novels and slave narratives leads directly to a reading of Irza as a participant in both scenarios.

20 Irza herself is acutely aware of the conflicting nature of the shelter the demon king can offer. When she first becomes aware that someone has come to save her from the dwarves, she expects a "pitying saint from high" and sees what she thinks is the "master-fiend." Her terror causes him to leave, at which point she is again attacked by the dwarves, and the demon king then returns, leaving her "[h]alf grieved, half grateful." When it becomes clear that she must return to his home with him or stay to be attacked by the dwarves yet again, we are told that "of ills she chose the best." She makes her way to the cave, and "sinking, prays she never more may rise" (pp. 169–70).

21 Fears of slave rebellion appear particularly in the later parts of the *Journal*. Lewis recounts a plot to murder "all the whites in the island" (p. 139), the "ringleaders" of which were "condemned . . . the one to be hanged, the other to transportation" (p. 138). Macdonald (1998) discusses this aspect of the journal; see especially pp. 201–5.

22 In making these remarks, I am thinking particularly of the arguments Sharpe (1993) makes in her introduction and in her third chapter, "The Civilizing Mission Disfigured."

23 Barash (1990: 410) has argued that, in colonial slave societies, "[w]omen's bodies and women's sexual conduct are . . . sites of cultural as well as sexual conflict, and ultimately means of placing white women and women of color politically and sexually at odds, yet invisibly joined in their oppression."

24 Bohls discusses this point in similar terms (2002: 69).

25 Such anxieties were common. Long, for example, implicitly acknowledges the same concern when he recommends not only rewarding the mother on the birth of the child, but that the plantation owner provide "a small annuity to be continued until its attaining the fourth or fifth year" of the child's life (1774: 2. 439–40).

26 To be quite fair to Lewis, he notes that children suffer not simply from maternal neglect, but from a "climate" that makes them "subject . . . to dangerous complaints" (p. 63).

27 Discussing the gothic horrors represented in Lewis's journal, Malchow (1996) implicitly reinforces my sense of Lewis's nervousness at the importance of reproduction in maintaining colonial life as he knew it. Drawing attention to a scene in which Lewis cuts a centipede in half and watches to see what will happen, he cites Lewis's comment that "The tail was evidently much more lively and full of motion than the head: perhaps the centipede was a female." Speculating that the insect might in part represent enslaved black females, he asks: "Does the black's womb also contain the thing that threatens to poison whites?" (Malchow 1996: 188)

28 For a history of the term "miscegenation," see Young 1995: 9–10, 144–6. Young's discussion of the range of thinking about mixed-race unions is focused largely on periods later than that in which the *Journal* was written, but makes clear the depth and complexity of this concern.

29 Talking about the period between abolition and emancipation, Higman states unequivocally that "[s]laves left the population when they reached the point of legal whiteness" (1976: 176). He then argues for complex and perhaps changing patterns

of manumission toward the end of that period (1829–32), arguing that the "chances of a slave gaining his freedom increasing with his whiteness" may well have characterized rural areas, while in towns "black manumissions outweighed coloured" (1976: 177). He attributes the difference to the fact that rural slaves were often manumitted by a benefactor, while urban slaves had the means to acquire the cash needed to purchase their own freedom, and "saw more to be gained from freedom than did [their] rural counterpart[s]" (1976: 178).

30 On his return trip to Jamaica, Lewis did sign manumission papers for Nicholas, who had paid £150 for a woman who could substitute for him on the plantation (p. 247).

31 In a related discussion, Malchow notes Lewis's fascination with "half breeds," attributing it in part to Lewis's own "ambiguous identity. That is (leaving aside the issue of his probable homosexuality), he was a cosmopolitan and liberal, a man of continental and British literary reputation, but who also, by inheritance, was an (absentee) slaveholder and plantation proprietor . . ." (1996: 186). Malchow argues more generally for "the racial half-breed as an essentially gothic type" that took shape in the "corrupted Eden" of Lewis's Jamaica (1996: 188), and that threatened the fundamental stability of the colonial order. See his chapter "The Half-Breed as Gothic Unnatural" (pp. 166–237).

32 Only a little later in the nineteenth century, what Young identified as "the *decomposition* thesis" did in fact take shape, arguing that, while "some 'amalgamation' between people may take place . . . any mixed breeds either die out or revert to one or other of the permanent parent 'types'" (1995: 18).

33 It is worth noting here Shyllon's comment that "[t]he early children of the union of black and white in Britain were objects of curiosity to the inquisitive" (1977: 103), as well as Malchow's similar remark that "[w]hite–black marriages and children from mixed-race unions were not unknown in eighteenth-century England," and that "the attention they drew seems commonly to have been that of the curious rather than the fearful" (1996: 185). In the article Shyllon cites, it seems significant that its author takes pains to show that mixed-race relationships manifest themselves in the marked bodies of the children they produce – to do away with the problem of passing before it is even raised, in other words – and so to suggest that such relationships should not inspire fear.

Chapter 8: Feminist, Postmodern, Postcolonial

1 For more on this, and an argument that complements mine, see Howells 1996.

2 Thanks to Tamar Heller for this observation. See also Howells, who notes the protagonist's "New World fascination with Europe" (1996: 72).

3 On Atwood's continuing interesting in the gothic, see also Howells (1996), who has a chapter on "Atwoodian Gothic: From *Lady Oracle* to *The Robber Bride*" (pp. 62–85). For a different view of Atwood's career – one that sees her writing "romance" through *Lady Oracle* and realistic novels thereafter, see Kolodny 1990.

4 On *Lady Oracle* as a comic novel, see Vincent 1983.

5 My reading differs superficially from Hite's insightful discussion of the female body in this novel. Hite notes that "this is a book in which fat is a feminist issue, and in which excess of body becomes symbolic of female resistance to a society that wishes to constrict women to dimensions it deems appropriate, using devices that range from exemplars to definitions to diets" (1989: 132). I do not disagree so much as think that this focus on the body as definitive of identity still indicates a form of entrapment.

6 Critical discussions of Joan's relationship to her mother especially, but also to her aunt, have been very strong and I have over the years learned from all I have read. See Godard (1983), Howells (1996), Sciff-Zamaro (1987), Hite (1989), and Wurst (1988).

7 Page references are to *Lady Oracle* (New York, 1976).

8 Cf. Hite (1989: 134–5, 141), who reads the novel's refusal to follow Radcliffe and explain away the supernatural as a strength, a way of accommodating the excess of women's experience that does not fit the "realist narrative" that in this novel is associated with the male characters.

9 For a complementary perspective on satire in this novel, see Hite (1989: 134), who notes that "the satire results not from an invasion of the real by the conventions of the artificial but from the clash of conventions belonging to different discursive practices."

10 Page references are to *The Blind Assassin* (Toronto, 2000).

11 This reading of Macdonald's novel began as a paper I presented at the annual meeting of the Rocky Mountain division of the Modern Language Association in October 2001, with the title "Displacing the Gothic: Genre and Identity in Contemporary Canadian Fiction." Page references in the text are to the New York 1998 edition.

12 For this insight, I am indebted to my former student Lauren Nishimura.

Bibliography

Alliston, April (1990) "The Value of a Literary Legacy: Retracing the Transmission of Value through Female Lines." *The Yale Journal of Criticism*, 4(1), 109–27.

——(2000) "Introduction" to Sophia Lee, *The Recess*. Ed. April Alliston. Lexington: University Press of Kentucky.

Armstrong, Nancy (1987) *Desire and Domestic Fiction: A Political History of the Novel*. Oxford: Oxford University Press.

Ashfield, Andrew, and Peter de Bolla (eds) (1996) *The Sublime: A Reader in British Eighteenth-Century Aesthetic Theory*. Cambridge: Cambridge University Press.

Atwood, Margaret (1976) *Lady Oracle*. New York: Fawcett Crest/Ballantine.

——(2000) *The Blind Assassin*. Toronto: McClelland & Stewart.

Auerbach, Nina (1995) *Our Vampires, Ourselves*. Chicago: University of Chicago Press.

Austen, Jane (1995[1798–9; 1st pub. 1818]) *Northanger Abbey*. Ed. Marilyn Butler. London: Penguin.

Avery, Simon (1998) "'Some strange and spectral dream': The Brontës' Manipulation of the Gothic Mode." *Brontë Society Transactions*, 23(2), 120–35.

Backus, Margot Gayle (1999) *The Gothic Family Romance: Heterosexuality, Child Sacrifice, and the Anglo-Irish Colonial Order*. Durham: Duke University Press.

Baldick, Chris (1989) "Introduction" to *Melmoth the Wanderer*. Oxford: Oxford University Press; 1st pub. 1968.

Barash, Carol (1990) "The Character of Difference: The Creole Woman as Cultural Mediator in Narratives about Jamaica." *Eighteenth-Century Studies*, 23, 406–24.

Barber, Paul (1994) *Vampires, Burial, and Death*. Albany: State University of New York Press.

Barnes, Elizabeth (2002) "Loving with a Vengeance: *Wieland*, Familicide and the Crisis of Masculinity in the Early Nation. In Milette Shamir and Jennifer Travis (eds), *Boys Don't Cry? Rethinking Narratives of Masculinity and Emotion in the U.S.*, pp. 45–63. New York: Columbia University Press.

Bartolomeo, Joseph F. (1993) "Subversion of Romance in *The Old Manor House.*" *Studies in English Literature,* 33, 645–57.

Bewell, Alan (1988) "An Issue of Monstrous Desire: *Frankenstein* and Obstetrics." *The Yale Journal of Criticism,* 2, 105–27.

Bhabha, Homi K. (1994) *The Location of Culture.* London: Routledge.

Birkhead, Edith (1921) *The Tale of Terror: A Study of the Gothic Romance.* London: Constable.

Bloom, Harold (1982) *Agon: Towards a Theory of Revisionism.* Oxford: Oxford University Press.

Bohls, Elizabeth A. (2002) "The Planter Picturesque: Matthew Lewis's *Journal of a West India Proprietor.*" *European Romantic Review,* 13, 63–76.

Botting, Fred (1996) *Gothic.* London: Routledge.

——(2000) "In Gothic Darkly: Heterotopia, History, Culture." In *A Companion to the Gothic.* Ed. David Punter. Oxford: Blackwell.

Brantlinger, Patrick (1988) *Rule of Darkness: British Literature and Imperialism, 1830–1914.* Ithaca: Cornell University Press.

Bronfen, Elisabeth (1992) *Over Her Dead Body: Death, Femininity and the Aesthetic.* New York: Routledge.

Brontë, Charlotte (1966[1847]) *Jane Eyre.* Ed. Q. D. Leavis. London: Penguin.

Brontë, Emily (1995[1847]) *Wuthering Heights.* Ed. Pauline Nestor. London: Penguin.

Brown, Charles Brockden (1991[1798]) *Wieland or the Transformation: An American Tale.* Ed. Jay Fliegelman. New York: Viking/Penguin.

——(1988[1799]) *Edgar Huntly.* Ed. and introd. Norman S. Grabo. Harmondsworth: Penguin.

Brown, Laura (1993) *The Ends of Empire: Women and Ideology in Early Eighteenth-Century English Literature.* Ithaca: Cornell University Press.

Bruhm, Steven (1994) *Gothic Bodies: The Politics of Pain in Romantic Fiction.* Philadelphia: University of Pennsylvania Press.

Burke, Edmund (1968[1757]) *A Philosophical Enquiry into the Origin of our Ideas of the Sublime and Beautiful.* Ed. James T. Boulton. Notre Dame, Ind.: University of Notre Dame Press.

Carson, James (1986) "Crime and Conscience in the Gothic Novel." Ph.D. diss., University of California, Berkeley.

Castle, Terry (1995[1987]) "The Spectralization of the Other in *The Mysteries of Udolpho.*" Repr. in Castle, *The Female Thermometer: Eighteenth-Century Culture and the Invention of the Uncanny,* pp. 120–39. Oxford: Oxford University Press.

Clery, E. J. (1995) *The Rise of Supernatural Fiction: 1762–1800.* Cambridge: Cambridge University Press.

——(2000) *Women's Gothic, from Clara Reeve to Mary Shelley.* Tavistock: Northcote House.

Craciun, Adriana (1997) "Introduction" to *Zofloya; or, The Moor: A Romance of the Fifteenth Century.* Ed. Adriana Craciun. Peterborough, Ont.: Broadview Press.

Culler, Jonathan (1988) *Framing the Sign: Criticism and its Institutions.* Norman: University of Oklahoma Press.

Dacre, Charlotte (1997[1806]) *Zofloya; or, The Moor: A Romance of the Fifteenth Century.* Ed. Adriana Craciun. Peterborough, Ontario: Broadview Press.

DeLamotte, Eugenia C. (1990) *Perils of the Night: A Feminist Study of Nineteenth-Century Gothic*. Oxford: Oxford University Press.

Deleuze, Gilles, and Félix Guattari (1987) *A Thousand Plateaus: Capitalism and Schizophrenia*. Trans. Brian Massumi. Minneapolis: University of Minnesota Press

Doody, Margaret Anne (1977) "Deserts, Ruins and Troubled Waters: Female Dreams in Fiction and the Development of the Gothic Novel." *Genre*, 10(4), 529–72.

Drew, Philip (1964) "Charlotte Brontë as a Critic of *Wuthering Heights*." *Nineteenth-Century Fiction*, 368–81.

Duncan, Ian (1992) *Modern Romance and Transformations of the Novel: The Gothic, Scott, Dickens*. Cambridge: Cambridge University Press.

Ellis, Kate Ferguson (1989) *The Contested Castle: Gothic Novels and the Subversion of Domestic Ideology*. Urbana, Ill.: University of Illinois Press.

Ellis, Markman (2001) *The Gothic Tradition*. Edinburgh: University of Edinburgh Press.

Engle, Lars (1989) "The Political Uncanny: The Novels of Nadine Gordimer." *The Yale Journal of Criticism*, 2, 101–27.

Fay, Elizabeth A. (1988) *A Feminist Introduction to Romanticism*. Oxford: Blackwell.

Ferguson, Frances (1992) *Solitude and the Sublime: Romanticism and the Aesthetics of Individuation*. New York: Routledge.

Filmer, Robert (1991) *Patriarcha and Other Writings*. Ed. Johann P. Somerville. Cambridge: Cambridge University Press.

Fleenor, Juliann E. (ed.) (1983) *The Female Gothic*. Montreal: Eden Press.

Fludernik, Monika (2001) "William Godwin's *Caleb Williams*: The Tarnishing of the Sublime." *Studies in Romanticism*, 68, 857–96.

Frayling, Christopher (1991) *Vampyres: Lord Byron to Count Dracula*. London: Faber & Faber.

Freeman, Barbara Claire (1995) *The Feminine Sublime: Gender and Excess in Women's Fiction*. Berkeley: University of California Press.

Freud, Sigmund ((1955)[1919]) "The Uncanny." In *The Standard Edition of the Complete Psychological Works of Sigmund Freud*. Translator and general editor James Strachey, in collaboration with Anna Freud, assisted by Alix Strachey and Alan Tyson, 24 vols. London: The Hogarth Press and the Institute of Psychoanalysis, 1953–74. Vol. XVII, pp. 217–56.

Frye, Northrop (1956) "Towards Defining an Age of Sensibility." *ELH* 23(2), 144–52.

Frye, Susan (1993) *Elizabeth I: The Competition for Representation*. Oxford: Oxford University Press.

Gamer, Michael (2000) *Romanticism and the Gothic*. Cambridge: Cambridge University Press.

Gelder, Ken (1994) *Reading the Vampire*. London: Routledge.

Gigante, Denise (2000) "Facing the Ugly: The Case of *Frankenstein*." *ELH* 67, 565–87.

Gilbert, Sandra M., and Susan Gubar (1979) *The Madwoman in the Attic: The Woman Writer and the Nineteenth-Century Literary Imagination*. Princeton, NJ: Yale University Press.

Godard, Barbara (1983) "My (m)Other, My Self: Strategies for Subversion in Atwood and Hébert." *Essays on Canadian Writing*, 26, 13–44.

Godwin, William (1976[1793]) *Enquiry Concerning Political Justice*. Ed. Isaac Kramnick. Harmondsworth: Penguin.

——(1988[1794]) *Caleb Williams*. Ed. Maurice Hindle. London: Penguin.

Bibliography

Gold, Alex, Jr. (1977) "It's Only Love: The Politics of Passion in Godwin's *Caleb Williams*." *Texas Studies in Literature and Language*, 19, 135–60.

Graham, Kenneth W. (1984) "The Gothic Unity of Godwin's *Caleb Williams*." *Papers on Language and Literature*, 20, 47–59.

Greenfield, Susan (2002) *Mothering Daughters: Novels and the Politics of Family Romance, Frances Burney to Jane Austen*. Detroit: Wayne State University Press.

Haggerty, George E. (1989) *Gothic Fiction/Gothic Form*. University Park: Pennsylvania University Press.

——(1998) *Unnatural Affections: Women and Fiction in the Later Eighteenth Century*. Bloomington: Indiana University Press.

——(1999) *Men in Love: Masculinity and Sexuality in the Eighteenth Century*. New York: Columbia University Press.

Halberstam, Judith (1995) *Skin Shows: Gothic Horror and the Technology of Monsters*. Durham: Duke University Press.

Heiland, Donna (1992) "Postmodern Gothic: *Lady Oracle* and its Eighteenth-Century Antecedents." *Recherches sémiotiques/Semiotic Inquiry*, 12, 115–36.

——(1997) "Historical Subjects: Recent Fiction about the Eighteenth Century." *Eighteenth-Century Life*, 21, 108–22.

——(2002) "The *Unheimlich* and the Making of Home: Matthew Lewis's *Journal of a West India Proprietor*." In Laura Rosenthal and Mita Choudhury (eds), *Monstrous Dreams of Reason: Body, Self, and Other in the Enlightenment*, pp. 170–88. Lewisburg: Bucknell University Press.

Heilman, Robert B. (1971) "Charlotte Brontë's 'New Gothic.'" In Ian Watt (ed.), *The Victorian Novel: Modern Essays in Criticism*, pp. 165–80. Oxford: Oxford University Press.

Heller, Tamar (1992) *Dead Secrets: Wilkie Collins and the Female Gothic*. New Haven: Yale University Press.

Hertz, Neil (1985) *The End of the Line: Essays on Psychoanalysis and the Sublime*. New York: Columbia University Press.

Higman, B. W. (1976) *Slave Population and Economy in Jamaica, 1807–1834*. Cambridge: Cambridge University Press.

Hite, Molly (1989) *The Other Side of the Story: Structures and Strategies of Contemporary Feminist Narrative*. Ithaca: Cornell University Press.

Hoeveler, Diane Long (1998) *Gothic Feminism: The Professionalization of Gender from Charlotte Smith to the Brontës*. University Park: Pennsylvania State University Press.

Hoffman, E. T. A. (1967) "The Sand-man." Trans. J. T. Bealby. In *The Best Tales of Hoffman*. Ed. E. F. Bleiler. New York: Dover Publications.

Homans, Margaret (1986) *Bearing the Word: Language and Female Experience in Nineteenth-Century Women's Writing*. Chicago: University of Chicago Press.

Howells, Coral Anne (1978) *Love, Mystery, and Misery: Feeling in Gothic Fiction*. London: Athlone Press/University of London.

——(1996) *Margaret Atwood*. New York: St. Martin's Press.

Huet, Marie-Hélène (1993) *Monstrous Imagination*. Cambridge, Mass.: Harvard University Press.

Isaac, Megan Lynn (1996) "Sophia Lee and the Gothic of Female Community." *Studies in the Novel*, 28, 200–11.

Johnson, Claudia (1995) *Equivocal Beings: Politics, Gender, and Sentimentality in the 1790s – Wollstonecraft, Radcliffe, Burney, Austen*. Chicago: University of Chicago Press.

Kahane, Claire (1985) "The Gothic Mirror." In Shirley Nelson Garner, Claire Kahane, and Madelon Sprengnether (eds), *The (M)other Tongue: Essays in Feminist Psychoanalytic Interpretation*, pp. 334–51. Ithaca: Cornell University Press.

Kant, Immanuel (1952[1790]) *The Critique of Judgement*. Trans. James Creed Meredith. Oxford: Clarendon Press.

Kaufman, Robert (1997) "The Sublime as Super-Genre of the Modern, or *Hamlet* in Revolution: Caleb Williams and his Problems." *Studies in Romanticism*, 36, 541–74.

Kenner, Hugh (1968) *The Counterfeiters*. Baltimore: Johns Hopkins University Press.

Kiely, Robert (1972) *The Romantic Novel in England*. Cambridge, Mass.: Harvard University Press.

Kilgour, Maggie (1995). *The Rise of the Gothic Novel*. London: Routledge.

Kolodny, Annette (1990) "Margaret Atwood and the Politics of Narrative." In Arnold E. Davidson (ed.), *Studies on Canadian Literature: Introductory and Critical Essays*, pp. 90–109. New York: Modern Language Association of America.

Kristeva, Julia (1980) *Desire in Language: A Semiotic Approach to Literature and Art*. Ed. Leon S. Roudiez, trans. Thomas Gora, Alice Jardine, and Leon S. Roudiez. New York: Columbia University Press.

Lee, Sophia (2000[1783–5]) *The Recess, or A Tale of Other Times*. Ed. April Alliston. Lexington: University Press of Kentucky.

Lewis, Jayne Elizabeth (1995) " 'Ev'ry Lost Relation': Historical Fictions and Sentimental Incidents in Sophia Lee's *The Recess*." *Eighteenth-Century Fiction*, 7, 165–84.

——(1998) *Mary Queen of Scots: Romance and Nation*. London: Routledge.

Lewis, Matthew (1973[1796]) *The Monk*. Ed. Howard Anderson. Oxford: Oxford University Press (pbk. edn 1980).

——(1999[1815–16]) *Journal of a West India Proprietor*. Ed. and introd. Judith Terry. Oxford: Oxford University Press.

Locke, John (1988[1690]) *Two Treatises of Government*, student edn. Ed. Peter Laslett. Cambridge: Cambridge University Press.

Logan, Peter (1997) *Nerves and Narratives: A Cultural History of Hysteria in 19th-Century British Prose*. Berkeley: University of California Press.

Long, Edward (1774) *History of Jamaica*, 3 vols. London: T. Lowndes.

Lydenberg, Robin (1997) "Freud's Uncanny Narratives." *PMLA* 112, 1072–86.

Lydon, James (1998) *The Making of Ireland: From Ancient Times to the Present*. London: Routledge.

Macdonald, Ann-Marie (1998) *Fall on Your Knees*. New York: Scribner/Simon & Schuster.

Macdonald, D. L. (1998) "The Isle of Devils: The Jamaican Journal of M. G. Lewis." In Tim Fulford and Peter J. Kitson (eds), *Romanticism and Colonization: Writing and Empire, 1780–1830*, pp. 189–205. Cambridge: Cambridge University Press.

Malchow, H. R. (1996) *Gothic Images of Race in Nineteenth-Century Britain*. Stanford: Stanford University Press.

Marshall, David (1988) *The Surprising Effects of Sympathy: Marivaux, Diderot, Rousseau, and Mary Shelley*. Chicago: University of Chicago Press.

Massé, Michelle A. (1992) *In the Name of Love: Women, Masochism, and the Gothic*. Ithaca: Cornell University Press.

Maturin, Charles (1968[1820]) *Melmoth the Wanderer*. Ed. Douglas Grant. Oxford: Oxford University Press (pbk. edn 1989).

McKeon, Michael (1995) "Historicizing Patriarchy: The Emergence of Gender Difference in England, 1660–1760." *Eighteenth-Century Studies*, 28, 295–322.

Mellor, Anne K. (1988) "Possessing Nature: The Female in *Frankenstein*." In Anne K. Mellor (ed.), *Romanticism and Feminism*. Bloomington: Indiana University Press.

——(1993) *Romanticism and Gender*. New York: Routledge.

Meyer, Susan (1996) *Imperialism at Home: Race and Victorian Women's Fiction*. Ithaca: Cornell University Press.

Michasiw, Kim Ian (1997) "Introduction" to *Zofloya, or the Moor*. Ed. Kim Ian Michasiw. Oxford: Oxford University Press.

Milbank, Alison (1993) "Introduction" to Ann Radcliffe, *A Sicilian Romance*. Ed. Alison Milbank. Oxford: Oxford University Press.

Miles, Robert (1993) *Gothic Writing 1750–1820: A Genealogy*. London: Routledge; pbk. edn. Manchester: Manchester University Press, 2002.

——(1995) *Ann Radcliffe: The Great Enchantress*. Manchester: Manchester University Press.

Mishra, Vijay (1994) *The Gothic Sublime*. Albany: State University of New York Press.

Moers, Ellen (1985). *Literary Women: The Great Writers*. New York: Oxford University Press; 1st pub. Doubleday, 1976.

Moglen, Hélène (2001) *The Trauma of Gender: A Feminist Theory of the English Novel*. Berkeley: University of California Press.

Moore, Leslie E. (1990) *The Beautiful Sublime: The Making of Paradise Lost, 1701–1734*. Stanford: Stanford University Press.

Morris, David B. (1985) "Gothic Sublimity." *New Literary History*, 16, 299–319.

Noble, David (1992) *A World Without Women: The Christian Clerical Culture of Western Scienice*. New York: Knopf.

Nussbaum, Felicity (1995) *Torrid Zones: Maternity, Sexuality, and Empire in Eighteenth-Century English Narratives*. Baltimore: Johns Hopkins University Press.

O'Quinn, Daniel (1997) "Trembling: Wollstonecraft, Godwin and the Resistance to Literature." *ELH* 64, 761–88.

Pateman, Carole (1988) *The Sexual Contract*. Stanford: Stanford University Press; 1st pub. Polity Press, 1988.

Patterson, Orlando (1969) *The Sociology of Slavery: An Analysis of the Origins, Development and Structure of Negro Slave Society in Jamaica*. Rutherford: Fairleigh Dickinson University Press.

——(1982) *Slavery and Social Death: A Comparative Study*. Cambridge: Harvard University Press.

Paulson, Ronald (1983) *Representations of Revolution (1789–1820)*. New Haven: Yale University Press.

Polidori, John (1997[1819]) *The Vampyre and Other Tales of the Macabre*. Ed. and introd. Robert Morrison and Chris Baldick. Oxford: Oxford University Press.

Poovey, Mary (1979) "Ideology and 'The Mysteries of Udolpho'." *Criticism*, 21, 307–30.

——(1984) *The Proper Lady and the Woman Writer: Ideology as Style in the Works of Mary Wollstonecraft, Mary Shelley, and Jane Austen*. Chicago: University of Chicago Press.

Praz, Mario (1956). *The Romantic Agony*. Trans. Angus Davidson. Cleveland: Meridian Books/The World Publishing Company; 1st pub. 1933.

Punter, David (1981) *The Literature of Terror*, 2 vols. London: Longman; 2nd edn 1996.

——(ed.) (2000) *A Companion to the Gothic*. Oxford: Blackwell.

Radcliffe, Ann (1966[1794]) *The Mysteries of Udolpho*. Ed. Bonamy Dobree. Oxford: Oxford University Press (pbk. edn 1980).

——(1968[1797]) *The Italian, or the Confessional of the Black Penitents. A Romance*. Ed. Frederick Garber. Oxford: Oxford University Press (pbk. edn 1981).

——(1986[1791]) *The Romance of the Forest*. Ed. Chloe Chard. Oxford: Oxford University Press.

——(1993[1790]). *A Sicilian Romance*. Ed. Alison Milbank. Oxford: Oxford University Press.

Railo, Eino (1927) *The Haunted Castle: A Study of the Elements of English Romanticism*. London: Routledge.

Rajan, Tillottama (2000) "Framing the Corpus: Godwin's 'Editing' of Wollstonecraft in 1798." *Studies in Romanticism*, 39, 511–31.

Reeve, Clara (1967[1777]) *The Old English Baron: A Gothic Story*. Ed. and introd. James Trainer. London: Oxford University Press.

Richardson, Ronald Kent (1987) *Moral Imperium: Afro-Caribbeans and the Transformation of British Rule, 1776–1838*. Contributions in Comparative Colonial Studies 22. New York: Greenwood Press.

Richter, David (1996) *The Progress of Romance: Literary Historiography and the Gothic Novel*. Columbus: Ohio State University Press.

Rollins, Hyder Edward (ed.) (1958) *The Letters of John Keats, 1814–1821*, 2 vols. Cambridge, Mass.: Harvard University Press.

Rombes, Nicholas (1994) "'All was lonely, darksom, and waste': *Wieland* and the Construction of the New Republic." *Studies in American Fiction*, 22, 37–46.

Rosenthal, Laura (1996). *Playwrights and Plagiarists in Early Modern England: Gender, Authorship, Literary Property*. Ithaca: Cornell University Press.

——and Mita Choudhury (eds) (2002) *Monstrous Dreams of Reason: Body, Self, and Other in the Enlightenment*. Lewisburg: Bucknell University Press.

Rosowski, Susan J. (1981) "Margaret Atwood's *Lady Oracle*: Social Mythology and the Gothic Novel." *Research Studies* 49, 87–98.

Rymer, James Malcolm [misidentified in this edition as Thomas Preskett Prest] (1970[1845–7]). *Varney the Vampire, or, The Feast of Blood*, 3 vols. Ed. Devendra Varma. Arno Press.

Samuels, Shirley (1996) *Romances of the Republic: Women, the Family, and Violence in the Literature of the Early American Nation*. Oxford: Oxford University Press.

Sandiford, Keith A. (1996) "'Monk' Lewis and the Slavery Sublime: The Agon of Romantic Desire in the Journal." *Essays in Literature*, 23, pp. 84–98.

Bibliography

Schmitt, Cannon (1997) *Alien Nation: Nineteenth-Century Gothic Fictions and English Nationality.* Philadelphia, Pa.: University of Pennsylvania Press.

Sciff-Zamaro, Roberta (1987) "The Re/Membering of the Female Power in *Lady Oracle.*" *Canadian Literature,* 112, 32–8.

Sedgwick, Eve Kosofsky (1985) *Between Men: English Literature and Male Homosocial Desire.* New York: Columbia University Press.

——(1986) *The Coherence of Gothic Conventions.* Repr. New York: Methuen; 1st pub. 1980.

Seltzer, Mark (1978) "Saying Makes It So: Language and Event in Brown's *Wieland.*" *Early American Literature,* 13, 81–91.

Sharpe, Jenny (1993) *Allegories of Empire: The Figure of Woman in the Colonial Text.* Minneapolis: University of Minnesota Press.

Shelley, Mary (1994) *Frankenstein or The Modern Prometheus* [1818 text]. Ed. and introd. Marilyn Butler. Oxford: Oxford University Press.

Showalter, Elaine (1977) *A Literature of their Own: British Women Novelists from Brontë to Lessing.* Princeton, NJ: Princeton University Press.

Shyllon, Folarin (1977) *Black People in Britain, 1555–1833.* London: Oxford University Press for the Institute of Race Relations.

Smith, Andrew (2000) *Gothic Radicalism: Literature, Philosophy and Psychoanalysis in the Nineteenth Century.* Houndmills, Basingstoke: Macmillan.

——and William Hughes (eds) (2003) *Empire and the Gothic: The Politics of the Genre.* Houndmills, Basingstoke: Palgrave/Macmillan.

Smith, Charlotte (1969[1793]) *The Old Manor House.* Oxford: Oxford University Press (pbk. edn 1989).

Sowerby, Robin (2000) "The Goths in History and Pre-Gothic Gothic." In David Punter (ed.), *A Companion to the Gothic,* pp. 15–26. Oxford: Blackwell.

Spacks, Patricia Meyer (1972) *The Female Imagination.* Toronto: Knopf.

Spivak, Gayatri (1985) "Three Women's Texts and a Critique of Imperialism." *Critical Inquiry,* 12, 243–61.

Stevenson, John Allen (1988) "'Heathcliff is me!' *Wuthering Heights* and the Question of Likeness." *Nineteenth-Century Fiction,* 43, 60–81.

Summers, Montague (1969) *The Gothic Quest: A History of the Gothic Novel.* London: Fortune Press; 1st pub. 1938.

Sussman, Charlotte (1993) "The Other Problem with Women: Reproduction and Slave Culture in Aphra Behn's *Oroonoko.*" In Heidi Hutner (ed.), *Rereading Aphra Behn: History, Theory, and Criticism,* pp. 212–31. Charlottesville: University Press of Virginia.

Todd, Janet (1988) *Sensibility: An Introduction.* London: Methuen.

Todorov, Tzvetan (1975) *The Fantastic: A Structural Approach to a Literary Genre.* Trans. Richard Howard. Ithaca: Cornell University Press; 1st pub. in French 1970; 1st pub. in English 1973.

Tompkins, J. M. S. (1932) *The Popular Novel in England.* London: Constable.

Trumpener, Katie (1997) *Bardic Nationalism: The Romantic Novel and the British Empire.* Princeton: Princeton University Press.

Varma, Devendra P. (1957) *The Gothic Flame: Being a History of the Gothic Novel in England: Its Origins, Efflorescence, Disintegration, and Residuary Influences.* London: Arthur Baker.

Vincent, Sybil Korff (1983) "The Mirror and the Cameo: Margaret Atwood's Comic/Gothic Novel, *Lady Oracle.*" In Juliann E. Fleenor (ed.), *The Female Gothic*, pp. 153–63. Montreal: Eden Press.

von Mücke, Dorothea (1996) " 'To Love a Murderer' – Fantasy, Sexuality, and the Political Novel: The Case of *Caleb Williams.*" In Deirdre Lynch and William B. Warner (eds), *Cultural Institutions of the Novel*, pp. 306–34. Durham, NC: Duke University Press.

Walpole, Horace (1982[1764]) *The Castle of Otranto.* Ed. W. S. Lewis. World's Classics. Oxford: Oxford University Press.

Walvin, James (ed.) (1982) *Slavery and British Society, 1776–1846.* Baton Rouge: Louisiana State University Press.

——(1992) *Black Ivory: A History of British Slavery.* London: HarperCollins.

Watt, James (1999) *Contesting the Gothic: Fiction, Genre and Cultural Conflict, 1764–1832.* Cambridge: Cambridge University Press.

Weldon, Roberta F. (1984) "Charles Brockden Brown's *Wieland*: A Family Tragedy." *Studies in American Fiction*, 12, 1–11.

Weiskel, Thomas (1986[1976]) *The Romantic Sublime: Studies in the Structure and Psychology of Transcendence.* Baltimore: Johns Hopkins University Press.

Williams, Anne (1995) *Art of Darkness: A Poetics of Gothic.* Chicago: University of Chicago Press.

Winter, Kari (1992) *Subjects of Slavery, Agents of Change: Women and Power in Gothic Novels and Slave Narratives, 1790–1865.* Athens: University of Georgia Press.

Wollstonecraft, Mary (1975[1792]) *A Vindication of the Rights of Woman.* Ed. Miriam Brody Kramnick. Harmondsworth: Penguin.

——(1976) *Mary and The Wrongs of Woman* [1788 and 1798]. Ed. Gary Kelly. Oxford: Oxford University Press.

Wurst, Gayle (1988) "Cultural Stereotypes and the Language of Identity: Margaret Atwood's *Lady Oracle*, Maxine Hong Kingston's *The Woman Warrior* and Alice Walker's *The Color Purple.*" In Mirko Jurak (ed.), *Cross-Cultural Studies: American, Canadian, and European Literatures 1945–1985*, pp. 53–64. Ljubljana: University of Ljubljana.

Yaeger, Patricia (1989). "Toward a Female Sublime." In Linda Kauffman (ed.), *Gender and Theory: Dialogues on Feminist Criticism.* Oxford: Basil Blackwell.

Yeazell, Ruth (1979) "More True than Real: Jane Eyre's 'Mysterious Summons.'" *Nineteenth-Century Fiction*, 29, 128–43.

Young, Robert (1995) *Colonial Desire: Hybridity in Theory, Culture, and Race.* New York: Routledge.

Index

Where two sequences of notes occur on one page, note references below are differentiated by the addition of a or b; thus 187 n.1a, 194 n.3b.

Index

politics (cont'd)
  and the sublime 32
  in Wollstonecraft 81
Poovey, Mary 74, 94–5, 192 n.15
Pope, Alexander, *The Rape of the Lock* 55
power
  in Atwood 166, 167
  in the Brontës 117, 128
  the Church 51–2
  in Dacre 44, 46, 48
  in Lee 20–3
  in Lewis 37–9, 41
  in Maturin 51–2
  in Radcliffe 69
  in Reeve 12, 13, 15
  in Shelley 103
  and the sublime 32, 35–6, 58
  in Walpole 12–14
Praz, Mario 182
Prest, Thomas Preskett 194 n.8
psychoanalysis, and gothic fiction 184
public sphere, women in 58, 60–1, 71
Punter, David 185

race
  and gender 28, 47, 144, 150, 170
  and miscegenation 153–5
  and passing 126, 155
Radcliffe, Ann
  and Austen 92, 157–8, 163
  and female sublime 62–3
  influence 6, 36, 57, 181–2
  and inheritance 71, 72, 73–6, 99
  The Italian 58, 63–8
  and mother–daughter relations 58,
    61–4, 67, 68, 71, 73–4, 170
  The Mysteries of Udolpho 65–6, 68, 71–6,
    184, 191 n.4
  and resistance to patriarchy 58–60,
    68–71, 75–6, 81
  The Romance of the Forest 57, 68–71
  A Sicilian Romance 58–63, 67, 68
  and the sublime 5, 6, 58–69, 71–2, 83,
    163

and "terror gothic" 34, 36–7, 66–7,
    69–70, 72–3, 157
Railo, Eino 181–2, 183
Rank, Otto 79
rape
  incestuous 170, 172, 179
  interracial 149–50
  in Lewis 40–1, 144
  male 51
realism
  and gothic fiction 4, 6, 15, 114–15,
    157–8
  and the novel 4
  in Reeve 15
  and romance 132–3
reality
  and appearance 163–4, 166
  and fiction 164–5, 169
reason, female 70, 91
Recess, The, see Lee, Sophia
Reeve, Clara 4
  literary lineage 20, 181–2
  and male friendships 17–19
  The Old English Baron 12–13, 15–20
  and patriarchy 12–13, 15–20
  and Walpole 15, 17
relationships
  between men 17–19, 83, 87–8, 107–9,
    140, 171
  between women 28, 44, 96–7, 158–60,
    168–9, 172, 189 nn.20, 25
  and class structure 87
  father–daughter 25–6, 59–60, 74–6,
    170, 171–4, 177
  father–son 17–18, 78–9, 101
  heterosexual 17, 19, 21, 94–6, 128, 184
  mother–daughter 25, 158–63, 166,
    173–4, 177–8, 184; *see also* Radcliffe,
    Ann
religion
  and Brown 139–41
  and corruption 37, 41–2, 52–3, 67,
    140–1
  and Lee 20–1, 24, 27–8

218

Index compiled by Meg Davies (Registered Indexer, Society of Indexers)